Interrogating Inequality

Interrogating Inequality

Essays on Class Analysis, Socialism and Marxism

ERIK OLIN WRIGHT

VERSO
London · New York

First published in this form by Verso 1994

© Erik Olin Wright

Verso
UK: 6 Meard Street, London W1V 3HR
USA: 29 West 35th Street, New York, NY 10001–2291

Verso is the imprint of New Left Books

ISBN 0 86091 408 9
ISBN 0 86091 633 2

British Library Cataloguing in Publication Data
A catalogue record for this book is available from the British Library

Library of Congress Cataloging-in-Publication Data
Wright, Erik Olin.
Interrogating inequality : essays on class analysis, socialism,
and Marxism / Erik Olin Wright.
p.   cm.
Includes bibliographical references and index.
ISBN 0–86091–408–9 — ISBN 0–86091–633–2 (pbk.)
1. Social classes.   2. Communism and society.   3. Socialism.
4. Capitalism.   I. Title.
HT609.W713   1994
305.5—dc20

Typeset by York House Typographic Ltd, London
Printed in Great Britain by Biddles Ltd

To My Mother and Mentor, Beatrice A. Wright

Contents

Preface

When I discussed the proposed title of this book, *Interrogating Inequality*, with various friends and family, some people proclaimed that the title was ridiculous, that it didn't mean anything. *Interrogating Inequality*, they argued, makes no more sense than *Shaking Hands with Contradiction*, or *Speaking to Triangles*. Various alternatives were suggested: *Investigating Inequality*; *Studying Inequality*; *Examining Inequality*. None of these was quite right. They each suggested that inequality as such was the main topic of the book – that the book was either an empirical study of inequality, or that it explored various theoretical and philosophical problems with various kinds of inequality. This is not really what the book is about.

Interrogating Inequality is meant to evoke a different image. Inequality is a witness in a criminal investigation, perhaps even the prime suspect. It is being questioned to get at some underlying truth about the crime, an injustice that has been committed. Our concern is not simply with the witness itself, but with what we can learn about broader issues by probing the witness. The book, then, is as much about the kinds of questions we need to ask in this interrogation, and the concepts we need to use in asking them, as it is about inequality itself. It is about class analysis as a way of asking questions about inequality, about socialism as a way of challenging inequality, and about Marxism as a broad framework for linking the moral concerns with inequality to the theoretical tasks of explanation and the political tasks of transformation. Perhaps it would have been better to have used as a title the more straightforward message of the subtitle of the book, *Essays on Class Analysis, Socialism and Marxism*, but that seemed too boring. So, at the risk of sounding a bit post-modernist, I settled on *Interrogating Inequality*.

The twelve essays gathered together in this volume were written between 1979 and 1993. Four of them were commissioned for specific purposes. "Inequality" (chapter 1) was prepared for *The New Palgrave*, edited by John Eatwell (London 1987) and was written with an eye to explaining to economists what was distinctive about a Marxist approach to inequality. "Class and Politics" (chapter 5) was written for the *Oxford Companion on Politics* (Oxford 1993) and was designed to serve a similar function for political scientists. "Marxism as Social Science" (chapter 9) was written as an invited response to a series of critiques of a previously published exchange between me and Michael Burawoy which appeared in the *Berkeley Journal of Sociology*. The set of critiques and my reply were then published as a symposium in the *BJS* in 1989. "Falling into Marxism; Choosing to Stay" (Prologue) was written for a conference celebrating the 100th anniversary of the founding of the Sociology Department at the University of Kansas. A number of sociologists with some kind of connection to K.U. were invited to give sociological talks on their own careers. My connection was that I grew up in Lawrence, Kansas, and both of my parents were professors at K.U. (although in psychology, not sociology). My essay is an attempt at understanding the trajectory of choices I have made that have generated the kind of academic Marxist scholarship I try to produce. This essay subsequently appeared in 1991 in a journal published by the K.U. Sociology Department, *The Midwest Review of Sociology*.

Several of the essays were written as direct engagements with the work of fellow members of the annual London Analytical Marxism meeting (this group is described in the Prologue). "The Status of the Political in the Concept of Class Structure" (chapter 3) was my first encounter with the work of John Roemer. It was eventually published in a special issue of the journal *Politics and Society*, vol. 11, no. 2, 1982, devoted to Roemer's work on class and exploitation. "Why Something Like Socialism is Necessary for the Transition to Something like Communism" (chapter 7) grew out of discussions about a paper, "A Capitalist Road to Communism," presented by Robert Van der Veen and Philippe Van Parijs for the 1986 Analytical Marxism meeting. It was later published in an issue of the journal *Theory & Society*, vol. 15, 1987, along with the Van der Veen and Van Parijs paper and a series of other commentaries. Finally, "Coercion and Consent in Contested Exchange" (chapter 4, written with Michael Burawoy) is a response to a paper, "Contested Exchange," by Sam Bowles and Herb Gintis, discussed at the 1989 meeting. Both papers were published in the June 1990 issue of *Politics & Society*.

All of the rest of the chapters in the volume were originally conceived as talks, given at various universities and conferences. "Capitalism's Futures" (chapter 6) was first presented at a conference on "The Theory of the State in Contemporary Capitalism," at Puebla University, Puebla, Mexico, in October 1979, and at a conference on "New Developments in the Theory of the State," University of Toronto, December 1979. After many revisions (mainly because of theoretical and, perhaps, political disagreements with the editors of the journal), it was published in *Socialist Review*, no. 69, in 1983. "What is Analytical Marxism?" was prepared as the Keynote Talk at the Brazilian Sociological Association Meetings in Rio di Janeiro in June 1989. It was also published in *Socialist Review*, no. 4, 1989. Sections of this essay were later embodied in parts of the first chapter of my book with Andrew Levine and Elliott Sober, *Reconstructing Marxism* (London 1992).

"Explanation and Emancipation in Marxism and Feminism" (chapter 10) was first presented at the American Sociological Association annual meeting in August 1990, and later at the University of Capetown, South Africa, in June 1992. Of all of the papers reprinted in this book, I had the greatest difficulty in originally getting this one published. I first submitted it to the *New Left Review* in 1990. It was sent back to me with many comments and a request for revisions. After making substantial changes which I thought dealt with all of the important objections, I resubmitted the paper. This time it was rejected outright. The members of the editorial board apparently felt that in the paper I unfairly characterized Marxism as having a largely deterministic view of the self-destructive trajectory of capitalism, and that I denigrated feminism by seeing its emancipatory goals as less problematic than those of Marxism. I then submitted the paper to the *Socialist Review* and in relatively short order it was rejected. While the paper was seen as "provocative," many of the members of the editorial board had strong objections to its arguments. My next try was the *American Sociological Review*. I had never tried to publish a theoretical essay there and I thought that perhaps, since left-wing journals seemed not to like this piece, the bastion of establishment sociology would go for it. The rejection was prompt in coming. The paper, I was told, was insufficiently scholarly, lacking adequate references for its various claims about the nature of Marxism and feminism as theoretical traditions. The paper was eventually published in the journal *Sociological Theory* in March 1993.

"Marxism After Communism" (chapter 11) was first presented under this title at the American Sociological Association Meeting, August 1992, but various bits and pieces of it had been presented earlier as talks at various universities in South Africa and the United States. Some of the ideas appeared in an earlier form in the last chapter of *Reconstructing Marxism*. This version of the paper was published in the *New Left Review*, no. 202, November–December 1993.

Finally, "The Class Analysis of Poverty" (chapter 2) was prepared for a conference in October 1993 on "Measuring Social Inequalities in Health" at the National Institute of Child Health and Human Development in Bethesda, Maryland. I was invited in order to bring a "class perspective" to bear on the problem of inequalities of health and decided that the best I could do was to lay out the basic principles of a class analysis of poverty. This paper has not been previously published.

Over the nearly fifteen years that spanned the early drafts of the first of these essays and the final draft of the last of them, profound changes have occurred in both the immediate intellectual context and the broader social and political context within which Marxist scholarship has taken place. In the late 1970s, Marxism was still at the core of intellectual work on the left. Classical Marxist themes and concepts were still being hotly debated – the labor theory of value, historical materialism, the nature of the capitalist state – and many of the classical formulations were still given considerable credibility even by their critics. By the time the final essay, "The Class Analysis of Poverty," was written in the fall of 1993, Marxism no longer held center stage among critical scholars in the academy, and many of the core concepts of the Marxist tradition had either been abandoned or significantly transformed by many people who still considered themselves working within that tradition.

These changes in context are reflected in theoretical and rhetorical shifts across the essays. In some of the earlier essays, for example, discussions of the labor theory of value still appear. In the later essays, the labor theory of value does not figure at all, except occasionally in passing. The two chapters on socialism (chapters 6 and 7), one initially written in 1979 and the other in 1986, more or less take for granted the epochal alternatives of capitalism and socialism, whereas the two essays written in the early 1990s, which discuss the emancipatory project of Marxism (chapters 10 and 11), both treat socialism and communism as problematic concepts in need of serious defense.

It is tempting, given these historical changes in the parameters of intellectual debate, to edit the earlier essays to make them more in keeping with the preoccupations and sophistication of the current period. (In fact, in the initial plans for this book, three essays written in the early 1970s were considered for inclusion – "Recent Developments in Marxist Theories of the State," "Modes of Class Struggle and the Capitalist State," and "The Parsonsian and Structuralist-Marxist Theories of the State" – but I subsequently decided not to include them because they seemed so dated.) I have resisted this temptation and have not expunged the naïvety of any of the essays. The only editing that has been done is the removal of some sections from certain chapters which closely overlap discussions in other chapters and adding occasional short clarifications.

Many people have provided extensive comments, both written and verbal, on many of these chapters. I would particularly like to acknowledge the insightful and often sharp criticisms of Michael Burawoy, who constantly urges me not to give up too much ground in order to be respectable. Many of the papers were dissected at the annual meetings of the Analytical Marxism group attended by Sam Bowles, Robert Brenner, G.A. Cohen, Jon Elster, Adam Przeworski, John Roemer, Hillel Steiner, Robert van der Veen, and Philippe van Parijs. Periodic discussions during dog walks with Andrew Levine and Sunday breakfasts with Joel Rogers are also reflected in many of the pieces. Over the years the graduate students in the class analysis and historical change program within the Wisconsin Sociology Department have been the initial audience and critics for many of the ideas that eventually appeared in these essays.

Falling into Marxism;
Choosing to Stay

In 1968, as a senior at Harvard, I made a film called "The Chess Game" as part of a course I took in animation. Using "solid animation" techniques (i.e., moving a piece slightly and then shooting a frame of film), the film revolves around the action of a set of elaborately carved chess pieces who are playing a chess game. The basic story of the film was simple:

> The pieces march onto the board in military fashion. First the aristocracy enters, followed by the pawns flanked by the knights. Two pawns try to run away, but are captured and brought back to the board. The game starts. Right from the start, the mortality rate for the pawns is very high (from a chess point of view it is a terrible game). When a piece is taken, it falls over and is kicked off the board. The pawns gradually pile up next to the board. Eventually you see them talking to each other, the two sides mixed together. After a while, in a burst of action, they attack the aristocratic pieces playing the game. The soundtrack changes from baroque harpsichord music to Stravinsky's "The Rite of Spring." Before long, the elite are defeated and pushed from the board. The pawns then dance a Virginia Reel folk dance, light and dark pieces intermingled. The screen fades out. But is the story over? No. The picture comes back on and you see the pieces marching back onto the board. They line up to play a new chess game, only this time the pawns are on the back row and the old aristocratic pieces on the front row. The pawns now move like knights, queens, bishops; the elite of the *ancien régime* are reduced to the status of pawns. And the game begins again.

I made that film at a momentous time in the history of the left, in the Western world for sure. The following autumn I showed it at an international student center in Paris. People were still living in the aftermath of the events of May of that year. After the film was shown, a North Vietnamese student stood up and denounced it on the grounds that it represented the complete futility of the attempt at revolutionary change. In his view, the message of the film was *plus ça change, plus c'est la même chose* (the more things change, the more they stay the same). I replied that this was a misunderstanding of the message of the film. The point of the film is that you can't dance a revolutionary square dance on a chessboard. The mistake of the pawns in this fable was to imagine that by simply eliminating the ruling class from the board they could reconstruct a new society. The board was supposed to represent the social structure that produces the games that we play, not simply to provide a "natural" or neutral background for the action. Thus, what the pawns needed to do was to remove the board itself from the field, not just the previous players. In failing to do so, in the end, they recreated the same old game but with a reversal of the traditional roles. You can't dance a square dance for long on a chessboard.

I must admit that this articulate account of the film's message comes from later reflections on my own intuitions that were at work in making the film. Still, I think the film does show something about where my own thinking was at a time before I would have identified my own intellectual work as Marxist. It wasn't really until several years later, during the early 1970s when I was a graduate student, that I first began explicitly to identify my work in this way. Nevertheless, I had all the basic intuitions in place, at least it seems to me, prior to the recognition that, indeed, those intuitions were essentially Marxist intuitions. This is part of what I had in mind when I adopted the title for this chapter, "Falling into Marxism; Choosing to Stay." The allusion is, of course, a somewhat romantic one: you fall in love, but you choose to get married. (And increasingly you choose to stay married, given the ease with which one can get divorced.)

In my own biography, I think that what I learned in my first years in graduate school was that I was already in fact "Marxist" in my own views about the world. This was more of a *discovery* than a *choice*. Given this discovery, however, I have faced a series of more or less conscious choices at various junctures in my career. It is on the nature of these choices that I would like to focus in this discussion.

Reflecting upon the interplay of choice and context is basic bread-and-butter sociology: intended and unintended consequences; rational calculation and normative action; choices under constraints. The particular twist I would like to give to the notion of the dialectic between choice and constraint is found in the story of Ulysses and the Sirens – choices you make today are sometimes consciously made with an eye to constraining your future choices. (This use of the Ulysses and the Sirens metaphor comes from Jon Elster's book, *Ulysses and the Sirens*, Cambridge University Press.) Ulysses knew, as a form of meta-rationality, that he was going to face a situation shortly in which he did *not* want to be able to make choices. He wanted to be tied to the mast, and he instructed the sailors on the ship not to listen to his calls to be released because he knew that if he were free he would bring about his own downfall. At one point in time, therefore, he had the capacity to makes choices that would constrain his future choices.

A series of choices that I've made in the course of my career have this basic Ulysses and the Sirens character: in one way or another I made strategic choices with more or less understanding of how these choices would constrain the possibility of choices in the future. Choices made at five such junctures seem especially important to me. The first of these has to do with the choice to identify my work primarily as *contributing* to Marxism rather than simply *using* Marxism. The second concerns my choice to be a sociologist, rather than some other "ist." The third is the choice to become what some people describe as a multivariate Marxist: to be a Marxist sociologist who engages in grandiose, perhaps over-blown, quantitative research. The fourth choice is the choice of what academic department to be in. This choice was acutely posed to me in 1987 when I spent a year as a visiting professor at the University of California, Berkeley. I had been offered a position there and I had to decide whether I wanted to return to Wisconsin. Returning to Madison was unquestionably a choice. Finally, and the issue that I will spend more time on, is the choice to stay a Marxist in this world of post-Marxisms when many of my intellectual comrades have decided for various good, and sometimes perhaps not so good, reasons to recast their intellectual agenda as being friendly to, but outside of, the Marxist tradition.

To set the stage for this reflection on choice and constraint, let me tell you a little about the trajectory of my life that brought me into the arena of these choices.

I knew that I wanted to be a professor by about age ten. Both of my parents are academics; both of my siblings are academics; both of their spouses are academics. The joke in the family is, the only social mobility is interdepartmental. If you go one generation further back, that's no longer the case; but it was just obvious to me that being a professor was the thing to be. I never experienced that as a real choice. Literally, it never was an experience to decide to become a professor. As long as I can remember ever thinking about what I wanted to do with my life, that's what I wanted to do.

In a funny way being an undergraduate at Harvard was also not really a choice in the sense of a decision coming after a careful weighing of alternatives and thinking through consequences. I was a high-school student in Lawrence, Kansas, the home of the University of Kansas at which my parents taught. By the time I graduated from high school I had accumulated a bunch of credits at the university. All my friends were

going to K.U. It just seemed like the thing to do, to go to K.U. A friend
of the family, Karl Hieder, gave me as a Christmas present in my senior
year in high school an application form to Harvard. He was a graduate
student at Harvard in anthropology at the time. I filled it out and sent it
in. Harvard was the only place to which I applied, not out of inflated self-
confidence but because it was the only application I got as a Christmas
present. When I eventually got accepted (initially I was on the waiting
list), the choice was thus between K.U. and Harvard. I suppose this was a
choice, since I could have decided to stay at K.U. However, it just
seemed so obvious; there was no angst, no weighing of alternatives, no
thinking about the pros and cons. Thus going to Harvard, like becoming
a professor, in a way just *happened*, rather than being *chosen*.

I could list a number of other things of this character: I got a
scholarship to study at Oxford for two years after I finished at Harvard.
Well, for a young intellectual who loved to study and read and liked new
settings, it just seemed ridiculous not to go to Oxford. It was, again, not a
real choice. I didn't weigh the consequences. It was just the obvious thing
for me to do.

My career, however, does not entirely consist of a meandering walk
through non-choices of obvious alternatives, and what I would like to
focus on now is a series of junctures which did have more of the character
of choices in which there was real deliberation and thought about the
implications of different options.

Becoming a Marxist: Accountability and Eclecticism

When I began graduate school in Berkeley in 1971 I was already quite
radicalized intellectually and politically. The previous year I had spent as
a student at a Unitarian seminary in Berkeley, the Thomas Starr King
School of the Ministry. I enrolled in the seminary not out of a deep and
abiding commitment to the ministry as a possible vocation – that never
occurred to me as something I would actually do – but because it was the
only way I could think of at the time to keep out of the army in the
context of the Vietnam war. The enrollments in seminaries, especially in
Unitarian seminaries, increased dramatically in the late 1960s. During
the year I spent at the Unitarian seminary in Berkeley, I was a student
chaplain at San Quentin prison and became actively involved in something called the Prison Law Project. This was an activist organization,
particularly (but not exclusively) linking radical black prisoners with left-
wing lawyers, devoted to challenging prison conditions through litigation
and other forms of activism. In the context of my work with the Prison
Law Project and my role in the prison, I decided with my friends in the

Project to write a book about San Quentin which eventually became published as *The Politics of Punishment*, about half of which was written by myself, and the rest by prisoners and others connected with the Prison Law Project.

The Politics of Punishment was the first context in which I had to deploy systematically my emerging theoretical perspective in an academic context of writing a sustained analysis. I wrote that book during my first year of graduate school in sociology at Berkeley. It was really in that context that it became clear to me that not only were my ideas compatible with Marxism, but indeed that, in terms of my own intellectual commitments, I was a Marxist. There was a discovery, in effect, that there existed an ongoing intellectual tradition which accorded very closely with my views. I came to that understanding not through a deep study of Marx. I hadn't at that point read *Capital*, for example. I had had the typical kind of Harvard undergraduate exposure to certain classic bits of Marxism, and I did a little more of that when I was studying history at Oxford. But basically the discovery that my ideas could properly be labeled "Marxist" was not the result of insights informed by a careful reading of the classics, but rather of an exposure to the central themes and current debates of Marxism as an ongoing intellectual tradition. I thus came to Marxism more through the contemporary substantive arguments of class analysis and political economy than through classical texts.

While I discovered that my ideas fell firmly within the Marxist tradition, there was still a basic choice to be made. This is the first crucial branch point that I want to identify. Among radical intellectuals there is an important distinction between defining one's work as *drawing from the Marxist tradition* on the one hand, or seeing one's work as *contributing to the reconstruction of Marxism* on the other. Many scholars acknowledge that their work is, in important ways, inspired by Marxism without taking the additional step of seeing it as contributing to Marxism. One can, if you will, *do* Marxism without *being* a Marxist.

Most of what I have written, if you strip away certain rhetorical parts which make a big deal about how this is contributing to Marxism, could almost as well have been written in the softer spirit of Marxist inspiration. I could have framed my arguments by saying something like "the Marxist tradition is a rich and interesting source of ideas. We can learn a lot from it. Let's see where we can go by taking these traditional notions of class and massaging them, changing them, combining them with other elements in various ways." I could have cast my class analysis this way without any commitment to Marxism *per se* as a tradition worth reconstructing.

Many sociologists in the late 1960s and early 1970s, radical intellec-

tuals of my generation, made the opposite choice. Take as an example
Theda Skocpol's work, especially her first book, *States and Social
Revolutions*. This book could have been written as a Marxist work with
no change in any substantive thesis in it. It could have been written as a
book that was amending and reconstructing certain weaknesses in the
Marxist tradition in order to rebuild and strengthen that tradition.
Instead she chose, for reasons that she would have to explain in her own
set of intellectual and personal coordinates, to treat the book as a
dialogue with the Marxist tradition but firmly, rhetorically, outside it. I
made the opposite choice. The question is, why did I do this, what was
my thinking behind it?

Let me give you a vignette which I think helps to reveal what's at issue
here. In 1986 I gave a talk in Warsaw called "Rethinking Once Again,
Alas, the Marxist Concept of Class" or some pretentious title like that. In
the talk I discussed such things as contradictory class locations, exploitation and post-capitalistic society, the role of control over different kinds
of assets for constructing new kinds of exploitation, and so on. After-
wards, the first question was the following: "Professor Wright, I find
your ideas very interesting and very compelling. I think there is a lot to be
discussed about them, but why do you call this *Marxist*? Why deflect
attention from what you are really talking about by saying that this has
anything to do with Marxism?" What is at issue here is a dramatic
difference in the contexts for pursuing radical intellectual work. In the
Polish context to declare that this was a reconstruction of Marxism meant
something utterly different from what the same statement means, the
same words mean, when they are declared in the context of American
sociology. In Poland, to reconstruct Marxism is to salvage the ideology of
state repression. In the United States, to embed one's work in a rhetoric
of reconstructing Marxism means something entirely different.

Thus I think the first motivation behind the declaration of my work as
contributing to Marxism centers around a point in the sociology of
knowledge. What does it mean to define one's work as integral to an
oppositional current within an established set of institutions? This is very
close to what sociologists mean when they talk about "reference
groups," although I think this is not simply a question of the *people* to
whom one feels connected and to whom one feels responsible. What
really was at stake for me was the nature of the *constituency* or audience
to whom I wanted to feel accountable. Whose criticisms did I want to
worry about, and whose did I want to simply be able to dismiss?

This issue of active constituency or reference group is reflected in the
gut reaction I get when a paper of mine is rejected by the *American
Sociological Review*, which happens quite regularly, in contrast to the
way I feel when I get a paper rejected by the *New Left Review*, which

happens less regularly, but does happen. (As noted in the Preface, the paper on Marxism and feminism on which chapter 10 of this book is based was rejected by *New Left Review* after it had been carefully revised in light of the editorial board's criticisms.) When I get a paper rejected by the *ASR* I am basically pissed off. I'm annoyed and frustrated by the amount of additional work, usually of a boring technical character which will have no consequences for any substance of knowledge, that I'm forced to do to deal with the objections that have been raised. When I have a paper rejected by the *New Left Review* I get worried, it makes me very anxious. I need a bigger space of time even to think through the criticisms. In the case of my paper on Marxism and feminism I got ten single-spaced pages of criticisms back from the board of the *NLR*. I couldn't even read them until I had a period of a couple of days uncluttered by other work; it was too anxiety-provoking for me even to contend with the ideas and issues they were raising. That never happens when I get rejected from the *ASR*. I just get mad about it and go about my business.

These psychological issues are an important part of what is at stake in making the choice to see my work as embedded in the Marxist tradition, as contributing to the reconstruction of that tradition rather than simply drawing on it. Defining my work this way establishes whom I am accountable to, whose opinions are going to matter. The issue of reference group, however, is not just psychological, since reference groups are also social networks that dispose of real resources and impose real pressures of various kinds. Choosing a reference group, then, has the effect of creating a set of constraints which one faces in the future.

In the decision to describe my work as contributing to Marxism, then, there is a kind of Ulysses and the Sirens story at work. It is an attempt, however imperfect, at blocking certain pressures of co-optation which one experiences once one enters a profession. It is an attempt to make life *more* difficult for oneself. The same holds true for feminist sociologists today. Some feminists say that their work is contributing to feminism as such. Rather than just contributing to sociology inspired by feminism, they see their work as contributing to building Feminist Theory. Such declarations make life more difficult, since you could say most of the same things without framing your agenda in this more provocative manner. Making one's life more difficult in this way, however, is not a sign of masochism; it is a strategy which makes it harder to slide inadvertently into a theoretical and intellectual practice which is overwhelmed by its acceptability. The pressures for mild, non-confrontational, acceptable scholarship are enormous, and situating one's work firmly in a radical oppositional current is one way of partially neutralizing those pressures.

*

There is another side to the choice to contribute to building Marxism as an intellectual tradition rather than simply to use it, which entered my own decisions and which has become increasingly important in my subsequent ongoing decision to stay in Marxism rather than to become, as is fashionable these days, post-Marxist. This second aspect of the choice raises philosophy of science rather than sociology of knowledge issues. What is the best way to contribute to the enhancement of our knowledge of social life? Is the most productive strategy to work within what one considers the best available paradigm, or is it better to take a more eclectic approach, avoiding any strong commitment to a single perspective but instead picking and choosing from different traditions as is appropriate for different particular questions one might ask? In a somewhat stylized way we can contrast two stances towards these issues: a stance which places great value on ambitious programs for theoretical coherence and integration in the form of a sustained paradigm, and a stance, which is sometimes referred to as a more empiricist approach, which argues that what we want to do is deeply and intensively describe the world while eclectically drawing from different sorts of ideas as we see fit for different problems.

My views on this contrast of intellectual practices are not the conventional ones for someone who is committed to a paradigmatic view of knowledge in his own work. Most people who are committed to some kind of effort at building strong paradigms are anti-eclectic: eclecticism is viewed as the enemy of paradigm-building. I believe, to the contrary, that there is a symbiotic relationship between paradigm-mongers and carefree eclectics. The optimal intellectual terrain for radical theory – or for any sociological knowledge for that matter – is a mixture of people who are committed eclectics and people who are committed paradigmists. If I could snap my fingers and make every radical intellectual a committed Marxist, I wouldn't do it. I think it would be bad for Marxism, and certainly bad for the left. If I could snap my fingers and make everybody a committed eclectic, if that's not an oxymoron, I would also not do it. Eclecticism is in a certain sense parasitic on committed paradigms. To be an effective eclectic, you've got to have some other scholars around who are worrying obsessively about how to rebuild paradigms and maintain the maximum coherence possible within them. But if that's what everyone did, it would reduce the possibility of effectively reconstructing paradigms because the puzzles and worries and anomalies that a reconstructive project faces often come from the insights generated by the eclectics.

The environment of intellectual work which I see as optimal, and which I try to achieve to the extent possible in the intellectual circles within which I work, thus values an intellectual pluralism in which no one is holier-than-thou about meta-theoretical principles. Dialogue between the doubts of the eclectics and the commitments of the paradigmists strengthen both. These issues hold for contemporary feminism as well as Marxism. In the feminist tradition radical feminism is crucial for healthy feminism, even though I think radical feminism is the least plausible version of feminism. Still, it would be a shame for the feminist tradition if radical feminists were somehow persuaded to abandon the most radical and extreme forms of feminism. Similarly for the socialist tradition of intellectual work, it is important to have a body of scholarship and intellectual work which remains committed to rebuilding, rather than simply drawing from, the Marxist tradition.

Becoming a Sociologist: Non-disciplines and Intellectual Pluralism

The second choice was the fateful decision to become a sociologist. I still consider myself as being in sociology rather than of sociology. I see sociology as a platform on which to do my work rather than a discipline to which I feel any great commitment as such (although I have to admit that over time my sense of loyalty to the field has grown a bit). As an undergraduate I majored in an interdisciplinary social science program (social studies), after which I studied history for two years at Oxford. I see myself as a social scientist and social theorist rather than a capital 'S' Sociologist. Why, then, did I choose sociology as an academic home?

Of all the available social sciences, sociology seemed to me to be the *least disciplinary*; it had the fuzziest boundaries. But even more significantly, sociology has valued its own marginal traditions in a way that other social sciences don't. In economics, Marx is described as a third-rate post-Ricardian. (That's a famous quote by Paul Samuleson, the Nobel prize-winning economist.) Even anti-Marxist sociologists recognize the importance of Marx as one of the intellectual founders of what has become sociology. All graduate courses in theory contain at least some reading of Marx. There are economic departments in which the name Marx would never be mentioned. The only social science discipline that might have served as well as sociology was political science, and I suppose if I had been at some other university I might have become a political scientist. But at Berkeley I felt that sociology was a more congenial place in which to be a radical, and in general I now think that political science tends to be somewhat less hospitable to radicalism because of the tight relationship between political science and the state. Political science is a breeding place for government advisers and policy analysts, and that aspect of political science as a discipline would be a constraint that I did not want to choose. So, I chose sociology.

Becoming a Multivariate Marxist: Legitimating Marxism and Careerism

Very quickly in graduate school, even in a place like Berkeley, it becomes clear where the intellectual core of the discipline lies. Having decided to be a sociologist and having as a mission the reconstruction of Marxism as a social science, I saw as a crucial task of my work to try to increase the credibility of Marxism within the academy, and I felt that quantitative research would accomplish this. As I wrote in an essay published in the *Berkeley Journal of Sociology* in 1987, reflecting on my early theoretical ambitions: "I originally had visions of glorious paradigm battles, with lances drawn and the valiant Marxist knight unseating the bourgeois rival in a dramatic quantitative joust. What is more, the fantasy saw the vanquished admitting defeat and changing horses as a result."

My decision to launch a series of projects at the core of which were sophisticated statistical techniques was not driven by any epistemological conviction that these techniques generated deeper or more reliable knowledge. Indeed, on that score I have found nearly always that I learn more from good qualitative and historical research than from research by quanto-maniacs. But I felt that at that point in the history of Marxism in sociology (the mid 1970s), establishing the credibility of Marxism within a quantitative methodology had the greatest chance of making a difference in the intellectual space Marxists could occupy within the academy.

To be honest, there was also, from the start, a darker side to the appeal of quantitative research. Just as it became clear where the intellectual core of sociology was going in the 1970s, it was also clear what kinds of research were likely to generate grants and acclaim. All academic disciplines as institutions contain a system of rewards and sanctions that channels work in particular directions, and there were clearly more resources to be had through quantitative research. I was very ambitious as a young scholar – ambitious in my search for what I considered to be the "truth," but also ambitious for status, recognition, influence, world travel. Embarking on a line of research anchored in conventional survey research thus offered tangible rewards.

I cannot reconstruct exactly what the balance of these motives was in the mid 1970s when I did my dissertation research – a quantitative study of class structure and income determination – or the late 1970s when I began my still ongoing comparative project on class structure and class consciousness. But whatever the balance between grantsmanship and intellectual purpose, the choice to direct my research in this way has been enormously consequential, and not always in ways to my liking. It has resulted in a narrowing of askable questions and divergence between much of my best theoretical work and my empirical research. Originally, the idea in 1978 when I began the comparative class analysis project was to do a survey of class structure and class consciousness in the US, Italy, and Sweden. This was meant to be a brush-cleaning operation: settling and clarifying a range of empirical issues before returning to the problems I cared about the most – the state, politics, social change. It is now fifteen years later. The survey has been done in sixteen countries, including much of Western Europe, the USA, Canada, Australia, New Zealand and Japan, as well as most recently Russia, South Korea, Taiwan and a second USA survey. Because of the scale of the enterprise, I have created a set of expectations and commitments that cannot be easily (or responsibly) abandoned, and yet the work does not always yield intellectual insights in proportion to the time and resources the project absorbs.

Choosing a Department: Professional vs. Intellectual Sociology

I initially went to the University of Wisconsin without a great deal of thought and deliberation. I had some graduate school friends there and the department actively recruited me, so I never really went on a national job search to explore all options. In 1987–8, however, I spent a year at the University of California in Berkeley, and by the end of the year was clearly faced with a genuine, unmistakable choice, a choice laden with "road not taken" potentials.

Here is how I would characterize the big difference between these two departments. If you think of the famous people in the Berkeley department, what comes to mind are titles of books. When you think of the famous people in the Wisconsin department, what comes to mind is the journals in which they publish and the topics which they pursue. Philip Selznick is *TVA and the Grass Roots*; Bob Hauser is Mr. Mobility. Wisconsin is an article-writing department and Berkeley is a book-writing department.

This contrast between the two departments is also reflected in the nature of their graduate programs: at Wisconsin a significant number of graduate students write dissertations that are spin-offs in one way or another from large, ongoing research projects. The model of education is that of an apprenticeship, and while students are expected to do original and innovative work, the core model is to do so within the context of some professor's research shop. At Berkeley, it is quite rare for students to play this apprenticeship role. Students are expected to be autonomous intellectuals; dissertations are supposed to be first drafts of books. While graduate students may get systematic feedback from their professors, it is rare that dissertations are in any direct way derivative of the data and projects of their advisers.

In agonizing about the choice of where to be, I stylized the contrast between these two settings by saying that Berkeley was one of the leading intellectual departments in which I would be on the discipline-oriented wing, whereas Wisconsin was one of the leading discipline-oriented departments in which I would be on the intellectual wing. Which of these settings, I thought, do I want to be in? Which would provide the most creative context for my future work? The irony was that although I actually found the intellectual climate of Berkeley more interesting in many ways than that of Wisconsin, I felt that I would be more challenged and pushed in more interesting ways if I was more an intellectual maverick in a disciplinary department than a disciplinary maverick in an intellectualized one. I felt that at this point in history and at this point in my life, perhaps, the creative tension would be more constructive in Madison. At Berkeley I would be constantly arguing with the post-structuralist, post-modernist currents about the relevance of culture for everything and the impossibility of explaining anything. In Madison I would be arguing for the importance of an open and dialectical perspective on the relationship between social change and social action and the need for unconventional voices in sociology. So, for better or for worse, I returned to Wisconsin.

Staying a Marxist

Increasingly in the 1980s there have been many divorces in the intellectual tradition of Marxism. These divorces have a name now – post-Marxism. Post-Marxism is very different from earlier ex-Marxisms. In the 1950s, the people who abandoned Marxism often became apologists for the established order. The anti-communist ex-Marxists of those years became enemies of Marxism. Post-Marxism is a very different phenomenon and really shouldn't be viewed in the same way at all. When I became radicalized and first began my intellectual work, Marxism really was the only game in town and if you were serious as an intellectual and really wanted to develop theory, in some way or another you had to find a home in or make peace with the Marxist tradition, whether or not you then used the label as a self-designation. That's just not true any longer; there are many currents of radical thought which, to a greater or lesser extent, break with Marxism. Feminism, of course, is the most vibrant of these on the contemporary American scene, but many other kinds of theoretical currents exist as well. Many erstwhile Marxists have thus opted for some variety of post-Marxism. Sometimes this occurs in the form of a declaration in an article or book in which they announce their break; sometimes the shift occurs simply by drifting into a different mode of writing and thinking.

Well, I've remained stubbornly working inside of Marxism and continue to work for the reconstruction rather than abandonment of this intellectual tradition. I do so primarily for the two reasons I described earlier – that this continues to be a way to remain accountable to a radical intellectual constituency and that in a pluralist environment of models of theoretical work, the eclecticism of others requires the reconstruction of theoretical paradigms.

I have not, however, pursued this goal simply as an individual project of my own. Reconstructing Marxism is not the lonely task of an isolated, ivory-towered intellectual. To sustain these commitments and to hope to accomplish these goals requires embedding oneself in a particular set of social networks, a particular circle of people whose work one reads and with whom one discusses issues. A "reference group" is not just an impersonal audience defined by some social category; it is also a circle of people with names and addresses who constitute the active, ongoing basis for the intellectual interactions which spur one's own intellectual development.

In my case, there are two such concrete reference groups that anchor my work. The first "group" consists of a single person, Michael Burawoy, a professor of sociology at Berkeley. Michael and I have read nearly every page that either of us has written in the past fifteen years or so. He is constantly reminding me not to lose sight of the ultimate point of it all by becoming preoccupied with analytical rigor at the expense of political relevance; I am constantly telling him to be more precise in his formulations, to be clearer about the underlying logic of the conceptual distinctions he makes. Our intellectual styles are quite at odds with one another in many ways. He does ethnographic research of an extra- ordinarily fine-grained character; my research has been quantitative, typically obliterating much of the nuance and texture of the subjects I study. He is generally skeptical of claims about "objective" truth; I have generally defended rather conventional philosophical views of the scientific aspirations of Marxism and sociology. We have discussed these issues and their bearing on our respective work while walking my dog in the woods and looking for open restaurants in Moscow. (This dialogue has been made public in the form of a series of published exchanges between the two of us in the 1987 and 1989 issues of the *Berkeley Journal of Sociology*. The first of these exchanges is reprinted in my 1990 book, *The Debate on Classes*; the second appears as chapter 9 in this volume.) The particular way in which personal loyalty and closeness is combined with intellectual difference in our relationship has been for me a vital source of intellectual challenge and encouragement. It is also, surely, at least part of the personal dimension of "staying" Marxist.

My deep and abiding relationship with Michael Burawoy acts as a kind of antidote to the second powerful reference group in which I am embedded, a group of scholars that has been at the core of an intellectual current known since the mid 1980s as "Analytical Marxism." (See chapter 8 for a discussion of some of the core principles which guide the discussions of the group.) The group has a less high-blown name that it gives to itself: the NBSMG – the Non-Bullshit Marxism Group. (Actually there was a discussion once in the group as to whether this was *non*-bullshit or *no* bullshit, there being a very subtle nuance in the distinction, but I can't reconstruct the philosophical debate.) The NBSMG is a group of scholars from five or six different countries that meets every September in London for a three-day conference. Some of the names are relatively familiar – Jon Elster, Adam Przeworski, G.A. Cohen, John Roemer, Robert Brenner, Sam Bowles – and a few others may be less so to American sociologists – Robert Van der Veen, Philippe Van Parijs, Pranab Bardhan and Hillel Steiner. The group formed in 1979 with no intention of becoming an on-going event. I became a part of it in 1981 and have met with them every year since but one. We meet in the same room every year. We eat the same festive dinner every year. Mostly, we only see each other on this three-day period and it's like a little chunk of the year snipped out, reserved for this special world. You have the rest of the year, then you have your three-day, no-bullshit meeting in London.

Here's how the meetings work. Usually, of the ten or eleven people who attend a meeting, about half will write papers. These get distributed five or six weeks in advance. At the meeting itself, one person is assigned to introduce a given paper; participants do not present their own papers. We spend roughly an hour and a half to two hours demolishing/discussing the paper in a no-holds-barred manner. The group is, as one might predict, all men. The intellectual style is intense and analytically exhausting. To an outsider, many of the discussions might seem destructive, but I think this is a mistake. The interactions involve a particular form of masculine intellectual aggressiveness that is not inherently invalidating; the very act of taking each other's work so seriously is itself an affirmation of respect and support. An outsider wouldn't necessarily see this. If you saw the behavior, you might think this was a gladiatorial combat in which death was the only possible outcome. But from the inside it is an enormously exciting setting for coming to terms with the subtle problems and gaps in one's ideas and gaining insights about the inner workings of other people's work.

[*Digression*: We have discussions in the group from time to time about gender issues, both as a topic – I presented my paper on Marxism and feminism at the 1991 meeting – and as an issue in the group's composition. For better or worse, nobody in the group knew well any women scholars who both shared an interest in the substantive topics about which we were concerned and engaged those topics in the intellectual style that marked the group. To be honest, I suppose, many members of the group probably felt that the kind of intensity of the group would also be harder to sustain if it were gender mixed. In any event, no women have been recruited as members of the "club," although several have been invited at various times. In these terms the NBSMG raises important, and troubling, issues in the sociology of gender. Networks of this sort are the real sites where productive intellectual development occurs, where ideas are forged and refined. While the NBSMG does not control any financial resources – it gives no grants and until 1993 everyone always paid for his own travel – nevertheless as a vigorous interpersonal network of intellectual exchange, it is influential and valuable. Undoubtedly the gender composition of the network both reflects the historically marginalized role of women intellectuals in the Marxist tradition and contributes in some way to sustaining such gender inequality.]

Since the early 1980s, the NBSMG has been the organized reference group that has mattered most to me. When I write a paper, the ghosts who sit in the back of my room and periodically jump up to tell me that what I have written is ridiculous, and make me worry about whether I got it right, are mainly from this group (or, perhaps, kindred spirits of this group). The group has unquestionably given my work a particular direction and cast because I have to worry, by virtue of this reference group, about certain issues while others seem less pressing.

The chapters which follow are all products of this intellectual and personal trajectory. They embody the tensions of that trajectory, tensions between radical egalitarian values and elite academic professionalism; between the commitment to Marxism as a vibrant intellectual and political tradition and the fear of being trapped in indefensible, outmoded assumptions; between being relevant to real struggles and devoting my energies to refinements of abstract concepts. These tensions are impossible to escape, at least for me, but I hope in the end that they have been creative tensions that have pushed my ideas forward and kept me from sliding into comfortable complacency.

PART I

Class Analysis

Introduction

Class analysis is at the heart of Marxism as a tradition of social theory. In one way or another, class figures in nearly all explanations Marxists produce, whether of conjunctural problems or broad historical tendencies. And at the core of class analysis is a specific way of thinking about the problem of economic inequalities: inequalities among people are seen not mainly as the consequence of their individual attributes (intelligence, education, motivation, etc.), but of the way the system of production is organized around mechanisms of exploitation.

The chapters in Part I explore a variety of different problems in class analysis. Chapter 1, "Inequality," attempts to define a variety of different types of inequality that social scientists study, and then to give precision to class analysis as a way of understanding inequalities in material welfare. The central argument of the chapter involves clarifying the contrast between explanations of inequality that focus on variations in individual achievement and the obstacles to "equal opportunity," and explanations that focus on class exploitation.

The second chapter, "The Class Analysis of Poverty," carries the argument further by focusing more intensively on the specific problem of poverty. The first part of the chapter gives greater precision to a class analysis of poverty by formally distinguishing it from three other types of explanations prevalent both in the popular imagination and in scholarly works. The second part then elaborates the substance of a class analysis of poverty by developing the contrast between *non-exploitative economic oppression* and *exploitation* as ways of distinguishing different forms of poverty.

Chapter 3, "The Status of the Political in the Concept of Class Structure," and chapter 4 (written with Michael Burawoy), "Coercion and Consent in Contested Exchange," both concern the problem of domination in the analysis of class relations. The first of these chapters engages John Roemer's influential work on class and exploitation.

19

Roemer argues forcefully that while domination may be important in protecting property rights, it is not important in understanding exploitation and class since exploitation can occur without the exploiters directly dominating the exploited. I argue that domination remains an essential part of the very definition of class relations. The second of these chapters discusses the very interesting work of Sam Bowles and Herbert Gintis on surveillance and coercion within the labor process. They are interested in showing that under conditions in which it is impossible to specify fully the criteria for the fulfillment of a contract and contracts cannot be costlessly monitored, exchange relations will have an essentially contested character. This has important implications for the nature of domination within what they call the "labor extraction function" – basically, exploitation – in the production process. In our critique, Michael Burawoy and I argue that various mechanisms which generate consent to exploitation are as important as domination in understanding how labor effort is extracted within production. We try to show how sociological attention should focus on the forms of variability of coercion and consent within contested exchange rather than exclusively emphasizing one or the other.

Chapter 5, "Class and Politics," shifts the focus from a discussion of the internal logic of class analysis and its differences from other forms of social theory, to the problem of using class analysis to understand politics. Building on the conceptual distinctions Robert Alford and Roger Friedland make between situational power, institutional power, and systemic power, the chapter explores three clusters of mechanisms through which class shapes politics: the class-based access to resources which can be strategically deployed for political purposes; the institutionalization of certain class-biases into the design of state apparatuses; and the way in which the operation of the economic system as a whole universalizes certain class interests.

1

Inequality

To speak of a social inequality is to describe some valued attribute which can be distributed across the relevant units of a society in different quantities, where "inequality" therefore implies that different units possess different amounts of this attribute. The units can be individuals, families, social groups, communities, nations; the attributes include such things as income, wealth, status, knowledge, and power. The study of inequality then consists of explaining the determinants and consequences of the distribution of these attributes across the appropriate units.

This chapter has four principal objectives: first, I will propose a general typology of *forms of inequality*. This typology will help to map out the conceptual terrain of the discussion. Second, I will examine debates on the conceptual status of one particular type of inequality within this typology: inequality in material welfare. In particular, I will examine the debate over whether or not material inequalities in contemporary societies should be viewed as rooted in *exploitation*. Third, I will examine the implications of these contending views of material inequality for strategies for empirical research on income inequality. Finally, I will discuss the relationship between contending accounts of income inequality and the analysis of social classes.

A Typology of Inequalities

Social inequalities can be distinguished along two dimensions: first, whether the unequally distributed attribute in question is a *monadic* attribute or a *relational* attribute; and second, whether the process of acquisition of a particular magnitude of this attribute by the individual can be considered a monadic or relational *process*.

Monadic and relational attributes

A monadic attribute is any property of a given unit (individual, family, community, etc.) whose magnitude can be defined without any reference to other units. Material consumption is a good example: one can assess how much an individual unit consumes in either real terms or monetary terms without knowing how much any other unit consumes. This does not mean that the attribute in question has no social content to it. Monetary income, for example, is certainly a social category: having an annual income of $30,000 only represents a source of inequality given that other people are willing to exchange commodities for that income, and this implies that the income has an irreducibly social content to it. Nevertheless, income is a monadic attribute in the present sense in so far as one can measure its magnitude without knowing the income of other units. Of course, we would not know whether this magnitude was high or low – that requires comparisons with other units. But the magnitude of any given unit is measurable independently of any other unit.

Relational attributes, in contrast, cannot be defined independently of other units. "Power" is a good example. As Jon Elster writes: "In one simple conceptualization of power, my amount of power is defined by the number of people *over whom* I have control, so the relational character of power appears explicitly."[1] To be powerless is to be controlled by others; to be powerful is to control others. It is impossible to measure the power of any unit without reference to the power of others.

Monadic and relational processes

Certain unequally distributed attributes are acquired through what can be called a monadic process. To describe the distribution process (as opposed to the attribute itself) as monadic is to say that the immediate mechanisms which cause the magnitude in question are attached to the individual units and generate their effects autonomously from other units.

A simple example of a monadic process that generates inequalities is the distribution of body weight in a population. The distribution of weight in a population of adults is certainly unequal – some people weigh three times the average weight of the population, some people weigh half as much as the average. An individual's weight is a monadic

---

1. Jon Elster, *Making Sense of Marx*, Cambridge 1985, p. 94.

attribute – it can be measured independently of the weight of any other individual. And the weight acquisition process is also essentially monadic: it is the result of mechanisms (genes, eating habits, etc.) directly attached to the individual. This is not to say, of course, that these mechanisms are not themselves shaped by social (relational) causes: social causes may influence genetic endowments (through marriage patterns – e.g. norms governing skinny people marrying fat people) and social causes may shape eating habits. Such social explanations of body weight distributions, however, would still generally be part of a monadic process in the following sense: social causes may help to explain why individuals have the weight-regulating mechanisms they have (genes, habits), but the actual weight of any given individual results from these individual weight-regulating mechanisms acting in isolation from the weight-regulating mechanisms of other individuals. The empirical distribution of weights in the population is therefore simply the sum of these monadic processes of the individuals within the distribution.

Now, we can imagine a social process through which weight was determined in which this description would be radically unsatisfactory. Imagine a society in which there was insufficient food for every member of the society to be adequately nourished, and, further, that social power among individuals determined how much food each individual consumed. Under these conditions there is a *causal* relation between how much food a fat (powerful) person eats and how little is consumed by a skinny (powerless) person. In such a situation, the immediate explanation of any given individual's consumption of food depends on the social *relations* that link that individual to others, not simply on monadic mechanisms. Such an inequality-generating process, therefore, would be described as a relational rather than a monadic process. More generally, to describe the process by which inequalities are generated as relational is to say that the mechanisms which determine the magnitude of the unequally distributed attribute for each individual unit causally depends upon the mechanisms generating the magnitude for other individuals.

Taking these two dimensions of inequality together, we can generate a typology of ideal-typical forms of inequality. This typology is deliberately a simplification: the causal processes underlying the distribution of most inequalities will involve both monadic and relational mechanisms. Nevertheless, the simplification will help to clarify the conceptual map of inequalities which we have been discussing (see Table 1.1).

"Power" is perhaps the paradigmatic example of a relationally determined relational inequality. Not only is power measurable only rela-

Table 1.1   Typology of Forms of Inequality

		Form of the Unequal Attribute	
		Relational	*Monadic*
Form of the Process of Distribution of Attributes	*Relational*	Power, Status	Income
	Monadic	Talent	Health, Weight

tionally, but power is acquired and distributed through a relational process of competition and conflict between contending individuals, groups, nations, etc.[2]

Power is not, however, the only example. Social status is also generally an example of a relationally determined relational attribute. Status is intrinsically a relational attribute in that "high" status only has meaning relative to lower statuses; there is no absolute metric of status. The process of acquisition of such high status is also generally a relational process of exclusion of rival contenders for status through competitive and coercive means. (Under special circumstances status-acquisition may be a largely monadic process. In artistic production, for example, one could imagine a situation in which each individual simply does the best he or she can and achieves a certain level of performance. There is nothing in one person's achievement of a given level of performance that precludes anyone else achieving a similar level. The status that results from that achievement, however, is still relational: if many people achieve the highest possible level of performance, then this level accords them less status than if few do, but the acquisition process would not itself be a relational one. In general, however, since the process by which the level of performance itself is achieved is a competitive one in which people are excluded from facilities for learning and enhancing performance, status acquisition is itself a relational process.)

The distribution of health is a largely a monadic process for the distribution of a monadic attribute. In general, as in the weight acquisition case, the mechanisms which determine an individual's health –

---

2. For discussions of power as a term of inequality, see Steven Lukes, *Power: a Radical View*, London 1974 and Gerhard Lenski, *Power and Privilege*, New York 1966.

genetic dispositions, personal habits, etc. – do not causally affect the health of anyone else. There are, however, two important kinds of exceptions to this monadic causal process, both of which imply a relational process for the distribution of health as a monadic inequality. First, contagious diseases are clearly an example of a process through which the mechanisms affecting health in one person causally affect the health of another. More significantly for social theory, where the distribution of health in a population is shaped by the distribution of medical services, and medical services are relatively fixed in quantity and unequally distributed, then the causal mechanism producing health in one person may well affect the health of another in a relational manner.

Talent is an example of a relational attribute that is unequally distributed through a monadic process. A "talent" can be viewed as a particular kind of genetic endowment – one that enhances the individual's ability to acquire various skills. To be musically talented means to be able to learn to play and compose music easily, not actually to play and compose music well (a potential prodigy who has never seen a piano cannot play it well). Talents are caused through a monadic process, since the causal mechanism which determines one person's latent capacities to acquire skills does not affect anyone else's. (Obviously, parents' talent-generating mechanisms – genes – can affect their children's through inheritance. This is identical to the effect of parents' genes in the weight example. The point is that the effectivity of one person's genes is independent of anyone else's.) The attribute so produced, however, is clearly relational: a talent is only a talent by virtue of being a deviation from the norm. If everyone had the same capacity to write music as Mozart, he would not have been considered talented.

Income inequality, at least according to certain theories of income determination (more on this below), could be viewed as an example of a relational process for distributing a monadic attribute. Income is a monadic attribute in so far as one individual's income is definable independently of the income of anyone else. But the process of acquisition of income is plausibly a relational one: the mechanisms by which one person acquires an income causally affects the income of others.

Inequalities in Material Welfare: Achievement versus Exploitation

More than any other single kind of inequality, inequalities of material welfare have been the object of study by social scientists. Broadly speaking, there are two distinct conceptualizations which have dominated the analysis of this kind of inequality in market societies. These I will call the achievement and exploitation perspectives.

Achievement models

The achievement model of income determination fundamentally views income acquisition as a process of individuals acquiring income as a return for their own efforts, past and present. The paradigm case would be two farmers on adjacent plots of land: one works hard and conscientiously, the other is lazy and irresponsible. At the end of a production cycle one has twice the income of the other. This is clearly a monadic process producing a distribution of a monadic outcome.

The story then continues: the conscientious farmer saves and reinvests part of the income earned during the first cycle and thus expands production; the lazy farmer does not have anything left over to invest and thus continues production at the same level. The result is that over time the inequality between the two farmers increases, but still through a strictly monadic process.

Eventually, because of a continually expanding scale of production, the conscientious farmer is unable to farm his/her entire assets through his/her own work. Meanwhile the lazy farmer has wasted his/her resources and is unable to adequately support him/herself on his/her land. The lazy farmer therefore goes to work as a wage-earner for the conscientious farmer. Now, clearly, a relational mechanism enters the analysis, since the farm laborer acquires income in a wage paid by the farmer-employer. However, in the theory of wage-determination adopted in these kinds of models in which the laborer is paid exactly the marginal product of labor, this wage is exactly equivalent to the income the laborer would have received simply by producing the same commodities on his/her own account for the market. The relational mechanism, therefore, simply mirrors the initial monadic process.

In such achievement models of income acquisition genuinely relational processes may exist, but generally speaking these have the conceptual status of deviations from the pure model reflecting various kinds of disequilibria. In the sociological versions of achievement models – typically referred to as "status attainment" models of stratification – these deviations are treated as effects of various kinds of ascriptive factors (race, sex, ethnicity) which act as obstacles to "equal opportunity." Similarly, in the economic versions of such models – generally referred to as "human capital" models – the deviations either reflect transitory market disequilibria or the effects of various kinds of extra-economic discrimination.[3] In both the sociological and economic versions, these relational mechanisms of income determination that produce deviations from the pure achievement models mean that certain kinds of people are prevented from getting full income pay-off from their individual efforts. The inner logic of the process, in short, is monadic with contingent relational disturbances.

Exploitation models

Exploitation models of income inequality regard the income distribution process as fundamentally relational. The basic argument is as follows: in order to obtain income, people enter into a variety of different kinds of social relations. These will vary historically and can be broadly classified as based in different "modes of production." Through a variety of different mechanisms, these relations enable one group of people to appropriate the fruits of labor of another group.[4] This appropriation is called exploitation. Exploitation implies that the income of the exploiting group at least in part depends on the efforts of the exploited group rather than simply their own effort. It is in this sense that income inequality generated within exploitative modes of production is intrinsically relational.

There are a variety of different concepts of exploitation contending in current debates. The most promising, in my judgment, is based on the work of Roemer.[5] In Roemer's account, different forms of exploitation are rooted in different forms of property relations, based on the ownership of different kinds of productive assets. Roemer emphasizes two types of property in his analysis: property in the means of production (or alienable assets) and property in skills (or inalienable assets). Unequal distribution of the first of these constitutes the basis for capitalist exploitation; unequal distribution of the second constitutes the basis, in his analysis, for socialist exploitation.

While Roemer criticizes the labor theory of value as a technical basis for analyzing capitalist exploitation, nevertheless his basic defense of the logic of capitalist exploitation is quite in tune with traditional

---

3. The classic account of human capital theory is given by G.S. Becker, *Human Capital*, New York 1975. For his analysis of discrimination, see G.S. Becker, *The Economics of Discrimination*, Chicago 1971.

4. G.A. Cohen, "The Labor Theory of Value and the Concept of Exploitation," *Philosophy and Public Affairs*, no. 8, 1979.

5. John Roemer, *A General Theory of Exploitation and Class*, Cambridge, Mass. 1983. For a debate over Roemer's formulation, see *Politics and Society*, vol. II, no. 3, 1982.

Marxist intuitions: capitalists appropriate part of the surplus produced
by workers by virtue of having exclusive ownership of the means of
production. Socialist or skill exploitation is a less familiar notion. Such
exploitation is reflected in income returns to skills which is out of
proportion to the costs of acquiring the skills. Typically this dispropor-
tion – or "rent" component of the wage – will be reproduced through
the institutionalization of credentials. Credentials, therefore, constitute
the legal form of property that typically underwrites exploitation based
in skills.

Two additional assets can be added to Roemer's analysis. Unequal
distribution of *labor-power* assets can be seen as the basis for feudal
exploitation, and unequal distribution of *organization* assets can be
viewed as the basis for state bureaucratic exploitation (i.e. the distinctive form of exploitation in "actually existing socialism"). The argument
for feudalism is basically as follows: in feudal society, individual serfs
own less than one unit of labor-power (i.e. they do not fully own their
own labor-power) while the lord owns part of the labor-power of each
of his serfs. The property right in the serf's labor-power is the basis for
the lord forcing the serf to work on the manor land in the case of
corvée labor or paying feudal rents in cases where corvée labor has
been converted into other forms of payment. The flight of peasants to
the cities, in these terms, is a form of theft from the lord: the theft of
the lord's labor-power assets. The argument for state bureaucratic
societies is based on the claim that control over the organizational
resources of production – basically, control over the planning and
coordination of the division of labor – is the material basis for appropriation of the surplus by state bureaucrats.[6] In all of these cases, the
ownership and/or control of particular types of productive assets
enables one class to appropriate part of the social surplus produced by
other classes.

In exploitation models of income distribution, monadic processes
can have some effects. Some income differences, for example, may
simply reflect different preferences of individuals for work and leisure
(or other trade-offs). Some of the income difference across skills may
simply reflect different costs of acquiring the skills and therefore have
nothing to do with exploitation. Such monadic processes of income
determination, however, are secondary to the more fundamental relational mechanisms.

---

6. For a detailed discussion of these additional types of assets and their relationship
to exploitation, see Erik Olin Wright, *Classes*, London 1985.

Implications for Empirical Research Strategies

As one would suspect, rather different empirical research strategies follow from monadic versus relational conceptions of the process of generating income inequality. In a strictly monadic approach, a full account of the individual (non-relational) determinants of individual income is sufficient to explain the overall distribution of income. This suggests that the central empirical task is first to assemble an inventory of all of the individual attributes that influence the income of individuals and, second, to evaluate their relative contributions to explaining variance across individuals in income attainment. In the case of the example of the two farmers discussed above this would mean examining the relative influence of family background, personalities, education and other individual attributes in accounting for their different performances. The sum of such explanations of autonomously determined individual outcomes would constitute the basic explanation of the aggregate income distribution.

It follows from this that the heart of statistical studies of income inequality within an achievement perspective would be multivariate micro-analyses of variations in income across individuals. The study of overall income distributions as such would have a strictly secondary role.

In exploitation models of income distribution, the central empirical problem is to investigate the relationship between the variability in the form and degree of exploitation and income inequality. This implies a variety of specific research tasks, including such things as studying the relationship between the overall distribution of exploitation-generating assets in a society and its overall distribution of income, the different processes of income determination within different relationally defined class positions,[7] and the effects of various forms of collective struggle which potentially can counteract (or intensify) the effects of exploitation-mechanisms on income inequalities.

This does not imply, of course, that achievement models of income inequality have no interest in macro-studies of income distribution, nor that exploitation models have no interest in micro-studies of individual income determination. But it does mean that the core empirical agendas of each model of income inequality will generally be quite different.

---

7. See Erik Olin Wright, *Class Structure and Income Determination*, New York 1979.

Material Inequality and Class Analysis

Sociologists are interested in inequality of material welfare not simply for its own sake, but because such inequality is thought to be consequential for various other social phenomena. Above all, material inequality is one of the central factors underlying the formation of social classes and class conflict.

The two models of income inequality we have been discussing have radically different implications for class analysis. In achievement models of income distribution, there is nothing intrinsically antagonistic about the interests implicated in the income determination process. In the example we discussed, the material interests of the lazy farmer are in no sense intrinsically opposed to those of the industrious farmer. The strictly economic logic of the system, therefore, generates autonomous interests of different economic actors, not conflictual ones.

Contingently, of course, there may be conflicts of interests in the income determination process. This is particularly the case where discrimination of various sorts creates non-competitive privileges based on ascriptive characteristics such as sex and race. These conflicts, however, are not fundamental to the logic of market economies and they do not constitute the basis for conflicts between economic classes as such. Conflicts between classes in capitalist societies, therefore, basically reflect either cognitive distortions on the part of economic actors (e.g. misperceptions of the causes of inequality) or irrational motivations (e.g. envy). Conflicts do not grow out of any objective antagonism of interests rooted in the very relations through which income inequalities are generated.

Exploitation models of income inequality, in contrast, see class conflict as structured by the inherently antagonistic logic of the relational process of income determination. Workers and capitalists have fundamentally opposed interests in so far as the income of capitalists depends upon the exploitation of workers. Conflict, therefore, is not a contingent fact of particular market situations, nor does it reflect ideological mystifications of economic actors; conflict is organic to the structure of the inequality-generating mechanisms themselves.

These different stances towards the relationship between interests and inequality in the two approaches means that for each perspective different social facts are treated as theoretically problematic, requiring special explanations: conflict for achievement theories, consensus for exploitation theories. Both models, however, tend to explain their respective problematic facts through the same kinds of factors, namely combinations of ideology and deviations from the pure logic of the competitive market. Exploitation theories typically explain cooperation between antagonistic class actors on the basis of "false consciousness" and various types of "class compromises" between capitalists and workers, typically institutionalized through the state, which modify the operation of the market.[8] Achievement theories, on the other hand, use discriminatory preferences and market imperfections to explain conflict.

---

8. Adam Przeworski, *Capitalism and Social Democracy*, Cambridge 1985.

2

The Class Analysis of Poverty

The objective of this chapter is to explain the underlying logic of what might be termed the "class analysis of poverty." To understand the distinctiveness of this approach, it will be useful to contrast four general ways of explaining poverty found in both the scholarly literature and popular consciousness. These four approaches differ along two dimensions: first, whether they see the *individual* or *society* as the central unit of analysis for the most salient causes of poverty,[1] and second, whether they see poverty as an unfortunate *by-product* of certain causes or as an *inherent feature* of the system in question. As illustrated in Table 2.1, I will refer to these four kinds of explanations of poverty as the genetic inferiority approach (individual/inherent), the culture of poverty approach (individual/by-product), the ravages of social change approach (societal/by-product), and the class exploitation approach (societal/inherent).

Of course, many scholars mix and match these approaches in an eclectic manner; there is no reason to believe that any one of them will be better than the others for explaining all aspects of poverty. Nevertheless, most sociological thinking about poverty emphasizes one or another of these four modes of analysis and, in any case, it will be useful to clarify the differences in order to understand the specific contribution of class analysis to the study of poverty. In what follows I will first elaborate, in a somewhat stylized manner, the salient differences among these four general ways of thinking about poverty and then turn to a more systematic discussion of the class exploitation approach.

---

1. Other "units of analysis" are possible, especially families or households. Generally when the family is the unit of analysis for discussions of poverty, the *explanations* that are proposed are either about the individuals in the family or about the societal conditions faced by the family.

Table 2.1   General Types of Explanations of Poverty

		Nature of the Explanation	
		Unfortunate By-product	*Inherent feature*
Site of the Explanation	*Individual Attributes*	Culture of poverty	Genetic/Racial inferiority
	Social Systems	Ravages of social change (liberal reformist)	Class exploitation (Marxist class analysis)

The Four General Approaches to Explaining Poverty

Poverty as the result of inherent individual attributes

This form of explanation constitutes a special kind of "blaming the victim": the poor are poor because they individually suffer from some inherent flaw, generally linked to genetic inferiority affecting their intelligence. These days, relatively few scholars lay much importance on genetic factors in explaining poverty, except for arguments that attempt to link racial differentials in poverty to alleged racial differences in IQ. Still, even though genetics-based explanations of poverty do not find favor in the academy, they remain relatively popular with the public at large. Table 2.2 presents the results of two surveys of adults in the United States in which, among other things, attitudes towards poverty were explored.[2] In 1980 just over 50 per cent of Americans said that they either strongly agree or somewhat agree with the statement "One of the main reasons for poverty is that some people are simply not intelligent enough to compete in this modern world."[3] In the 1991 replication of this survey the figure had declined considerably to about 40 per cent.

---

2. These results come from the 1980 US survey in the Comparative Class Analysis Project and the 1991 replication of that survey. See Erik Olin Wright, "The Comparative Project on Class Structure and Class Consciousness: an Overview," *Acta Sociologica*, spring 1989, for details about the original project.

3. While the phrase "compete in this modern world" introduces a social element into this explanation, nevertheless its real thrust explains poverty in terms of the genetic attributes of individuals.

Table 2.2   Attitudes towards Explanations of Poverty

	% Who Strongly Agree or Somewhat Agree	
	1980	*1991*
1. One of the main reasons for poverty is that some people are just not intelligent enough to compete in this modern world.	51.7	40.6
2. One of the main reasons for poverty is that many poor people simply do not want to work.	69.3	54.9
3. One of the main reasons for poverty is lack of education and job opportunities for the poor.	77.0	81.0
4. One of the main reasons for poverty is that the economy is based on private ownership and profits.	49.1	not asked
5. One of the main reasons for poverty is bad government policies.	not asked	67.1

Poverty as the by-product of contingent individual characteristics

A more common approach to explaining poverty among social scientists sees the central cause of poverty as various *contingent* attributes of individuals which render them incapable of effectively functioning in contemporary society. These attributes are not inherent in the individual; they are by-products of various social and cultural processes. Nevertheless, the most salient explanation for why the poor are poor is that they lack the right values, they are lazy or in other ways have flawed motivation, they are too present-oriented and unable to delay gratification, they have low self-esteem, etc.

Because of its emphasis on values and norms, this approach to poverty is generally referred to as the "culture of poverty thesis." In its strongest versions, the explanation of poverty centers on cultural socialization, the intergenerational transmission of a set of values that perpetuate endless cycles of poverty.[4] Somewhat more moderate versions place more stress on current conditions of life and how these may generate certain kinds of preferences, habits, and values. Long-term deprivations, for example, may explain short time horizons. Or, as William Julius Wilson has emphasized, the lack of role models of success through hard work for inner city black youth may explain low self-esteem, fatalism, low motivation for work, and other traits which reproduce poverty.[5] In any event, for either the strong or moderate version of the culture of poverty thesis, once generated, these values and personality traits are seen as embedded in the individual, not simply as superficial correlates of poverty.

This view of poverty suggests that solving poverty requires changing these values and motivations, changing the people themselves. This can be a daunting task, especially for the strong versions of the culture of poverty thesis which see these values as deeply embedded in personality traits through early patterns of socialization. As Edward Banfield stated:

Lower-class poverty . . . is "inwardly" caused (by psychological inability to provide for the future, and all that this inability implies). Improvements in external circumstances can affect this poverty only superficially, one problem of a "multiproblem" family is no sooner solved than another arises. In principle, it is possible to eliminate the poverty (material lack) of such a family, but only at great expense, since the capacity of the radically improvident to waste money is almost unlimited. Raising such a family's income would not necessarily improve its way of life, moreover, and could conceivably even make things worse.[6]

In such a view there is not much that can really be done other than to provide modest relief to soften the most deleterious effects of poverty.

As in the case of the genetic-flaw view of poverty, the culture of poverty thesis has significant popular appeal. In the survey results reported in Table 2.2, almost 70 per cent of the respondents in 1980 and

---

4. The emphasis on intergenerational transmission of poverty-inducing values is associated with the many works of Oscar Lewis, e.g. *Five Families: Mexican Case Studies in the Culture of Poverty* (New York 1959); *La Vida: A Puerto Rican Family in the Culture of Poverty*, New York 1966. See also Edward Banfield, *The Unheavenly City*, Boston 1970. There are numerous systematic critiques of the culture of poverty perspective. See, for example, William Ryan, *Blaming the Victim*, New York 1971 and *Equality*, New York 1981.

5. See Wilson, *The Truly Disadvantaged: The Inner City, the Underclass and Public Policy*, Chicago 1987.

6. Banfield, *The Unheavenly City*, p. 126.

55 per cent of the respondents in 1991 agreed with the statement that "One of the main reasons for poverty is that some people are simply too lazy to work hard." While this statement does not directly attribute laziness to culture, this kind of statement nevertheless suggests the kind of explanation supported by defenders of the culture of poverty thesis.

Poverty as a by-product of social causes

This is undoubtedly the most popular kind of explanation of poverty found among liberal social scientists. While individual attributes may play some role in explaining poverty, the main explanation is sought in the nature of the opportunity structure that disadvantaged people face. Consider the core of William Julius Wilson's explanation for the deep poverty of "underclass" blacks in contemporary American inner cities. Wilson sees the most important cause centering on the changes in the American job structure since the 1960s. As Paul Peterson states, Wilson explains poverty as "the social by-product of a changing economy whose uneven impact was leaving inner cities with extraordinarily high levels of unemployment."[7] The decline of manufacturing, and in particular the decline of job structures containing the diverse mix of skilled, semi-skilled and unskilled jobs available to previous generations of unskilled immigrants, has virtually destroyed the possibility of routes out of poverty for significant segments of the black population. This general tendency in the American economy has been exacerbated by the massive evacuation of jobs from the inner city and the flight of the black middle class from the ghetto, so the general decline in opportunity has been compounded by severe social isolation. No one intended this calamity and no one really benefits from it, but it has the consequence of significantly deepening the problem of poverty.

With this diagnosis of the causes of poverty, the solution is generally seen as twofold. First, a massive effort needs to be devoted to the problem of skill formation and education so that disadvantaged children are equipped to participate actively in the labor market. Secondly, serious jobs programs, generally assumed to require considerable expansion of public works, need to be created to employ people with marginal skills. Both of these solutions require an expansion of the "affirmative state."

While social by-product views of poverty tend to be associated with liberal reformists, there are conservatives who adopt a version of this approach. Charles Murray, for example, sees the problem of the under-

---

7. Paul E. Peterson, "The Urban Underclass and the Poverty Paradox," in Christopher Jencks and Paul E. Peterson (eds), *The Urban Underclass*, Washington 1991, p. 16.

class in the United States as an unfortunate by-product of well-meaning welfare policies instituted in the 1960s and expanded in the 1970s.[8] He argues that AFDC programs have the effect of creating incentives for people to act irresponsibly and to engage in strategies which perpetuate their poverty. He does not believe that this creates deep-seated personality flaws, but simply that poor people are acting rationally when they exploit the generosity of the welfare system. The solution, he argues, is to eliminate virtually all welfare programs and thus radically change the incentive structure facing poor people. With these altered incentives they will begin to work hard, act responsibly and thus "raise themselves out of poverty."[9]

In terms of public opinion, there is more support for the social by-product view of poverty than for the views that attribute poverty primarily to individual attributes. Seventy-seven per cent of the respondents in our survey in 1980 and 81 per cent in 1991 agreed with the statement that "One of the main reasons for poverty is lack of adequate education and job opportunities," and 67 per cent of the respondents in 1991 agreed with the statement that "One of the main reasons for poverty is bad government policies." The latter, of course, does not distinguish between conservative and liberal views of which social causes generate poverty, but it does affirm a social by-product view of the causes of poverty.

Poverty as a result of the inherent properties of the social system

The least familiar approach to explaining poverty among Americans is the view that poverty should be seen as an inherent attribute of the functioning of certain kinds of social systems. The most prominent version of this view is identified with the Marxist tradition, and sees poverty in contemporary capitalism as generated by the core dynamics of class exploitation. Poverty is not an accident; it is not a by-product. It is an inherent, and crucial, feature of a society whose economic structure is

---

8. See Charles Murray, *Losing Ground*, New York 1984. For a strong critique of Murray's views see Christopher Jencks, *Rethinking Social Policy: Race, Poverty and the Underclass*, Cambridge, Mass. 1992.

9. Murray's full argument is actually a combination of individual/inherent arguments, individual/by-product arguments and social/by-product arguments. Males, he argues, are genetically disposed to be irresponsible, to live for the moment. They can be induced to act in a responsible manner – work hard, save, care for others – only when their impulses are tamed by family obligations. The current welfare system encourages single motherhood and unstable families among poor people by making it unprofitable for people to marry. AFDC has the effect of inducing a set of values and norms which perpetuate irresponsibility, and thus poverty, because they reinforce the genetically determined irresponsibility of males.

grounded in class and exploitation. The pivotal idea (which we will elaborate more systematically in the next section of this chapter) is that there are powerful and privileged actors who have an active interest in maintaining poverty. It is not just that poverty is an unfortunate consequence of their pursuit of material interests; it is an essential *condition* for the *realization* of their interests. To put it bluntly, capitalists and other exploiting classes benefit from poverty.

This view of poverty has crucial political implications. In the social by-product view of poverty, the political condition for solving the problem of poverty mainly involves trying to convince people that certain kinds of programs are necessary and will work. No one has a stake in maintaining poverty. Everyone would like to see it eliminated. The political problem is lack of knowledge and enlightenment, with perhaps a dose of myopia, but not malice. In the class exploitation view of poverty, on the other hand, to reduce poverty requires the *defeat* of powerful, privileged social forces, not their conversion. The persistence of extreme levels of poverty occurs not because powerful elites have mistaken ideas of what is in their interests and what would solve poverty, nor because they are short-sighted or unenlightened, but because they benefit from the existence of poverty and have unchallenged power.

There are two principle variants of this general view of poverty. The first, identified with revolutionary Marxism, argues that the only way to reduce poverty significantly is to eliminate capitalism altogether. It is not just that poverty is *good* for capitalism; it is *essential* for its very survival. Thus, there is no real prospect for significantly reducing poverty inside of capitalism. The second variant, generally associated with social democracy, argues that capitalism can be significantly tamed, that while capitalists have real, material interests in sustaining poverty, significant redistribution of income is compatible with the survival of capitalist institutions. As a result, if the power of capitalists and their allies can be effectively challenged *inside of capitalism*, significant inroads against poverty can be achieved. In these terms, Sweden is often held up as an exemplary case where bourgeois forces were politically defeated or forced to compromise with powerful defenders of the underprivileged. Swedish capitalists did not want to help the poor; they were forced to help the poor by the combined forces of the Swedish labor movement and the Social Democratic Party. As a result, wealthy people live less well in Sweden than in the United States. This means that there are losers – that there is a zero-sum aspect to meaningful solutions to poverty. And, because there are real losers, it is unlikely that serious solutions will be politically based purely on consensus across social classes.

As in the case of the other three kinds of explanations of poverty, there is some popular support for explanations that attribute poverty to the inherent functioning of capitalism. Forty-nine per cent of the respondents in 1980 said that they agreed with the statement that "One of the main reasons for poverty is that the economy is based on private ownership and profits." It is also interesting that there are much larger class differences in those who support this explanation of poverty than there are in those who support the others: 61 per cent of respondents in the working class agree with the statement that an economy based on private profits significantly contributes to poverty, compared to only 11 per cent of the capitalists in the sample.

Elaboration of a Class Exploitation Analysis of Poverty

So far, I have only gestured at the substantive arguments of a class analysis of poverty. In this section I will fill out the argument. To do this it is necessary to define carefully three key concepts: economic oppression, economic exploitation, and class. Once these concepts are defined, I will explain how they generate a social system in which poverty plays a crucial functional role.

Oppression and exploitation

Economic oppression can be defined as a situation in which three conditions are satisfied:

(a) The material welfare of one group of people is causally related to the material deprivations of another.

(b) The causal relation in (a) involves coercively enforced exclusion from access to productive resources.

(c) This exclusion in (b) is morally indictable.

This is a fairly complex definition. Without (c), a fair competition between two people for a prize in which the ownership of the prize is backed by property rights (and thus by coercion) would count as a form of economic oppression. Without (b), simple cheating would be considered a form of oppression (assuming that the cheating in question was viewed as morally indictable). Without (a), we have economically gratuitous exclusion – exclusion from resources from which no one derives material benefit. "Economic oppression" is thus a situation in which the material benefits of one group are acquired at the expense of another, and in which morally indictable coercive exclusion from resources is an essential part of the process by which this occurs. The introduction of (c), of course, renders judgments of the oppressive nature of a particular inequality highly contentious, since there will generally be disputes about the moral standing of the exclusions that back up the inequalities in question.

Economic oppression defined in this way can take many forms. Of particular salience to class analysis is the distinction between exploitative and non-exploitative economic oppression. Economic exploitation is a specific form of economic oppression defined by a particular kind of mechanism through which the welfare of exploiters is causally related to the deprivations of the exploited. In exploitation, *the material well-being of exploiters causally depends upon their ability to appropriate the fruits of labor of the exploited.* The welfare of the exploiter therefore depends on the *effort* of the exploited, not merely on the deprivations of the exploited. In non-exploitative economic oppression there is no transfer of the fruits of labor from the oppressed to the oppressor; the welfare of the oppressor depends on the exclusion of the oppressed from access to certain resources, but not on their effort. In both instances, the inequalities in question are rooted in ownership of and control over productive resources.

The crucial difference between exploitation and non-exploitative oppression is that in an exploitative relation, the exploiter *needs* the exploited since the exploiter depends upon the effort of the exploited. In the case of non-exploitative oppression, the oppressors would be happy if the oppressed simply disappeared. Life would have been much easier for the European settlers in North America if the continent had been uninhabited by people.[10] Genocide is thus always a potential strategy for non-exploitative oppressors. It is not an option in a situation of economic exploitation because exploiters require the labor of the exploited for their material well-being. It is no accident that culturally we have the saying, "the only good Indian is a dead Indian," but not the saying "the only good worker is a dead worker." The contrast between South Africa and North America in their treatment of indigenous peoples reflects this difference poignantly: in North America, where the indigenous people were oppressed (by virtue of being coercively displaced from the land) but not exploited, genocide was the basic policy of social control in the face of resistance; in South Africa, where the European settler population heavily depended upon African labor for its own prosperity, this was not an option.

---

10. This is not to deny that in certain specific instances the settlers benefited from the knowledge of native Americans, but simply to affirm the point that the displacement of the indigenous people from the land was a costly and troublesome process.

Exploitation, therefore, does not merely define a set of *statuses* of social actors, but a pattern of on-going interactions structured by a set of social relations, relations which mutually bind the exploiter and the exploited together. This dependency of the exploiter on the exploited gives the exploited a certain form of power, since human beings always retain at least some minimal control over their own expenditure of effort. Social control which relies exclusively on repression is costly and, except under special circumstances, often fails to generate the required levels of diligence and effort on the part of the exploited. As a result, there is generally systematic pressure on exploiters to moderate their domination and in one way or another to try to elicit some degree of consent from the exploited, at least in the sense of gaining some level of minimal cooperation from them. Paradoxically perhaps, exploitation is thus a constraining force on the practices of the exploiter. This constraint constitutes a basis of power for the exploited.

The non-exploited oppressed may also have some power, but it is generally more precarious. At a minimum oppressed people have the power that comes from the human capacity for physical resistance. However, since their oppressors are not economically constrained to seek any kind of cooperation from them, this resistance is likely very quickly to escalate into quite bloody and violent confrontations. It is for this reason that the resistance of Native Americans to displacement from the land led to massacres of Native Americans by white settlers. The pressure on oppressors to seek accommodation is very weak; the outcomes therefore tend to become simply a matter of the balance of brute force between enemies.

The concepts of both exploitation and non-exploitative oppression involve moral indictments against certain social arrangements, but the moral textures of the two are different in important respects. On the one hand, situations of non-exploitative oppression have been accompanied by the most monstrous moral outrages. Since the oppressor has no material need for the oppressed, and since the oppressed often resist the conditions of their oppression, murderous repression is always an attractive solution.[11] In the case of exploitation there is at least some material incentive for the exploitative oppressor to refrain from the most extreme forms of violence against the exploited.

On the other hand, exploitation contains within its structure a kind of

---

11. Of course, individual oppressors may be committed to moral principles of decency for religious or other reasons, and thus may refrain from maximum repression for moral reasons extrinsic to their relation to the oppressed. The point here is that there is nothing endogenous to the relation between non-exploitative oppressor and oppressed to encourage such moral restraint.

Table 2.3 Preference Orderings for Distribution of Manna from Heaven

Preference Ordering	Non-exploitative Oppressor	Exploiter	Oppressed and Exploited
1	All manna to oppressors	All manna to exploiters	All manna to oppressed/exploited
2	Evenly divide to everyone	Destroy the manna	Evenly divide the manna
3	All manna to the oppressed	Evenly divide the manna	Give manna to the exploiters
4	Destroy the manna	Give manna to the exploited	Destroy the manna

mean-spiritedness that is absent from simple oppression. Suppose that the gods decreed that manna from Heaven would descend on a community that would be sufficient, *if evenly divided* among people, to provide everyone with an adequate, if not luxurious, standard of living without expending any labor. What would be the preferences of different people in different classes for the distribution of this boon? On the assumption of selfishness and rationality, the relevant preference orderings are listed in Table 2.3.

If we assume purely self-regarding interests and rationality, both exploiters and non-exploitative oppressors would prefer all of the manna to go to themselves.[12] But they have different second-best preferences: exploiters would prefer to see the manna destroyed and go to no one rather than for it to be evenly divided among everyone, whereas non-exploitative oppressors prefer the oppressed to get their per capita share of manna rather than for it to be destroyed. If they cannot monopolize the manna for themselves, oppressors would in general have no material interest in preventing the oppressed from gaining access to the manna.[13] Exploiters, on the other hand, would be materially hurt by the dramati-

12. Purely self-regarding interests exclude "spite" as a motivation. If actors were spiteful then they might prefer the manna to be destroyed if they cannot have it, just to spite the other group. We are ruling out such motivations in the present discussion. The actors are not motivated by spite or envy, but simply by their self-regarding interests in their own material well-being.

13. Of course, there might be some specific situations in which oppressors would rather destroy the manna than have it fall into the hands of the oppressed. This would be the case if, for example, the manna would increase the capacity of the oppressed to fight back against the oppressor. But in terms of the direct material consequences of the manna, the oppressor would have no incentive to destroy it.

cally improved living standards of the exploited since the exploited would no longer have to work for the exploiter in order to gain access to subsistence. To have a positive interest in perpetuating and deepening the material deprivations of other human beings creates a particularly degraded moral climate.

A digression

The Li'l Abner comic strips of 1948, in which "shmoos" come to Dogpatch, is a story that captures the basic moral logic of exploiters having a positive interest in the deprivations of the exploited.[14] Shmoos are creatures who multiply rapidly and whose sole desire in life is to please humans by transforming themselves into material things human beings need for an adequate standard of living. They do not provide humans with luxuries, but with all the basic necessities of life. A rich capitalist, P.U., does a study to identify the poorest place in America in order to be able to hire cheap labor for a new factory. The place turns out to be Dogpatch. P.U. and his manager come to Dogpatch to recruit employees for the new factory. Once they discover shmoos and realize how seriously shmoos threaten their capacity to exploit the poor, they resolve to destroy them. The story unfolds in some strips from 1948 (see Figure 2.1).[15]

Class

Underlying both the concept of simple material oppression and the concept of exploitation is the idea that there are various kinds of productive resources which are important for material welfare and which have the property that one's welfare is enhanced by excluding others from access to the resource. Oppression occurs when one group illegitimately excludes another from access to those resources.[16] Exploitation occurs when such exclusion from resources also gives the owners of the resource the capacity to appropriate the fruits of labor of others. If I kick the peasants off the land and let them fend for themselves in the bush,

---

14. The use of the Shmoos as an illustration for moral critique of capitalism was introduced to me by G.A. Cohen in a lecture on British television in August 1986.

15. These strips are reprinted in Al Capp, *Li'l Abner Meets the Shmoo*, Princeton, Wisconsin 1992.

16. The modifier "illegitimate" is necessary since there may be circumstances in which the exclusive use of a resource by one group may be justified. This proviso, again, makes judgments of oppression highly contested.

Figure 2.1   Capitalism Meets the Shmoo

then I have merely oppressed them materially; if I use my ownership of the land as a basis for hiring them back to work the fields, then I exploit them.

The concept of class, within the Marxist tradition, is closely tied to this understanding of exploitation. Classes are categories of social actors defined by the property relations which generate exploitation. In the above example, the landowner and the peasant are in different classes because (a) they are bound together through a specific set of social property relations (or, as they are often called, social relations of production) and (b) the landowner exploits the peasant. Homeowners and the homeless, on the other hand, would generally not constitute two classes.

More generally, one can define a range of different kinds of class relations in terms of the pivotal form of productive resources that provides the basis for exploitation. Marxists have traditionally focused on two such resources: capital and labor. Slavery is based on a form of class relations in which the slavemaster owns the slave and by virtue of that ownership exploits the slave. Capitalism is based on a form of class relations in which the capitalist owns the means of production, the worker owns labor-power, and by virtue of these property rights in capital and labor, the capitalist is able to exploit the worker through the employment relation.

More recently, a variety of suggestions have been made about how this map of potential class relations might be expanded. John Roemer has suggested that skills or expertise might constitute a third productive asset, the ownership of which could constitute the basis for exploitation in which skill-owners are able to appropriate labor effort (embodied in the social surplus product) from the unskilled.[17] I have argued in various places that this might be a useful way of understanding the specificity of the class situation of the "middle class." The middle class can be thought of as "contradictory locations within class relations" in so far as they are

---

17. The argument that skill-owners are able to appropriate surplus products from the unskilled is rather complicated and problematic. The basic idea is that skill-owners are able to receive a "monopoly rent" within their earnings because of their control over a scarce productive resource (skills). This rent component of the wage enables them to consume part of the "social surplus," where the "surplus" is defined as production above the costs of reproducing all the factors of production. In effect this means that the *price* of skilled labor-power is above its *costs* of production. The problem with this description of skill-owners is that it is ambiguous whether they should be viewed as exploiting the unskilled (i.e. appropriating the effort of the unskilled) or simply as being less exploited than unskilled workers (i.e. they appropriate some of the surplus which they themselves produce).

simultaneously exploited through capitalist mechanisms and exploiters through skill or other secondary mechanisms.[18] Philippe Van Parijs has argued that the *de facto* ownership of jobs in advanced welfare state capitalism might also be seen as a basis of class differentiation.[19]

Whether or not these extensions of the basic idea of class and exploitation are satisfactory, the core idea of a class analysis of inequality remains powerful. To the extent that classes exist in exploitative and oppressive relations, there will be powerful actors with a positive interest in the deprivations of others. Poverty is one specific consequence of this logic of interests and power.

Class, exploitation and poverty

The concepts we have been exploring suggest that the general problem of poverty needs to be broken down into two sub-problems: poverty generated inside exploitative relations, and poverty generated by non-exploitative oppression. The former corresponds to what in contemporary policy discourse is called "the working poor"; the latter corresponds to the "underclass."

The working poor

If one takes a static view of the economy, then it is easy to attribute the existence of the working poor to the intersection of two facts: (1) many firms have low levels of productivity and in order to compete they can only offer low wages; and (2) many workers have low levels of skills or limited possibility of geographical mobility and thus are constrained to accept such poor-paying jobs. Within a class analysis framework, however, the existence of a sizeable population of working poor in an otherwise affluent society can be viewed, to a significant extent, as one of the many dynamic consequences of a weak, fragmented, and relatively conservative labor movement. A strong, solidaristic labor movement is likely to be committed to reducing wage inequalities within the working class. When such a movement is closely linked to a political party capable of using the power of the state to back up such egalitarian commitments,

18. See John Roemer, *A General Theory of Exploitation and Class*, Cambridge, Mass. 1982 for the exposition of the idea of skill exploitation. The relationship of this idea to the problem of the middle class is explored in Erik Olin Wright, *Classes*, London 1985.

19. Philippe Van Parijs, "A Revolution in Class Theory," in Erik Olin Wright et al., *The Debate on Classes*, London 1989, pp. 191–212.

then one would predict a long-term disappearance of impoverished employed workers.

The "solidarity wage" policy in Sweden, for example, was a deliberate policy of the labor movement to raise the wages of the most poorly paid sectors of the working class as a way of reinforcing the long-term solidarity of the labor movement. This strategy was complemented by the well-known "active labor market policy" of the social democratic state, which was committed to retraining workers when firms became uncompetitive by virtue of rising wages. The distribution of income among workers, and in particular the extent to which a stratum of impoverished employed workers exists, therefore, should not be viewed simply as a spontaneous result of "natural" market forces, but as the result of the exercise of power by social forces with different interests.

The concept of the "working poor," in this context, should not be seen as only referring to the stratum of poor employed workers within a rich country. The employment of poor Mexican workers in U.S. automakers' factories in northern Mexico also follows the same logic. In this case the issue of class power is the absence of a solidaristic international labor movement capable of constraining the capacity of multinational firms to pay Third World workers miserable wages. The existence of the working poor employed by multinational firms in Third World countries thus, in part, reflects power relations, not simply impersonal market forces.[20]

The underclass

The term "underclass" is used in a variety of ways in contemporary policy discussions. Sometimes it is meant to be a pejorative term rather like the old Marxist concept of "lumpenproletariat"; other times it is used more descriptively to designate a segment of the poor whose conditions of life are especially desperate and whose prospects for

---

20. This does not mean that the capitalist class has a general interest in workers as a whole being as poor as possible. There are two reasons why capitalists, even in the absence of an organized working class, have some interest in workers not being maximally impoverished. First, as we will see in more detail in chapter 4, employers need to pay workers a wage sufficiently above what they would have if they were fired if the threat of being fired is to have any bite. What economists call an "efficiency wage" is thus induced by problems of social control within production. Second, workers are also consumers who buy the products capitalists produce, and if workers are universally maximally impoverished, capitalists may face problems of inadequate aggregate demand for their products. Both of these factors are counter-tendencies to the tendency for capitalist exploitation to generate a category of "working poor." In the context of global capitalism, however, these tendencies are certainly weak relative to the tendency of the capitalist class to pay workers as little as they can profitably get away with.

improvement are particularly dismal.[21] One way of giving this concept a
more precise theoretical status is to link it to the concepts of exploitation
and oppression: and "underclass" can be defined as a category of social
agents who are economically oppressed but not consistently exploited
within a given class system.

Different kinds of class structures will tend to have different forms of
an "underclass." In many parts of the world today and throughout much
of human history, the pivotal resource which defines the underclass is
land. Landlords, agrarian capitalists, peasants, and exploited agrarian
producers all have access to land; people who are excluded from such
access constitute the underclass of agrarian societies. In these terms,
Native Americans were transformed into an underclass in the nineteenth
century when they were pushed off the land into the reservations.

In contemporary advanced capitalism, the key resource that defines
the predicament of the underclass is labor-power itself. This might seem
like an odd statement since in capitalism, at least since the abolition of
slavery, everyone supposedly owns one "unit" of labor-power, him or
herself. The point is that some people do not in fact own productively
usable labor-power. The situation is similar to that of a capitalist owning
outmoded machines. While the capitalist physically controls these pieces
of machinery, they cease to be "capital" – a productive resource – if they
cannot be deployed within a capitalist production process profitably. In
the case of labor-power, a person can physically control his or her own
laboring capacity, but that capacity can cease to have economic value in
capitalism if it cannot be deployed productively. This is the essential
condition of the "underclass." They are oppressed because they are
denied access to various kinds of productive resources, above all the
necessary means to acquire the skills needed to make their labor-power
saleable. As a result, they are not consistently exploited.

It is perhaps controversial to amalgamate the exclusion of the contemporary urban underclass from human capital and other job resources
with the exclusion of native Americans from the land. In the latter case
there was a zero-sum character to access to the resource in question and
massive coercion was used to enforce the exclusion, whereas in the case

21. This is the essential way that the term is used by William Julius Wilson in his analysis
of the interconnection between race and class in American society. Wilson argues that as
legal barriers to racial equality have disappeared, and as class differentiation within the
black population has increased, the central determining structure of the lives of many
African-Americans is no longer race as such, but class. More specifically, he argues that
there has been a substantial growth of an urban "underclass" of people without marketable
skills and with very weak attachments to the labor force, living in crumbling central cities
isolated from the mainstream of American life and institutions. See William Julius Wilson,
The Declining Significance of Race, Chicago 1982, and William Julius Wilson, *The Truly
Disadvantaged*, Chicago 1987.

of education, skills, and even good jobs, it is not so obvious that the resources in question are a fixed quantity and that access is being denied through force. Thus the factual inequalities of access to these resources may not in fact be instances of coercively enforced "exclusion." For present purposes, therefore, it should be viewed as an hypothesis that the underclass is "economically oppressed," i.e. that there is indeed a process of morally indictable exclusion from access occurring here, an exclusion which has the effect of benefiting certain groups of people at the expense of others.[22]

Understood in this way, the underclass consists of human beings who are largely expendable *from the point of view of the rationality of capitalism*. As in the case of native Americans, who became a landless underclass in the nineteenth century, repression rather than incorporation is the central mode of social control directed towards them. Capitalism does not need the labor-power of unemployed inner-city youth. The material interests of the wealthy and privileged segments of American society would be better served if these people simply disappeared. However, unlike in the nineteenth century, the moral and political forces are such that direct genocide is no longer a viable strategy. The alternative, then, is to build prisons, to cordon off the zones of cities in which the underclass live. In such a situation the main potential power of the underclass against their oppressors comes from their capacity to disrupt the sphere of consumption, especially through crime and other forms of violence, not their capacity to disrupt production through their control over labor.

Poverty, Politics and Class Analysis

This chapter has argued that in order to understand more fully the nature of poverty it is important to see it as, in part, the result of inherent features of the social system. This does not mean that no individuals are poor because of lack of innate intelligence, or that cultural factors of various sorts do not create obstacles for some groups and prevent them improving their lot in life, or that the disjunction between the supply of labor and the demand for jobs does not intensify the plight of the poor in the inner cities. But it does mean that each of these approaches to understanding poverty is incomplete. Each of these partial factors inter-

---

22. This, of course, leaves open the crucial question of who, precisely, is benefiting from this exclusion. Some people argue that it is workers with secure jobs who benefit from the economic oppression of the underclass; others argue it is high-earning employees and capitalists who would otherwise have to pay for providing adequate training, retraining, education, public service jobs, etc.

acts with the underlying class structure to generate the empirical patterns of poverty which we confront.

Adding a class analysis perspective to the analysis of poverty is not just adding another variable to a laundry list of factors in a multivariate model. It changes the way we think about the political dynamics at stake in attempts to do something about the problem. Specifically, since a class analysis of poverty argues that there are significant numbers of privileged[23] people with a strong, positive material interest in maintaining poverty, significant advances towards reducing poverty in the United States must place the problem of power and struggles over power at the center of the political agenda.

This does not imply rejecting the content or objectives of many of the reforms proposed by liberals working within an "unfortunate social by-product" view of poverty. The proposals by Liberal Democrats for life-long processes of skill formation and retraining, for equalizing educational resources by channeling funds to inner-city schools, for government-provided jobs in the face of persistent failures of private employers to provide jobs for people in the "underclass," and so on, are fine proposals. The mistake is the view that these proposals can be effectively achieved primarily by demonstrating their usefulness, by trying to convince powerful groups that these proposals will significantly help solve the problems of poverty. So long as powerful, privileged groups are willing to use their power to maintain their privileges, such proposals for reform can only be achieved through deep and pervasive popular mobilization of pressure which challenges the power of dominant classes in the United States. This does not mean that capitalism as such has to be destroyed before inequalities can be significantly reduced; but it does mean that the power of capitalists and other privileged elites cannot go unchecked if there are to be significant inroads on poverty. The necessary reforms cannot be achieved simply through a politics of perpetual harmony which always seeks consensus among conflicting parties. They can only be achieved through victories and defeats in which there will be losers who will have to pay.

---

23. The term "privilege" is a convenient way of identifying the material advantages of groups that are either simple (non-exploitative) oppressors or exploiters. As I use the term, an economically privileged group is not simply materially advantaged compared to other groups; its advantages are rooted in processes of oppression and exploitation.

The Status of the Political in the Concept of Class Structure

In rethinking the basic categories within Marxist theory over the past twenty years, Marxists have devoted considerable attention to the concept of class. They have both reconceptualized the place of "class" in the overall Marxist theory of society and social change and transformed the concept itself.[1]

Many of the attempts at reconceptualizing have revolved around the relationship between the political and the economic in class relations. Traditionally, Marxists have regarded class structure as an economic category. Whether defined by property relations or by production relations, class structure was understood in strictly economic terms. Capitalists appropriated surplus-value because of their location within economic relations; workers produced surplus-value because they did not own their own means of production and had to sell their labor-power to capitalists. In this notion of a "class-in-itself," politics entered the analysis explicitly in only two ways: first, the state was seen as essential for reproducing this structure of economic class relations and for setting its legal presuppositions (guaranteeing contracts, enforcing property rights, and so forth); and second, politics was seen as central to how classes became organized in the class struggle. Indeed, the transition from a "class-in-itself" to a "class-for-itself" was traditionally viewed as a movement from the purely economic existence of classes to their political existence.

More recent Marxist analyses have stressed the importance of political relations in the very definition of class relations. Not only does the state establish the legal preconditions of property relations, but in a deep

---

1. For an overview of alternative perspectives on class within current Marxist debates, see Erik Olin Wright, "Varieties of Marxist Conceptions of Class Structure," *Politics & Society*, vol. 9, no. 3, 1981.

sense those relations themselves have a political dimension. Different theorists express that dimension in different ways – as power relations, relations of domination and subordination, relations of control – but in all cases they assert a notion of class relations that necessarily embodies a political aspect. Even at the most abstract level, they have argued, a purely economic understanding of class relations is unsatisfactory.

John Roemer challenges this recent trend in class analysis in his article, "New Directions in the Marxian Theory of Class and Exploitation."[2] His central argument is that, at the most abstract level, classes can be defined strictly in terms of ownership relations. Political factors enter into the story only at "lower" levels of abstraction, particularly in the institutional conditions necessary for maintaining the basic property relations. In this chapter I will critically examine Roemer's arguments in support of this thesis. I will argue that while, as Roemer argues, *exploitation* can be defined in purely economic terms, *class* cannot. Class is an intrinsically political concept and for it to serve its explanatory purposes it must have its political dimensions systematically represented within the concept itself. Before making these arguments, however, I will briefly situate the theoretical object of this discussion – class structure – within a broader context of class analysis and discuss what is meant by "political practices" and "political relations."

Class Structure as an Element in Class Analysis

It is useful in discussing the concept of class to distinguish three separate elements in a class analysis: *class structure*, *class formation*, and *class struggle*. While each of these presupposes the other two and can be defined only in terms of its connection with the other elements, it is nevertheless important to make the distinctions. Class struggle refers to the practices of individuals and collectivities in pursuit of class interests; class formation designates the social relations within each class that

---

2. John Roemer, "New Directions in the Marxian Theory of Exploitation and Class," *Politics & Society*, vol. 11, no. 3, 1982, pp. 253–87. This chapter will not address Roemer's innovative strategy for defining exploitation using game-theory models, nor his development and defense of the Class-Exploitation Correspondence Principle. I consider both of these to be extremely important contributions to the Marxist theory of exploitation and class. My critique is limited to the way Roemer deals with politics in his analysis. His claims about domination could be modified without any fundamental change in his general argument.

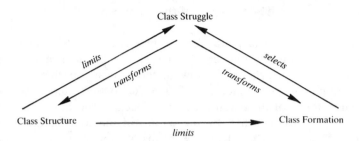

Figure 3.1 Interconnections among Core Elements of Class Analysis

determine its capacity to pursue its interests; and class structure is the social relations between classes that determine or shape basic interests over which classes-in-formation struggle. These three elements, then, are related as illustrated in Figure 3.1.[3] The underlying structure of class relations limits the possible forms of collective class organization and the possible forms of class struggle. Within these limits class struggle transforms both class structure and class formation. These transformations imply that the limits on class struggle (and on class formation) are not permanently fixed but change in response to the struggles themselves. It is in this sense that the model can be seen as "dialectical": struggles transform the conditions of their own determination.

This model is, of course, purely formal in character. There is no specific content given to any of the terms and no concrete propositions about the nature of the limits and transformations involved. The model provides a framework to specify a theory of class, but does not itself constitute such a theory.

One of the critical steps in developing a theory is to elaborate the logic of each of the elements in the model. In this chapter I will focus on the concept *class structure*, particularly on the role of political relations. I will not, except in passing, discuss the role of the political in class formation and class struggle. This is not to suggest that explicating the concept of class structure is somehow the key to the entire analysis, but simply that it is a necessary starting point.

---

3. This model is, of course, a radically incomplete picture. The state, ideology, nonclass relations and interests, and many other factors have been left out. It is not meant to show how all the aspects of class are determined but simply to explain the interrelationships among them. For a discussion of the precise meaning of "limits," "selection," and "transformation" in this diagram and for further elaboration on what constitutes class, see Erik Olin Wright, *Class, Crisis and the State*, London 1978.

The Concept of the "Political"

In order to define the political, it is first necessary to define social
practice. Following Althusser, "practice" can be defined as human
activity that transforms some raw material, using specific means of
production, into some product.[4] Practices are thus human activities
viewed in terms of their transformative effects in the world. Different
practices are distinguished by the nature of the transformation (the
nature of the raw material, of the means of production, of the transformative activity, and of the product). Economic practices can thus be
defined as those activities that produce and transform *use-values*; political practices can be defined as those activities that produce and transform
social relations; and ideological practices can be defined as those activities that produce and transform the *subjective experience* of those
relations. Concrete, observed activities of people typically involve each
of these types of practice. When workers work on an assembly line, they
simultaneously transform nature into useful products (an economic
practice) and produce and reproduce a particular structure of social
relations (a political practice) and particular forms of subjectivity (an
ideological practice).

These distinctions among practices correspond to distinctions among
social relations. Thus, economic relations can be defined as social
relations that shape or limit the activities of transforming nature; political
relations can be defined as those social relations that shape or limit the
activities of transforming social relations; and ideological relations can
be defined as those social relations that shape or limit the activities of
transforming subjectivity. Again, any concrete social relation may
involve all three types. Using the example of the factory, we might say
that the technical division of labor is primarily an economic relation in
that it systematically shapes the activities that transform nature; the
authority structure is primarily a political relation in that it systematically
limits the capacities of workers to transform the relations within which
they work; and the job structure (seniority, competition in internal labor
markets) is primarily an ideological relation in that it systematically
shapes the subjectivity of workers on the job.[5]

When we speak of "political practices" or "political relations," the
terms should be understood as a shorthand for practices or social

---

4. See Louis Althusser, "On the Materialist Dialectic," in Althusser, *For Marx*, New
York 1970, pp. 166 ff.

5. It would be incorrect, however, to say that such labels exhaust the character of
actual social relations within the factory. The technical division of labor also influences
capacities to transform social relations; authority relations also shape subjectivity; and so
on.

relations within which the political aspect is the most important. This may be quite difficult to determine empirically in specific cases, as in the debate over whether educational institutions should be viewed as primarily ideological (producing forms of subjectivity) or primarily economic (producing skilled labor-power). We must nonetheless acknowledge this complexity of practices and relations and set the agenda for investigating the relationships among the various types.

The focus here is on the political dimension of class structure (the structure of class relations). As already stated, a political relation is a relation (or that aspect of a relation) that shapes the practices of transforming social relations. In these terms, the relations of domination and subordination are quintessentially political. To say that A dominates B is to say that A not only tells B what to do or in other ways directs B's activities, but also that A has the capacity to constrain B's attempts at transforming the relationship between A and B. To be a subordinate is not simply to be in a position in which one is given orders, but to be unable to transform the relationship of command-obedience. This is what distinguishes following instructions or suggestions in a reciprocal relationship and following orders in a hierarchical relation. They may be behaviorally equivalent in a given instance, but they are structurally quite distinct.

The question at hand, then, is whether this particular political aspect of social relations – domination and subordination – is essential in defining class relations. I will show in the next section that as John Roemer argues, such relations of domination are not necessary for a definition of exploitation, but that they are necessary for a definition of class relations.

Roemer's Treatment of Domination in the Concepts of Class and Exploitation

In his discussions of class and exploitation, Roemer adopts two rather different stances toward domination. In the first part of his analysis he argues that both class and exploitation can be specified strictly in terms of the distribution of property rights, without any reference to domination relations. At the end of the paper, when he introduces a game-theory analysis of exploitation, he argues that there is an implied relation of domination in the concept of exploitation and thus in class as well. What I will argue is that each of Roemer's formulations is half right: class does require domination relations; exploitation does not.

Let us first examine the strategy Roemer employs to investigate exploitation and class as direct consequences of the distribution of property rights. His strategy is to examine several different economies that differ only in the kinds of markets that are allowed in them and in the character of the distribution of productive assets. In the course of these investigations he proves two propositions, both of which may at first glance seem quite surprising. First, he shows that exploitation can occur in situations in which all producers own their own means of production, and thus there is no domination whatsoever within the actual process of production; and, second, he shows that there is complete symmetry in the structure of exploitation in a system in which capital hires wage laborers and in a system in which workers rent capital. Let us look at each of these in turn.

Roemer demonstrates that exploitation can exist in an economy in which every producer owns his or her own means of production and in which there is consequently no market in either labor-power or means of production; the only things that are traded are final products of various sorts, *but* different producers own different amounts of productive assets. The result is that some producers have to work more hours than other producers to produce the exchange-equivalent of their own subsistence. What Roemer shows in this simple economy is that the result of trade among producers is not only that some producers work less than others for the same subsistence, but that the producers who work less are able to do so *because* the less-endowed producers have to work more. That is, an actual transfer of labor occurs from the asset-poor to the asset-rich. (The critical proof is that if the asset-poor person simply stopped producing – died – the asset-rich producer would be worse off than before and have to work longer hours.) Since in this economy the exploiter clearly does not in any way directly dominate the exploited – they both own their own means of production and use them as they please – this example shows that exploitation does not presuppose immediate domination relations. Of course, a repressive apparatus may be needed to guarantee the property rights themselves – to protect the asset-rich from theft of assets by the asset-poor – but no domination directly between the rich and poor is implied.

The second analysis is more complex. It compares the class structures on what Roemer calls a "labor market island" and a "credit market island." On both islands some people own no means of production, and other people own varying amounts of the means of production. The distribution of these assets is identical on the two islands. And on both islands people have the same motivations: they all are labor-time minimizers for a common level of subsistence. The two islands differ in only one respect: on the labor-market island, people are allowed to sell their labor-power, whereas on the credit-market island, people are not allowed to sell labor-power but are allowed to borrow, at some interest rate, the means of production. Roemer then demonstrates two things. First, that on each island there is a strict correspondence between class location (ownership of differing amounts of the means of production, including no means of production) and exploitation status (having one's surplus labor appropriated by someone else). This is his important "Class-Exploitation Correspondence Principle." Second, he demonstrates that the two class structures are completely isomorphic: every individual on one island would be in exactly the same class on the other island.

It is because of this strict functional equivalence of the labor-market island and the credit-market island that Roemer concludes that domination plays no essential role in the most abstract definition of classes. Roemer writes:

> Exploitation can be mediated entirely through the exchange of produced commodities and classes can exist with respect to a credit market instead of a labor market – at least at this level of abstraction. In this analysis, coercion is still necessary to produce Marxian exploitation and class. However, it suffices for the coercion to be at the point of maintaining property relations and not at the point of extracting surplus labor directly from the worker. . . . These results thus force some re-evaluation of the classical belief that the labor process is at the center of the Marxian analysis of exploitation and class. . . . I have demonstrated that the entire constellation of Marxian "welfare" concepts can be generated with no institution for the exchange of labor. Furthermore, this has been done at the level of abstraction at which Marxian value theory is customarily performed.[6]

Political relations are important for institutionally reproducing class and exploitation, but they are not essential in the very definitions of these concepts.

This is not, however, the only assessment of domination made in Roemer's analysis. Toward the end of the paper, when a game-theory approach is introduced, domination re-enters the analysis as a central feature. The idea is to compare the different systems of exploitation by treating the production system as a kind of game and asking if a coalition of players would be better off if they withdrew from the game under certain specified procedures. Different types of exploitation are defined by the withdrawal rules that would make certain kinds of agents better off. "Feudal exploitation" is defined as the situation in which agents would be better off if they withdrew from the game with only their

---

6. Roemer, "New Directions," p. 266.

personal assets (that is, if they were freed from relations of personal bondage). Capitalist exploitation is defined as the situation in which agents would be better off if they left the game with their per capita share of total social assets (not just personal assets).

Roemer's game is a clever and insightful device, but it immediately runs into problems without additional specifications. For example, under the rules laid out so far, the handicapped could be said to exploit the nonhandicapped feudalistically, since the nonhandicapped would be better off if they withdrew with their personal assets from the game in which the handicapped are aided. Even more damaging, perhaps, if two islands, one rich and one poor, are arbitrarily grouped together even though they have no relations with each other, the poor island would be considered "exploited" capitalistically by the richer one (that is, it would be better off if it withdrew from the game with its per capita share of the combined assets of the two islands).

It is to avoid these and related problems that Roemer added a number of further specifications of the game-theory approach in footnote 15 to the paper. There he states:

> a coalition S is said to be exploited at an allocation if two conditions hold: (1) that S does better than at the current allocation by taking its payoff as specified by the characteristic function of the game; and (2) that the complement of S (called S') does worse than at the current allocation by taking its payoff. . . . One way to pre-empt the invalid example might be to require a third condition for exploitation, namely, (3) that S' be in a relation of dominance to S. Since dominance is undefined and is as elusive a concept as exploitation, the addition of (3) is ad hoc . . . and reduces the sharpness of the game-theoretic characterization.[7]

This final criterion, Roemer's reluctance to include it notwithstanding, implies that a relationship of domination in some sense or other is required for the definition of exploitation and class. The handicapped do not dominate the nonhandicapped – indeed, if anything, the relations of domination are in the opposite direction – and thus even if they receive benefits from the assets of the nonhandicapped, they cannot be considered exploiters. Similarly, the poor island is not exploited by the rich one, since even though it would benefit from getting its per capita share

---

7. Ibid., p. 277.

of the two islands' combined assets, there is no social relationship between the people of the two islands.[8]

Why is it that, in the discussion of the game-theory strategy of analyzing class and exploitation, Roemer was compelled to introduce relations of domination into the basic definition of class, whereas in his earlier discussion he was not? It is because, I think, the initial discussion was confined to the problem of exploitation and class within commodity-producing economic systems, whereas the game-theory discussion was designed to explicate the problem across more fundamentally different economic systems, including non-commodity-producing economies. Since feudalism, for example, revolves around relations of bondage and since this is at the heart of the definition of feudal class relations, it is impossible to generate a purely economic definition of feudal classes. So-called extra-economic coercion must be considered part of the definition of class relations in feudalism, not simply an institutional boundary-setting political process. Within commodity-producing societies, however, it appears that political relations are separated from economic relations, and it becomes possible to talk about classes and property rights as if they did not imply domination.

This view of the relationship between class exploitation in commodity-producing systems is, I believe, incorrect. Let us return to Roemer's discussion of simple commodity production and the two market "islands." In each of these analyses Roemer convincingly shows that exploitation can be specified strictly in terms of property rights and their distributions. Domination enters the story of *exploitation* only externally, in the enforcement of property rights themselves.

But what about class relations? Here we notice that there is a critical difference between the analysis of simple commodity production and the two islands. In the simple commodity-producing case there are, in Roemer's view, no classes properly speaking, since all actors have the same relationship to the means of production, whereas in the two islands we do have classes: a class of owners and a class of non-owners. But why

---

8. I would want to add a fourth criterion to Roemer's three: the two groups not only must exist in a relationship of domination and subordination, but this relationship must in some sense causally explain the inequalities between the two groups. Prison guards, for example, dominate prisoners, and the prisoners would be better off materially (and in other respects) if they withdrew from the prison with their per capita share of the combined assets of guards and prisoners (or indeed with just their personal assets), but they are not necessarily exploited by the guards, since the income of the guards is not gained by virtue of their domination of prisoners (that is, they do not appropriate any surplus labor from prisoners). Roemer's second criterion – that S' be worse off – touches on this issue, but it is possible for S' to be worse off even if its position in the initial game did not explain the initial inequalities. (The situation in the prison example would be quite different, of course, if the guards obtained services from prisoners. Then part of the inequality between guards and prisoners would be causally explained by a relationship of domination and subordination.)

does owning matter to such an extent as to warrant the designation "class"? In the simple commodity-producing society depicted by Roemer there are people who may live a life of relative leisure because of the heavy toil of others. With relatively little modification of the conditions of his story we could also have people with very different levels of final consumption – rich and poor standards of living (rather than just high and low levels of toil). Why is not the distinction "rich" and "poor" itself a *class* distinction?

The reason is that the rich do not dominate the poor in the simple commodity-producing society. No social relationship binds them directly to each other in a relation of domination and subordination. In both the credit-market island and the labor-market island, however, the owners and non-owners are directly bound together in relations of domination and subordination. There is thus a crucial difference between having few assets, but still enough to produce one's own means of subsistence, and having no assets, and thus having to either sell one's labor-power or rent the assets of others. Rich asset-owners do not directly tell the poor asset-owners what to do – they do not directly dominate them. However, a new kind of social relation is generated between the asset-owner and the non-owner: owners do dominate non-owners.

This implies that the *property rights* have a different social content in the two cases. In the simple commodity-producing economy, property rights only specify a set of effective powers over *things* – productive assets. While of course such effective powers imply that one has the right to exclude other people from using those assets (or to prevent them from taking them), the right itself implies no ongoing relationship in which effective powers over people are exercised. In the credit-market and labor-market economies, property rights imply a set of effective powers over both things and people. The owner of assets not only has the right to use those assets but the right to control in specific ways the behavior of people who have no assets but who desire to gain access to assets. The labor contract and the credit contract both imply a relation of domination – an agreement on the part of those without assets to follow certain orders from those with assets.

Because property rights in the labor-market and credit-market islands entail such relations of domination and subordination, the exploitation relations in this case constitute a class relation and not simply a basis of inequality.[9] Exploitation without domination, or domination without

9. G. A. Cohen makes a similar point in his discussion of classes and subordination. He argues that the distribution of ownership rights specifies class relations only when combined with relations of subordination and domination. See G. A. Cohen, *Karl Marx's Theory of History: A Defense*, Princeton, N.J. 1979, pp. 69–70.

exploitation, do not constitute class relations. Domination by itself, such as that of prison guards over prisoners, may be a form of oppression, but not class oppression. Similarly, exploitation without domination is not a form of class relations. Children certainly appropriate the surplus labor of their parents, but do not (at least in the normal sense of the term) dominate them and thus cannot be considered a "ruling class" within a family.[10]

Roemer is thus correct when he asserts that analyzing the labor process is not essential to specify the minimum conditions for capitalist exploitation. But he is wrong when he asserts that the labor process is also not essential for an abstract understanding of class relations in capitalism. At a very minimum, the capitalist labor process must be understood as a structure of relations within which capitalists have the capacity to dominate workers. For ownership to be the basis of a class relation, ownership rights must imply domination over the activity of workers. And this is indeed what the analyses of the labor process are concerned with: the forms of domination that govern laboring activity within production.[11]

Implications for Class Analysis

The argument that the political is intrinsic to the concept of class at even the highest level of abstraction has a number of important implications

---

10. But note: where fathers both exploit and dominate their children, as is true in some societies, then the father–child relation could be considered a form of class relation.

11. As we will see in the next chapter, it can be argued that domination also enters the analysis of capitalist class relations because workers will generally prefer to labor at a lower intensity than desired by capitalists. Domination is thus needed in order to get workers to actually perform labor once they are hired, or in traditional Marxist terms, to transform labor-power into labor. Roemer, in a personal communication, has objected to this argument for the importance of domination on the grounds that the reduction of work effort by workers is parallel to the problem of capitalists "cheating" each other. Thus, just as Marx bracketed the problem of cheating in contracts among capitalists in his abstract analysis of capitalism, Roemer argues we should bracket the problem of "cheating" in the contracts between workers and capitalists, even though the problem of such cheating may be massively important in understanding the concrete institutions of hierarchy within production. Roemer's argument here hinges on the view that the labor effort problem is strictly analogous conceptually to capitalists cheating each other in exchange relations. There is, however, a fundamental difference in the two cases. Inter-capitalist exchanges are symmetrical, and thus cheating is equally likely to occur on both sides. Both parties to the exchange therefore have identical basic interests with respect to the problem of cheating. The capital–labor exchange is radically asymmetrical, and the problem of effectively extracting labor effort from workers is an inherent part of the relation created by the exchange. The actors have intrinsically different interests with respect to this issue. As a result domination is not a contingent property of the capital–labor relation that only enters at a lower level of abstraction; it is an essential aspect of the relation itself.

for class analysis. I will discuss several of these: implications for the labor theory of value; implications for the defense of the Marxist concept of class against its various bourgeois rivals; implications for the more concrete elaboration of the concept of class in capitalist societies; implications for the problem of classes in socialism; and implications for the general Marxist analysis of modes of production.

The labor theory of value

Roemer argues that the justification for choosing labor-power as the numeraire commodity for defining value and exploitation is that it is uniformly distributed throughout the population. This property is essential for a "proper" theory of exploitation, that is, a theory that classifies the poor as exploited and the rich as exploiters. Only labor-power, Roemer argues, has this property since "no produced commodity is uniformly distributed, since proletarians are dispossessed of all productive assets."[12] Furthermore, the purpose of the theory is to explain class struggle between capitalists and workers, and the use of labor-power does indeed generate a theory of exploitation that corresponds to the polarization between capitalists and workers.

Once we add domination relations directly into our idea of class, a different kind of argument can be built for the use of labor-power as the numeraire commodity or, equivalently, for the use of labor time as the metric for exploitation. Labor time, as opposed to any other metric for the surplus product, is simultaneously a measure of appropriation relations and domination relations. It is a measure of how much product is appropriated and how much human time is dominated through that appropriation. As appropriators, exploiting classes appropriate surplus *products* in one way or another, and if the appropriation relation was sufficient to define class relations, any basic good could provide a satisfactory metric for the quantitative aspect of class relations. But, as I have argued, the concept of class is intrinsically a political concept as well. The ideal metric of exploitation, therefore, should capture both aspects of class relations. Labor time does do this, for it identifies how much laboring activity is appropriated by virtue of domination in production.[13]

To justify the choice of labor time as the metric of exploitation we

---

12. Roemer, "New Directions," p. 274.
13. Labor time is, of course, only a *quantitative* measure of domination relations, not qualitative. Labor time by itself does not provide an adequate way of analyzing domination, but it is the one metric of value that expresses both the magnitude of the product and the magnitude of domination.

must argue that domination relations are as central to class relations as are appropriation relations. While I have shown that domination relations are implied in Roemer's analysis even though he relegates them to secondary importance, I have not yet provided a general argument in support of their importance in a class analysis. To do so, I will turn to a comparison of Marxist and non-Marxist concepts of class.

Marxist versus non-Marxist concepts of class

Non-Marxist concepts of class typically take one of two forms: either they are structured around categories of distribution without reference to domination, or they are structured around categories of domination without reference to distribution. In the first of these tendencies, class is defined either directly in terms of distributional outcomes (incomes) or in terms of the proximate determinants of those outcomes (occupation or "market capacity" – the Weberian approach). In either case, relations of domination are either absent from or incidental to the discussion. The second tendency, most explicitly found in the work of Ralph Dahrendorf, defines classes solely in terms of power, or authority relations. There are "command classes" and "obey classes" in every institutional sphere of the society, with no special status being given to economic institutions.

The Marxist account of class subsumes both of these images of class relations through the concept of exploitation. Class relations are the unity of appropriation relations (the Marxist way of theorizing categories of distribution) and domination. The justification for this view of class relations rests on two arguments. First, within production relations, domination without appropriation and appropriation without domination are unreproducible structures of social relations.[14] Second, the coincidence of domination and appropriation within production relations provides the basis for understanding collective actors in the epochal processes of social conflict and social change.[15] The first of these can be

---

14. This does not mean that in every social position, domination and appropriation perfectly coincide but that a complete non-correspondence cannot be stable. It is entirely possible in capitalist production for certain positions – middle and lower management for example – to be in a domination relation to workers without being in an appropriation relation. This kind of noncoincidence is the heart of the idea of "contradictory locations within class relations," a concept developed to decode the class logic of "middle strata." See Wright, *Class, Crisis and the State*, chapter 2. What I am excluding as a possible structure of production relations is one in which power is completely divorced from appropriation.

15. "Epochal social change" refers to fundamental, qualitative transformations of a society's social structure. In the Marxist tradition this revolves around a transformation from one mode of production to another.

termed the "conditions of existence" argument, the second, the "historical materialism" argument. Let us briefly examine each in turn.

The first thesis states that within the social relations of production any time the relations of domination and appropriation cease to correspond with each other the situation would be highly unstable and tend toward a restoration of correspondence. Imagine, for example, that as the result of a series of labor reforms, workers organized in militant trade unions won the capacity to collectively organize the process of work, including the capacity to allocate labor and the means of production to different purposes, but that the rights to the products produced with these means of production, and thus the appropriation of the surplus product, remained in private hands. Capitalists could not tell workers what to do or fire them, but because they owned the means of production and appropriated the surplus product they could effectively veto any investment decision made by workers (for example, they could decide to consume their surplus rather than let it be used productively). This would be a situation in which appropriation brought with it no immediate power of domination, and domination was unaccompanied by appropriation. In such a situation it seems likely that either workers would attempt to extend their powers to include actual appropriation *or* that the appropriators' capacity to block investments would become a new means of domination, thus undermining or limiting the apparent domination of production by workers.

A radical non-correspondence between appropriation and domination within the relations of production cannot endure for long periods of time. There are two basic reasons for this. First, the appropriation of surplus products requires power. Direct producers usually do not like to toil for the benefit of exploiting classes, and unless there are coercive mechanisms at the disposal of the exploiting class to force them to do so, the level of exploitation is likely to decline. Second, unless relations of domination enable people in positions of domination to command resources, that domination quickly reaches severe limits. In the end, it is the capacity to command the use of the social surplus that provides the material basis for effective domination within the relations of production.

A concept of class that unites the relations of domination and appropriation, therefore, is structured around the necessary conditions of existence of both domination and appropriation. But Marxist theoretical claims go beyond this kind of functional or reproductive argument. Historical materialism, in its various incarnations, is an attempt to understand the conditions and dynamics of epochal social change and social conflict, not simply the conditions for the reproduction of stable structures of social relations. To define class as the unity of domination and appropriation is meant also to provide a way of understanding these problems.

A defense of historical materialism (or more accurately, of a modified version of historical materialism) lies outside the scope of this chapter, but I will offer a few comments on the suitability of the concept of class being discussed here for the theoretical ambitions of historical materialism.[16] The heart of social change necessarily revolves around the transformations of the social use and allocation of productive time and resources. This has two important implications for the present discussion. First, since class struggles are structured by the social relations within which laboring time and resources are allocated and used, such struggles are always implicated in epochal social change (although this does not imply that all such change is reducible to class struggles; other kinds of conflict, involving other sorts of actors and determinations, may also be of great importance in specific historical circumstances).

Second, any social movement, whatever its social base and whatever its logic of development, that pursues projects of fundamental social change ultimately faces the problems of reorganizing how time and resources are controlled. If the system of class relations is left intact, then there are clear limits to the range of possible social changes. If those limits are to be surpassed, then the social movement must be a movement for the transformation of class relations. Ethnic, religious, nationalist, and other non-class movements are thus forced to engage in class-like struggles, struggles that systematically transform basic class relations.

To summarize: non-Marxist accounts of class stress either distribution (appropriation) or domination, but not the unity of these two within a concept of class exploitation. The Marxist attempt to combine these two elements within a single concept produces a much more powerful theoretical tool, both in terms of analyzing the conditions of the existence of classes (the relational requirements of their reproduction) and in terms of analyzing the conditions for epochal social transformation. For both of these purposes it is essential in analyzing class structures that classes be understood as having a political dimension even at the highest level of abstraction.

Implications for the concrete investigation of class structures

Abstract concepts are to be evaluated not only for their logical presuppositions and coherence, but for their usefulness in more concrete

---

16. For my views on classical historical materialism and its weaknesses, see Andrew Levine and Erik Olin Wright, "Rationality and Class Struggle," *New Left Review*, no. 123, 1980.

investigations. One of the advantages of a concept of class that is defined explicitly in terms of the unity of exploitation and domination relations is that it provides a strategy for examining capitalist class relations at more concrete levels.

For example, such a concept provides a way of understanding the class character of managerial positions within capitalist production. Managers can generally be understood as locations within the social relations of production that (1) dominate the working class, (2) are dominated by the bourgeoisie, and (3) are exploited by capital, but (4) are exploited to a lesser extent than are workers. Whereas the capitalist class and the working class are perfectly polarized on both the domination and exploitation dimensions, managers occupy what I have termed elsewhere a "contradictory location within class relations."[17] They are simultaneously in the capitalist class and in the working class, occupying class locations that have some of the relational characteristics of each class. If capitalist class relations are defined exclusively in terms of exploitation relations, then most managers would fall into the working class. The specification of class in terms of both exploitation and domination thus provides a strategy for more concrete analyses of class.

The analysis of socialist exploitation and class

One of the most promising lines of investigation opened up in Roemer's work is the strategy for analyzing exploitation in socialist societies. Roemer suggests that socialist exploitation should be understood in terms of inequalities generated by the distribution of "inalienable assets," that is, skills. The exploiters in socialism are those who possess skills; the exploited are the unskilled. Given Roemer's formal criteria for exploitation, this would be a reasonable way of characterizing the distributional outcomes of skill inequalities in socialist societies.

The question, however, is whether or not this kind of exploitation can be considered a class relationship. If, in addition to benefiting from an exploitive redistribution, the skilled also dominated the unskilled, then this relationship would constitute a class relation. However, unlike the possession of alienable assets, the sheer possession of skills does not

---

17. See Wright, *Class, Crisis and the State*, chapter 2. In subsequent work, especially in *Classes*, I critized this particular strategy for understanding the class location of managers. Instead of seeing managers as a special position defined by domination and appropriation, I argued that managers should be seen as exploiting workers through a distinctive mechanism based in their control of organizational resources. More recently, in "Rethinking, Once Again, the Concept of Class Structure" (chapter 8 in *The Debate on Classes*), I have criticized this second formulation and proposed a conception closer to the one discussed here. For a brief discussion of these issues see pp. 250–51 below.

logically entail domination of the skilled over the unskilled. Thus, it is possible to imagine a situation in which the skilled still received an exploitive redistribution of income, even though production was controlled by democratic bodies of workers that decide on production priorities and procedures and that give orders to both skilled and unskilled workers. This would be the case, for example, if the only way of inducing people to acquire skills is through heavy incentives that effectively redistribute income from the unskilled to the skilled. This does not imply, however, that within the actual organization of ongoing production it was the skilled workers who dominated the unskilled workers. In such a situation, the skilled could reasonably be regarded as a privileged stratum of workers, but not as a different class.

The two kinds of "socialist" societies we have described are likely to have very different forms of social conflict, even though they may share a similar pattern of distribution. If the skilled actually dominated the unskilled as well as exploited them, social conflicts would be likely to crystallize between the unskilled and skilled. If the skilled received exploitative redistributive benefits, but did not dominate the unskilled, conflicts would be less likely to take on a class-like character. Conflicts might develop over the motivational underpinnings of the incentive structures, but they would not necessarily develop between the skilled and unskilled. If, however, we fail to distinguish these two situations by failing to incorporate the notion of domination into the specification of class relations, then in both cases skilled and unskilled would have to be regarded as antagonistic classes.[18]

Modes of production

I argued earlier that to include the political in the structural definition of class would facilitate a class analysis of the social conflicts implicated in

---

18. The conditions under which socialist "exploitation" becomes crystallized as a new form of class structure bears directly on what Roemer terms "status exploitation." Although not analyzed extensively in his "New Directions," Roemer's status exploitation refers to situations in which a person receives exploitative net redistributions not by virtue of ownership of private property or skills, but by virtue of incumbency in some office, typically of a bureaucratic character. I would argue that when socialist exploitation as defined by Roemer becomes a form of class relations, that is, when it coincides with relations of domination, it will also tend to generate what Roemer calls status exploitation, but which might more apropriately be called "bureaucratic exploitation." While according to traditional Marxism, socialism is not a new mode of production but rather a transition from a class society (capitalism) to a classless one (communism), the concept of bureaucratic or status exploitation suggests the existence of a form of postcapitalist class relations, a new mode of production altogether. For a further elaboration of these issues, see chapter 6 below.

epochal social change. In this final section I will examine how this definition of classes affects the theoretical specification of the "epochs" themselves, that is, of "modes of production."

In distinguishing capitalism and feudalism as modes of production, Marxists have usually stressed that feudal exploitation required "extra-economic" coercion whereas capitalist exploitation was purely "economic." This formulation was typically accompanied by the claim that in feudalism politics and economics (or the state and production) were institutionally fused in the social organization of the feudal manor, whereas in capitalism the political and the economic are institutionally separated.

The argument of this chapter challenges this traditional view of the modes of production. Classes in both capitalism and feudalism imply domination, and not simply system-preserving coercion, but domination directly within the social organization of production itself. The issue is where the coercion is located, how it is organized, and how it is articulated to other aspects of the system of production (technical, ideological, and so forth). Instead of seeing the contrast between capitalism and feudalism as economic exploitation versus extra-economic coercion, the contrast should be formulated as follows: class exploitation based on non-coercion outside the labor process and on coercion inside the labor process versus class exploitation based on coercion outside the labor process and on self-determination inside. The issue, then, is how the political dimension of the production relations is linked to the economic dimension of those same relations.[19]

This way of understanding production suggests a simple typology of modes of production, as shown in Table 3.1.[20] I will briefly discuss three implications of this typology for class analysis: the problem of class formation, the analysis of politics in general, and the transition between

---

19. Ellen Meiksins Wood, in an important article, "The Separation of the Economic and Political in Capitalism," *New Left Review*, no. 127, May–June 1981, pp. 66–95, makes a similar argument. She characterizes capitalism as a social system in which politics are made private (that is, removed from the "public sphere") through the organization of "politics of production" within the private factory. In feudalism, the political dimension of production coincided with the political dimension of the state – both were united in the feudal lord, and thus the politics of production had a "public" character. In capitalism, it is not that the political and the economic are institutionally separated, but that the political dimensions of production are institutionally separated from the state. For related arguments on politics of production, see Michael Burawoy, "The Politics of Production and the Production of Politics," *Political Power and Social Theory*, vol. 1, ed. Maurice Zeitlin, Greenwich, Conn. 1979.

20. This typology is only a first approximation. To deal effectively with such modes of production as the "Asiatic mode of production" or (if it is a legitimate concept) the "state bureaucratic mode of production," various distinctions within the category "coercion outside of the labor process" would have to be made. I will not explore these issues here.

Table 3.1   Typology of Modes of Production

Mode of Production	Political Dimension Outside the Labor Process	Political Dimension Inside the Labor Process
Slavery	Domination	Domination
Feudalism	Domination	Self-determination
Capitalism	Self-determination	Domination
Communism	Self-determination	Self-determination

modes of production, particularly from capitalism to socialism and communism.

Class formation
Traditionally, Marxists have understood the process of class formation as a transition from a "class-in-itself," which was seen as an economic category, to a "class-for-itself," which was seen as a political category. The analysis presented here suggests that classes can never be seen as purely economic categories, even at their most disorganized and atomized. They are always political. This suggests that instead of seeing class formation as a one-dimensional process of political formation, we should develop a typology of class formations. Classes can be formed around the political dimensions of production relations, around the political dimensions of the state, or around both. Without attempting to defend the argument, I suggest the simple typology of working-class formations shown in Table 3.2.

Politics
Politics cannot be analyzed simply as state-centered political processes and practices, that is, as politics oriented toward and structured by the state apparatuses. Instead, political analysis should focus on the articulation of what Michael Burawoy has called "global politics" and "production politics" – politics organized around the state and politics organized within the process of production.[21] Burawoy, for example, analyzes the relationship between these two sites of politics in the transition from the colonial to the independent state in Zambia, paying particular attention to the politics of production in the mining sector.[22] The mode of

---

21. See especially Michael Burawoy, "Terrains of Contest," *Socialist Review*, no. 58, 1981.
22. See Michael Burawoy, "The Hidden Abode of Underdevelopment," *Politics & Society*, vol. 11, no. 2, 1982.

Table 3.2 The Political Dimension of Class Formation

Political Formation of Working Class	Formation Centered on Production Politics	Formation Centered on State Politics
Syndicalist	Yes	No
Reformist		
social democratic	No	Yes
Revolutionary	Yes	Yes

production in mining, Burawoy argues, can best be characterized as a "colonial mode of production," a variant of capitalism that depended upon coercive forms of labor control and on certain forms of extra-economic coercion outside of the labor process. The whole social organization of the mines was built around this particular form of production during the colonial period. Burawoy then observes what happens when there is a drastic change in the form of the state and an accompanying change in the character of global politics, while the structure of the production system in the mines remains relatively unchanged. This meant in Zambia that global politics and production politics no longer corresponded with but instead contradicted each other.

Transitions between modes of production
The classic Leninist position on the transition between capitalism and socialism was that the proletariat had to *smash* the capitalist state apparatus and construct a new kind of state – a proletarian form of the state – that would enable the working class to be stabilized as a ruling class. Expropriating the means of production from the capitalist class plus restructuring the state were sufficient to consolidate socialism and accordingly to ensure the transition to communism. As became clear in Lenin's praise of Taylorism (scientific management), one-man management, and so on, no fundamental restructuring of production politics was deemed necessary.

The argument of this chapter suggests that the transition from capitalism to socialism requires a change in production politics as well as in global politics. If workers are dominated within production relations, it is hard to see how they could become a dominant class in any meaningful sense of the word, even if private ownership of the means of production were abolished. Under such conditions a new class system is likely to emerge in which public appropriation of the surplus product would combine with new forms of domination over direct producers. It is only when the political dimension of production relations and thus of class relations is recognized that such a new class system can be adequately theorized. If forms of appropriation of surplus labor are the only criterion for class, and if modes of production are understood in purely economic terms, then the public appropriation of the surplus product becomes *ipso facto* socialist production.

John Roemer's work is one of the few genuinely novel contributions to the Marxist theory of exploitation and class to be produced in recent years. It opens up possibilities not only for deepening our understanding of exploitation within a Marxist perspective but for critically assessing the competing claims made by the different theoretical traditions. His analysis is less satisfactory when he extends his idea of exploitation to the problem of class. The value of the Marxist concept of class lies in the way it links together economic and political relations within a single category. Classes are not determined solely by relations of exploitation or by relations of domination, but by the two together. If domination is ignored or made marginal, as it is in some of Roemer's analysis, the concept of class loses much of its power in explaining social conflict and historical transformation.

4

Coercion and Consent in Contested Exchange

(with Michael Burawoy)

At the core of Sam Bowles and Herbert Gintis's paper, "Contested Exchange," is a classical problem in Marxist theory: what are the mechanisms that explain the capacity of capitalists to actually appropriate surplus labor from workers?[1] The simple fact of a labor contract between workers and capitalists is insufficient to explain real appropriation. In the labor contract, workers merely sell their capacity to work to capitalists – their labor-power. How is it, then, that capitalists manage to get workers to perform sufficient actual labor effort to produce a profit above the costs (wages) of that labor-power?

Bowles and Gintis's answer to this question revolves around a complex analysis of the relationship between surveillance, threats, and wages in capitalist firms. The basic strategy for employers to get workers to provide adequate labor effort, they argue, is threats of various sorts, especially the threat of being fired. In order for the threat of firing to be effective, however, workers have to believe that there is some chance that they will be caught if they shirk and they must care about being fired. The use of such threats, therefore, imposes two kinds of cost on employers. First, there is the obvious cost of surveillance itself. In order to punish workers for shirking, bosses have to be able to detect this behavior, and this requires hiring (and paying) supervisors of various sorts and adopting other costly monitoring techniques. Second, in order for workers to care about the threat of firing, they must face significant costs for losing their jobs. This means that the wages of workers must be significantly above their reservation wage – the income they would have if they lost their job. This means that employers have to pay workers what Bowles and Gintis call an "employment rent" – an increment of income above the "market clearing wage"– so that they will care about

---

1. Sam Bowles and Herbert Gintis, "Contested Exchange," *Politics & Society*, June 1990.

keeping their jobs. Employers, then, face a strategic trade-off in deciding on the level of surveillance and employment rents they will use to control their employees: the higher the employment rent, the lower the costs of direct monitoring, since workers with high wages will be more worried about losing their jobs than workers whose wages are closer to their reservation wage, and thus less surveillance will be needed to instill fear of firing.

Bowles and Gintis's analyses constitute an interesting contribution on at least two scores. First, radical political economists have paid relatively little attention to efficiency wage theory and the transaction costs approach to organizational economics. Bowles and Gintis systematically incorporate these theoretical traditions into the agenda of Marxism. This incorporation has important implications not only for Marxist treatments of exploitation (the transformation of labor-power into labor) but also for a range of other problems such as the structural bases for unemployment in a competitive economy, the rationing of credit in capital markets, or the forms of power that divide employed from unemployed workers. Secondly, in a complementary manner, neoclassical economists have not understood the implications of transaction cost theory for the relationship between power and exchange. In their development of the concept of short-side power, Bowles and Gintis demonstrate that in any arena of market exchanges in which there are significant transaction costs in monitoring compliance with the terms of the contract, real power relations are likely to be constructed within the exchange relation.

In our judgment, the central weakness in Bowles and Gintis's analysis is that they do not treat their models of contested exchange as simply specifying one particular mechanism among several for insuring the performance of labor, but as constituting the most general or characteristic mechanism in capitalist societies. In contrast, we will argue (1) that the surveillance-threat mechanism elaborated by Bowles and Gintis is only one of a variety of mechanisms for generating labor effort within capitalist labor contracts, (2) that, except in certain relatively limited historical situations, this is not the most important mechanism, and (3) that in certain contexts, particularly in the case of generating effective performance by managers and experts, heavy reliance on a surveillance-threat mechanism can actually reduce effective performance of labor. In short, we will argue that Bowles and Gintis operate within a too restricted theoretical appreciation both of the logic of strategic action by workers within production and of what we will call the "non-strategic elements of strategic action," and thus tend illegitimately to treat the specific mechanism of contested exchange as the general solution to the problem of surplus appropriation.[2]

___

2. The non-strategic elements of strategic action include, among other things, what

A Typology of Mechanisms for Eliciting Labor Effort

It will be useful to distinguish two dimensions on which mechanisms that generate labor effort within labor contracts vary. The first concerns the *cognitive mechanisms* underlying the explanation of behavioral compliance: *strategic rationality* and two kinds of *non-strategic norms* we will call *behavioral* and *evaluative*. By strategic rationality we refer to cognitive processes in which actions are the result of a cost/benefit assessment by the individual of the likely consequences of alternative choices. Bowles and Gintis's argument that workers exert labor effort because of the expectation that shirking will lead to being fired would be an example. In contrast, when compliance is the result of non-strategic norms, individuals do not exert effort as a result of a rational calculation of the costs and benefits of the consequences of compliance and non-compliance but rather because they feel they *ought* to exert effort, that it is the moral thing to do.[3] This could be because, for example, they feel that it would be unfair for them not to do so. In the case of *behavioral* norms, the normative principle in question is directly applied to one's own behavior. In the case of *evaluative* norms, the normative judgment is applied to the behavior of others. Thus, for example, to describe a person as complying with an order because of the belief in the legitimacy of the authority issuing the order is to say that the authority in question satisfied a particular evaluative norm we call "legitimacy."

In describing strategic rationality and non-strategic norms as distinct cognitive mechanisms, we are not suggesting that in any given situation only one of these could be operative. In general, social actions will involve both strategic and normative considerations. Thus, for example, when workers obey an order by a boss, this is likely to be due in part to a rational calculation of the consequences of non-compliance and in part to various kinds of norms operating in the situation (that is, norms of obedience to legitimate authority or norms of fairness). As we shall argue below, the stability and efficacy of the social practices within which strategic rationality operates in part depend upon the presence of appropriate, corresponding, non-strategic norms.

---

sociologists have called the "non-contractual elements of contract," but also, as we shall see, the various normative underpinnings of domination.

3. To describe norms as "non-strategic" does not mean that they do not indirectly enter into strategic action. For example, normative judgments can rule out certain alternatives among a feasible set and thus shape strategic choices. It can also be the case that there are strategic considerations that enter into the decision to apply a norm. Thus, frequently, if the costs of following a norm exceed some threshold, the norm may be ignored. For an interesting discussion of the interplay of normative and strategic dimensions of rational action, see Margaret Levi's discussion of "quasi-voluntary compliance" in *Of Revenue and Rule*, Berkeley 1988, chapter 1.

The second general dimension we will use to examine the problem of generating labor effort concerns its *immediate relational basis*: *domination* or *asymmetrical reciprocity*. By "*immediate* relational basis" we refer to the qualities of the social relations *within production itself* that directly impinge on the practices of workers and bosses. In the case of domination, labor effort is performed because of the continual presence of various kinds of threats by bosses that individuals face if they are caught shirking. In the case of asymmetrical reciprocity, labor effort is based on consent, on the positive agreement by each of the parties concerned over the mutual, if still unequal, benefits of the exertion of such effort.

This does not imply, it must be stressed, that coercion plays no role in generating such consent, but simply that coercion is not being directly applied routinely to generate effort. Coercion is linked to consent in two ways. First, because in the contexts we will discuss the relations are deeply asymmetrical, coercion remains essential for reproducing the rules of the game within which such agreements are forged. As Gramsci put it, consent is always surrounded by the armor of coercion. The point is that under conditions of asymmetrical reciprocity, direct coercion is not a ubiquitous mechanism for eliciting effort. Second, in order to sustain consent, coercion may also be applied to sanction certain forms of individual deviance not simply to maintain the rules of the game as such. In factories coercion is used to repress individual acts of theft, not simply to protect private property against collective appropriation. This is consistent with the fact that fear of punishment for theft may not be the central mechanism for explaining why most workers refrain from stealing (although such repression may be important in maintaining the norms against theft).[4] The claim that effort is elicited through consent under conditions of asymmetrical reciprocity, therefore, does not imply the complete absence of coercion but simply that individual effort is not a strategic response to direct surveillance and threats.

If we put these two dimensions together, we get the general typology

---

4. Margaret Levi elaborates the relationship between coercion and consent in an interesting way in her analysis of why people pay taxes. She argues that limited, rule-bound use of coercion plays a critical role in facilitating what she terms "quasi-voluntary compliance." In many situations, she argues, most people pay their taxes not primarily because of the threat of coercion. Nevertheless, coercion plays a crucial role since it helps to ensure some minimal level of tax payment in a population. Given that this level is above a critical threshold, many people will voluntarily pay their taxes on the normative grounds that they will pay their fair share given that other people are doing so. The coercion therefore serves to create the necessary context for the norms against free riding to generate voluntary compliance. See Levi, *Of Revenue and Rule*. Limited, rule-bound coercion may play a similar role in stabilizing the conditions for consent to labor effort within capitalist production.

Table 4.1   A Typology of Mechanisms for Extracting
Labor Effort from Labor-Power

| | | Immediate Relational Basis for Behavioral Compliance | |
		Domination	Asymmetrical Reciprocity
Cognitive mechanisms underlying explanation of behavioral compliance	*Strategic rationality*	Surveillance/ coercion models (Bowles and Gintis: contested exchange)	Hegemony/consent models
	Behavioral norms	Obedience (Bowles and Gintis: schooling)	Responsibility
	Evaluative norms	Legitimacy	Fairness

of mechanisms that generate labor effort illustrated in Table 4.1. The two columns in this table, "Domination" and "Asymmetrical Reciprocity," constitute two ideal types. Thus compliance within immediate relations of domination is likely to be the most stable when the surveillance and coercion that define the context of strategic rationality are complemented by strong behavioral norms of obedience and beliefs in the legitimacy of authority. Similarly, the strategic rationality that underwrites consent under conditions of asymmetrical reciprocity is likely to be much more stable in the presence of strong norms of responsible performance and beliefs in the fairness of bosses. The working-class aphorism "a fair day's work for a fair day's pay" embodies an evaluative norm (a fair day's pay) and a behavioral norm (a fair day's work) that help stabilize strategically rational consent. This constellation of mechanisms is generally referred to as a "hegemonic" system.

Several points of clarification of the logic of the categories in this typology are necessary. First, there is no implication from this typology that in concrete work settings only one set of effort-inducing mechanisms will be present. In some settings, different labor processes may be governed by different mechanisms (for example, when there are dual labor markets within factories); in other cases, single labor processes may be characterized by the coexistence of both hegemonic and non-hegemonic mechanisms. This means that we can talk about the *degree* to which hegemonic practices for generating consent are the basis for eliciting labor effort, rather than simply about the presence or absence of such practices.

Second, there is also no implication from the typology that the presence of consent within hegemonic practices implies the absence of conflict. The *reciprocity* in asymmetrical reciprocity is forged through struggle in which workers win concessions of various sorts in exchange for responsibly performing labor within production. Furthermore, such reciprocity is not maintained simply through social inertia but itself requires various forms of ongoing conflict. Consent and conflict should thus not be viewed as antinomies but rather as complements.

Third, the linkage between consent and conflict implies that consent within asymmetrical reciprocity is always conditional, subject to contestation, renegotiation, transformation. Underlying consent is some kind of *quid pro quo* bargain. Depending upon social and economic conditions, both employers and workers may be tempted to erode their side of the bargain, and in so doing the material basis for consent may also erode. Identifying the distinctive properties of this mechanism, therefore, does not imply any claim that once in place consent is self-reproducing and unconditional.

Finally, the typology of mechanisms for extracting labor effort does not imply that in actual work settings there is invariably a correspondence between the strategic and normative rows of the table. Workers, for example, may perform labor effort because of the surveillance and threats characteristic of strategic rationality under conditions of domination even in the absence of strong norms of obedience and beliefs in the legitimacy authority of the boss. Such a situation corresponds to what might be called a purely *despotic* system of labor compliance.[5] Alternatively, if less realistically, if the norms of obedience were incredibly strong and deeply internalized, then conceivably workers might perform adequate labor effort within a relation of domination even without significant surveillance and threats. Similarly for the case of asymmetrical reciprocity: workers may strategically consent to perform effort given an understanding of the benefits of such performance without necessarily believing that the employers are fair. The logic of the typology suggests that strategic consent is likely to be more effective and durable if the implicit bargain is viewed as fair by workers and if behavioral norms of responsible work are strong. When such normative mechanisms are present, both parties to the bargain are less likely to be tempted to opportunistically erode their side of the bargain. Nevertheless, some

---

5. Michael Burawoy's analysis of "market despotism" approaches such a situation. Compliance is enforced largely through a variety of mechanisms of surveillance and threats, with very limited normative backing. See *The Politics of Production*, chapters 2–3.

level of strategic consent is possible even without such normative backing.[6]

Bowles and Gintis's work has been firmly rooted in the domination side of this table. In their earlier, important study of education, *Schooling in Capitalist America*, one of the central themes revolved around the schooling practices that internalized norms of obedience to authority among working-class children.[7] Docile, obedient workers were workers suited to exploitation, and one of the goals of schooling, Bowles and Gintis argued, was to produce that kind of person.[8]

In "Contested Exchange," the analysis shifts decisively from cognitive mechanisms involving the socialization of behavioral norms to strategic rationality. But Bowles and Gintis remain firmly committed to understanding workers' effort as fundamentally a problem of compliance within relations of domination. The exertion of effort by workers is seen as resulting from external authority that deploys surveillance threats in such a way as to make compliance strategically rational for the individual. Unlike the analysis developed in *Schooling in Capitalist America*, the normative aspects of domination play no role in this explanation. And even more significantly, we will argue, the explanation does not entertain the possibility that effort is expended by workers through processes that elicit their active consent.

It is perhaps natural for Marxists to believe that if workers act on the basis of strategic rationality, they will exert effort in production only under conditions of externally imposed commands, surveillance, and sanctions. If the interests of workers and capitalists are radically polarized, it would seem, even asymmetrical reciprocity is impossible and their relationship must be characterized essentially as a relation of pure domination. And if, then, workers act on the basis of strategic rationality, they will not spontaneously initiate effort without threats from bosses. Such assumptions suggest the centrality of the surveillance/

---

6. There is, again, an analogy between our analysis of labor effort and Levi's analysis of tax paying. She argues that one of the pivotal conditions for quasi-voluntary compliance is that taxpayers see the tax system as fair and the state as responsibly providing the public goods contained in the *bargain* between taxpayers and the state.

7. Samuel Bowles and Herbert Gintis, *Schooling in Capitalist America*, New York 1976.

8. A secondary theme in *Schooling in Capitalist America* – and a dominant theme in much other radical literature on education – is the ways the competitive practices of schooling teach children the legitimacy of meritocratic authority and hierarchy. This, along with more direct affirmations of the legitimacy of private property, contributes to internalizing the critical evaluative norms linked to authority relations. A very different picture emerges from Paul Willis's study, *Learning to Labour*, New York 1981, in which neither obedience nor legitimacy, but rather *resistance* to schooling and to mental work leads working-class "lads" to embrace manual work, creating the normative foundations for consent to capitalist work relations.

coercion mechanisms of contested exchange to the extraction of labor from workers.

One of the significant contributions of the Gramscian tradition in Marxist theory is to argue that consent by workers based in part on strategic rationality (and not just on norms and delusions) is possible in capitalism. This is precisely what the concept of *hegemony* is meant to convey: a system in which the conflicting interests of workers and capitalists are coordinated in such a way that workers spontaneously consent to their own exploitation.

How is this possible? The presupposition of Gramscian approaches to class analysis is that the interests of workers and capitalists are *not* monolithically polarized. To be sure, *if* the conflict is over capitalism versus socialism, the interests of workers and capitalists may become radically polarized, but so long as conflicts are contained within capitalism itself, this is not usually the case. Under many circumstances, workers have positive interests in the profitability and survival of the firms for which they work. Unless there are many equally good jobs readily available, layoffs and unemployment represent costs to workers. Even if layoffs were random (that is, there was no system of seniority in place) and there were no surveillance by bosses at all (and thus an individual worker's own performance would not directly increase the probabilities of that individual worker being laid off when layoffs occurred), workers in most firms would have an interest in reducing the probabilities of layoffs. Furthermore, *if* workers can anticipate working for their current firm into the future and *if* they believe that the firm will pass some of the gains of productivity on to workers in the form of wage increases (that is, if there is a class compromise), their own welfare will improve if their firm thrives. Under such conditions, workers share with capitalists an interest in the prosperity of the firms in which they are employed.[9] And given such shared interests, some degree of real reciprocity in the relations between workers and capitalists becomes possible. As a result of these shared interests, workers will often spontaneously have an interest in the *collectivity* of workers exerting sufficient labor for the firm to be profitable. This does not imply either that the conflict of interests between workers and capitalists is completely obliterated or that domination is ever completely banished from production, but it does mean that such conflicts are partially neutralized by the

---

9. It should be stressed that workers do not have interests in the economic well-being of capitalists as such or in improvements in the income consumed by their employers. They have interests in the profitability of firms and in maximizing the reinvestment of those profits in ways that enhance the viability and productivity of the firm. Capitalist consumption is a deduction from reinvestable profits and is thus contrary to workers' interests.

nonzero-sum quality of material welfare in capitalism and that, as a result, domination becomes displaced as the central logic through which compliance is obtained.

Now it might still be the case that even if workers *collectively* have an interest in performing surplus labor, workers would nevertheless have an *individual* interest in shirking. Collective effort is a public good, and as we know, there is frequently a problem in the provision of such goods since individuals often free ride on the efforts of others.

But note that the problem has now shifted completely from one of contested exchange *between* classes as posed by Bowles and Gintis to a problem of contested solidarity *within* a class. The issue is no longer how bosses can ensure the terms of a labor contract among workers whose interests are strictly antagonistic to those of capitalists, but rather how workers can collectively minimize the free riding of individual workers. To be sure, managers and employers are still interested in preventing shirking, but the essential mechanisms for generating labor effort come from the processes that sustain solidarities among workers rather than from the surveillance and coercion of workers by bosses.

A variety of solutions to the problem of individual workers free riding on the effort of others develop in the practical operation of production. In particular, workers engage in mutual surveillance to insure that everyone is "doing their share," and norms against free riding develop in ways that reduce purely selfish rationality. In any event, the driving force of the process is not managerial domination as portrayed in Bowles and Gintis's models of contested exchange but interest-driven consent by workers themselves.[10]

Just as the surveillance/coercion mechanisms Bowles and Gintis emphasize are likely to be more effective if they are complemented by effective norms of obedience and belief in the legitimate authority of bosses, so the active, strategically rational consent of workers is likely to be more stable and effective if it is complemented by strong norms of

---

10. In a capitalist economy in which firms compete with one another, one can imagine that a quasi-Darwinian mechanism of selection could operate to reward those firms within which workers have managed to solve this kind of free-rider problem effectively. Imagine that we live in a world in which firms differ in the extent to which effective mutual surveillance and antifree-rider norms exist among workers. If it is the case that those firms within which workers can effectively reduce free riding will be the most profitable – and thus have the highest probability of reproducing themselves and expanding – then over time these practices and norms will become more common even if capitalists do nothing to encourage the practices. There is, of course, always a potential threat to capitalists posed by the strengthening of such norms of worker solidarity within production since under altered conditions these norms can contribute to forms of collective struggle rather than simply hegemonic cooperation. For a discussion of the contradictory logics of solidarity, see Rick Fantasia, *Cultures of Solidarity*, Berkeley, Calif. 1988.

responsibility (living up to one's bargains, doing one's fair share) and beliefs in the essential fairness of the employment relation. The real basis of such consent, however, is not the normative conditions as such – the non-contractual elements of contract – but the fact that, under conditions of partially complementary interests, it is strategically rational for workers to exert effort within production. We thus share with Bowles and Gintis a "materialist" understanding of the central mechanisms at work in explaining the transformation of labor power into labor: the normative (cultural) elements are to be understood as reinforcing or stabilizing the processes rooted in strategic, rational action over material interests rather than as constituting the fundamental explanation of labor effort. Where we differ is in their exclusive focus on strategic rationality under conditions of fully polarized interests (pure domination). We believe, first, that there is a great deal of historical variability in the importance of surveillance/coercion and second that, if anything, in much of the history of capitalism, the hegemonic models based on consent play at least as important a role in explaining labor effort as do pure surveillance models based on the direct use of coercion.

Historical and Contextual Variability

Three variables strongly affect the extent to which surveillance and threats constitute an effective mechanism for generating work effort.

1. *The degree of interdependence of workers within the labor process.* When there is a relatively low level of interdependence within the labor process, employers can generally relatively easily measure the output of each worker and thus monitor their level of labor effort. If a labor process is highly interdependent, on the other hand, while it is possible to monitor the collective productivity of the workers as a whole, it becomes difficult to assess each individual worker's own contribution to that productivity.

2. *The degree of skill/knowledge of workers.* An alternative to monitoring output is to directly observe the behavior of workers, the performance of laboring tasks within the labor process. If one knew what kinds of behavior constituted *effort* and if one could directly monitor that behavior, then, even if the labor process was highly interdependent (thus blocking output measures of contribution), one could still use surveillance as a social control device. Under conditions of high levels of deskilling, where the cognitive and physical tasks of production are highly simplified and accessible to bosses, this kind of behavioral monitoring may become possible. When workers

monopolize high levels of skill and knowledge on the other hand, it is generally quite difficult for bosses, who lack such knowledge, to monitor effectively the actual performance of workers.[11] They can, of course, monitor extreme deviations and active transgressions of the characteristic behavior of workers on the shop floor, but as countless studies of social control within production have demonstrated, it becomes quite problematic to systematically observe the degree of real effort under conditions of complex skills and knowledge.

3. *The costs of job loss to workers.* At the heart of the contested exchange model is the issue of the costs of job loss. Bowles and Gintis emphasize that in order for surveillance and the threat of firing to work, it has to hurt workers to be fired. One thing that shapes how much this hurts is how easy it is for workers to get a new job if they are fired. If there are extreme labor shortages, presumably the threat of firing is less salient. But more important than sheer labor supply is the issue of the provision of public welfare. In the absence of any real public provision of welfare or individual savings, workers face extreme deprivation if they lose their jobs. Under these conditions, if surveillance is feasible as a method of gaining information on individual productivity, the threat of being fired is a real threat and likely to increase labor effort.

The combination of a high level of atomization and deskilling in the labor process with the absence of public provision of welfare is likely to foster the greatest reliance on surveillance and coercion as instruments of social control within production. This is characteristic of what Burawoy has termed "market despotism."[12] These conditions were common in certain sectors in the early phases of the industrial revolution, and they remain common in industrial settings in the Third World today. But even in the heyday of the competitive capitalism of the industrial revolution, the conditions for an exclusive reliance on surveillance/coercion strategy of extracting surplus were not universally present. Many labor processes involved high levels of skills and collective interdependency that made monitoring by bosses very difficult. Furthermore, when the internal social structure of early factories was based on systems of internal subcontracting and forms of what Burawoy has called "patriarchal

---

11. This is not to deny that there are tacit skills that pose monitoring problems in virtually all labor processes. The point here is that these problems are considerably intensified and more clearly recognized by bosses when they are compounded by high levels of skills.

12. See Burawoy, *The Politics of Production*, chapter 2.

despotism," it often became difficult in practice for employers to impose systematic punishments on workers since the direct control over the labor process was in the hands of the patriarchal head of the subcontracting unit. Thus, even though there were many instances in which the surveillance/coercion of contested exchange was the central mechanism of extracting labor effort, even in the era of competitive capitalism this was by no means the dominant mechanism.

While there are certainly sectors and specific labor processes in advanced capitalist countries within which this model still has some real force, it is no longer the core mechanism through which effort is elicited in most capitalist firms. In one way or another, hegemonic processes play a more central role. There are several reasons for this. First, the highly interdependent character of many labor processes makes it exceedingly difficult for bosses to monitor the productivity of individual workers, and thus, except in cases of gross deviation from desired levels of effort, the surveillance/threat mechanisms are largely not useful. Second, under conditions of relatively high reservation wages (due to the existence of a welfare system), monitoring and threats will generally be less effective than they are in a situation where the alternative to employment is misery. Third, in any kind of complex system of production, monitoring, surveillance, and the use of threats are not actually exercised by capitalists as such but by their hired managers instead. There is thus a principal–agent problem linking capitalists to managers that intervenes between capitalists and workers. Managers face a particularly thorny problem in trying to *control* workers, since their own prospects in the firm depend in part on how effectively the workers under their control perform their jobs. Especially in complex labor processes, workers have considerable capacity to make life miserable for their supervisors. They can disrupt production by working to rule, consciously withhold cooperation, and in other ways jeopardize the careers of the managers who nominally control them. Under these conditions managers have an interest in gaining the active cooperation of workers and of eliciting their effort through interest-based consent.

These factors suggest that in developed capitalism hegemonic strategies are generally likely to be more effective than purely repressive ones. It might be thought, however, that under these conditions both strategies should be strongly present. Why not extract labor through heavy doses of both surveillance/coercion and hegemonic consent? The reason, we believe, is that significant reliance on the surveillance/coercion mechanisms is inconsistent with the use of hegemonic mechanisms, thus making it difficult for both to be strongly present within a given organization of production. On the one hand, the pervasive use of surveillance, threats, and coercion tends to subvert the normative basis for hegemonic strategies. Workers are less likely to honor norms against free riding and to develop a sense of their interests being tied to the success of their firm under conditions of heavy surveillance and threats by bosses. On the other hand, the development of hegemonic strategies undermines the efficacy of coercion. One critical aspect of the elaboration of hegemonic strategies is the institutionalization of various kinds of procedural safeguards within the workplace. In many workplaces it becomes much more difficult for bosses to summarily fire workers without going through elaborate due-process procedures, which are both time-consuming and costly. Given that the costs to the employer of invoking punishments goes up under these conditions, surveillance/coercion becomes a much less attractive option. In extreme cases, employers may choose to ignore even quite flagrant transgressions by employees because punishments are too costly. Bowles and Gintis's model of contested exchange recognizes the costs of *surveillance* – especially in terms of the costs of hiring guard labor – but generally treats punishment as such as costless. They thus ignore both the direct cost of deploying the procedures of dismissal, which may be substantial under institutionalized conditions of hegemonic relations, as well as the indirect costs of punishments resulting from the way punishment undermines other effort-inducing mechanisms. This means that once hegemonic strategies become economically effective they will tend to push out the more repressive surveillance–threat mechanisms of social control.[13]

As a result of these factors, collective self-surveillance by workers in which they initiate effort in pursuit of their interests is a much more pervasive mechanism in advanced capitalist firms than simple boss-initiated surveillance and sanctions. Unlike managerial surveillance, such collective self-surveillance is not costly: to the extent that work is highly interdependent, workers observe each other's performance as an essential by-product of their own activity, and because of their own knowledge and skills, they know how to assess the linkage between behavior and *effort*. And as countless industrial ethnographies have demonstrated, the punishments available to workers to impose on each

---

13. These arguments suggest that, in thinking about the social control strategies of employers, one needs a concept parallel to Adam Przeworski's notion of "optimal militancy" for the strategies of workers. Przeworski argues in his essay "The Material Bases of Consent" (chapter 4 in *Capitalism and Social Democracy*, Cambridge 1985) that a strategically rational worker will support a level of militancy considerably below "maximum militancy" when there are assurances that such restraint will result in new investments, increasing productivity, and rising wages over time. In the present context, employers must seek a level of "optimal coercion" – optimal "militancy" in the pursuit of capitalist interests, if you will – that balances off the costs of coercion against the long-term trajectory of effort in a low-coercion environment.

other, while not as dramatic as firing, can be just as effective: ostracism, petty hassles, sabotage, and so forth.

In the present period of capitalist development with increasing global competition, decreasing employment opportunities in the core industrial sectors of the economy, a decline in union power, and a reduction of welfare state provisions, one might expect that there would be a return to a heavier reliance on the kinds of surveillance–coercion mechanisms analysed in "Contested Exchange." It is certainly the case that the threat of job loss is more salient now than it was in the recent past, and it is also the case that the relatively easy coordination of interests between capitalists and workers characteristic of the "class compromise" of the post-Second World War period has become more problematic. Nevertheless, there is little evidence that the actual mechanisms for eliciting labor effort under these altered conditions in advanced capitalism constitute a return to the *market despotism* of earlier periods of capitalist development. The fear of plant closures and accompanying job loss are real, but they have led to an intensification of workers' collective self-surveillance, not to an intensification of managerial surveillance with threats of individual firing.

Counterproductive Surveillance

We have argued that in complex processes of production (involving skilled and/or interdependent labor), hegemonic strategies are more effective than surveillance–threat strategies. In some circumstances the situation is even worse for surveillance: it can actually reduce rather than increase the desired kinds of effort. This is especially the case when we turn our attention from the problem of eliciting effort by ordinary workers to the problem of eliciting effort on the part of employees in "contradictory locations within class relations," particularly managers and experts.

For both managers and experts, employers seek not simply raw effort but also the responsible and creative exercise of their duties. Surveillance and threats are unlikely to generate effectively that kind of performance. Heavy bureaucratic controls and monitoring are much more likely to generate conformity and caution, not responsible and innovative behavior. If all one wanted of a manager or expert was that they did not violate any rules and did what they were told, surveillance and threats might work. But this is hardly a recipe for a successful firm in a capitalist economy.

These problems of social control over managerial behavior are compounded by the fact there are many layers of managers in many firms.

Many, perhaps most, managers supervise other managers, not workers. This means that a strategy of social control over managerial behavior is needed that works across layers of the hierarchy.

The alternative to crass surveillance and coercion that is most widely used is to create *careers* for managers and experts within firms. Careers consist of a trajectory of promotions in which individuals receive increasing pay and status, and usually responsibilities, over time.[14] While career trajectories are sometimes used to facilitate consent for workers as well, they are particularly salient among *middle-class* employees. Such trajectories help to solve the problem of generating responsible performance of labor by managers and experts in several ways. First, to a far greater extent than is the case for most ordinary workers, a career trajectory of future earnings links the interests of managers and experts to the interests of the firm. Because their interests are more closely identified with those of the firm, the kinds of norms of obligation that characterize hegemonic integration of workers are likely to work even more strongly among managers.

Second, the critical basis for promotion up managerial and professional hierarchies is the *positive* demonstration to superiors of one's achievements and one's loyalty to the welfare of the organization (or, in some circumstances, loyalty to the superiors themselves).[15] The individual manager therefore assumes the role of a self-promoter, having to prove to superiors that he or she is worthy of promotion. In effect, much of the work of monitoring of performance is done by the person being monitored.[16]

Third, the existence of career trajectories creates a particularly valuable *asset* for managers and experts, their *reputations*. When managers and experts apply for new jobs, they are required to submit résumés with lists of achievements and names of people willing to write letters of

---

14. Careers, of course, are not logically inconsistent with a system of pervasive surveillance and threats, and there certainly do exist career structures within which behavioral compliance relies significantly on coercion. Nevertheless, as a solution to the problem of eliciting behavioral compliance, career structures tend to develop under conditions where direct domination is likely to be especially ineffective.

15. See Alvin Gouldner, *Patterns of Industrial Bureaucracy*, New York 1954 for a discussion of the distinction between *expertise* and *loyalty* as two logics of promotion up bureaucratic hierarchies.

16. In her study of the restructuring of American Security Bank, *Managing the Corporate Interest* (Berkeley, Calif. 1990), Vicki Smith shows how managers are persuaded to manage each other out of the corporation. Rather than monitoring middle managers, top managers organized an effective system of self-surveillance and self-monitoring that provided the justification for removing middle managers. This process was all couched in the terms of an elaborate corporate culture that emphasized the responsibility and autonomy of managers. Here we see the operation of a powerful hegemonic system supported by norms of *responsibility* and *fairness*.

reference. Since reputation depends not simply on the absence of transgression but also on the demonstration of *publicly recognizable* accomplishment, it also tends to generate active responsibility on the part of managers.[17]

This kind of career structure of social control generates what Wright has called "loyalty rents" in the wages of managers and experts. A loyalty rent is different from the employment rents in Bowles and Gintis's model of contested exchange. An employment rent is the amount of extra income needed for an employer to make the threat of firing credible to an employee. A loyalty rent, on the other hand, is the amount of extra income built into a forward-looking career trajectory needed to create a sense of obligation toward the firm. It is based on the normative principle of gifts and reciprocity in which managers and experts come to feel that they *owe* their firm something since the firm has been so *good* to them. Whereas initially the structure of prospective rewards is a way of tying the interests of managers to the firm and generating a particularly intense kind of strategic consent, once a person works within such a career trajectory obligations may be forged that generate stronger normative commitments to the welfare of the firm.

Contested exchange and the social practices that it entails are certainly a property of capitalist economies. Surveillance occurs in all firms in one form or another, and the threat of being fired is also ultimately available to deal with problems of serious social control. By elaborating the model of contested exchange in terms of short-side power, Bowles and Gintis have given considerably more precision to our understanding of this mechanism than existed previously. What is needed now is to elaborate an equally rigorous conceptualization of the other central mechanisms of extracting labor from labor-power and developing a deeper understanding of the concrete ways in which these various mechanisms are combined in different contexts of capitalist production.

---

17. In terms of the general model of "Contested Exchange," reputation could be considered another dimension of the "cost of job loss." Reputation functions rather like collateral in a financial loan: it assures that the individual will try to avoid default since this could lead to a loss of the critical asset. Reputation, of course, goes against the assumption of the model that all prospective employees are indistinguishable. In general, managers and experts with higher levels of reputation will have a higher probability of getting the good jobs. The critical issue in the present context is that the level of reputational assets is endogenous to the practices within the labor process.

5

Class and Politics

The concept of class has had an erratic career in the contemporary analysis of politics. There was a time, not so long ago, when class played at best a marginal role in explanations of political phenomena. In the 1950s and early 1960s the dominant approach to politics was pluralism. Political outcomes in democratic societies were viewed as resulting from the interplay of many cross-cutting forces interacting in an environment of bargaining, voting, coalition building, and consensus formation. While some of the organized interest groups on this playing field may have been based in constituencies with a particular class character – most notably unions and business associations – nevertheless, such organizations were given no special analytical status by virtue of this.

From the late 1960s through the early 1980s, with the renaissance of the Marxist tradition in the social sciences, class suddenly moved to the core of many analyses of the state and politics. Much discussion occurred over such things as the "class character" of state apparatuses and the importance of instrumental manipulation of state institutions by powerful class-based actors. Even among scholars whose theoretical perspective was not built around class, class was taken seriously and accorded an importance in the analysis of politics rarely found in the previous period.

While class analysis never became the dominant paradigm for the analysis of politics, it was a theoretical force to be reckoned with in the 1970s. Ironically, perhaps, in the course of the 1980s, as American national politics took on a particularly blatant class character, the academic popularity of class analysis as a framework for understanding politics steadily declined. The center of gravity of critical work on the state shifted toward a variety of theoretical perspectives which explicitly distanced themselves from a preoccupation with class, in particular "state-centered" approaches to politics which emphasize the causal importance of the institutional properties of the state and the interests of state managers, and cultural theories which place discourses and

88

symbolic systems at the center of political analysis. While the class analysis of politics has by no means retreated to the marginal status it was accorded in the 1950s, it is no longer the center of debate the way it was a decade ago.

This is, therefore, a good time to take stock of the theoretical accomplishments and unresolved issues of the class analysis of politics. As a prologue to the discussion, the next section briefly looks at the concept of class itself. This is followed by an examination of three different kinds of mechanisms through which class has an impact on politics. Using terminology adapted from the work of Robert Alford and Roger Friedland,[1] I refer to these as the *situational, institutional,* and *systemic* political effects of class. I then briefly examine the problem of variability in the patterns of class effects on politics. The chapter concludes with a discussion of the problem of explanatory primacy of class relative to other causal processes.

The Concept of Class

The word "class" has been used to designate a variety of quite distinct theoretical concepts.[2] In particular, it is important to distinguish between what are sometimes called *gradational* and *relational* class concepts. As has often been noted, for many sociologists as well as media commentators, "class" is simply a way of talking about strata within the income distribution. The frequent references in contemporary American politics to "middle-class taxpayers" is equivalent to "middle-income taxpayers." Classes are simply rungs on a ladder of inequalities. For others, particularly analysts working in the Marxian and Weberian theoretical traditions, the concept of class is not meant to designate a distributional *outcome* as such, but rather the nature of the underlying social relations which generate such outcomes. To speak of a person's class position is

---

1. Robert Alford and Roger Friedland, *The Powers of Theory*, Cambridge 1985.
2. For a more extended discussion of varieties of alternative class concepts, see Erik Olin Wright, *Class Structure and Income Determination*, New York 1979, chapter 1, and "Varieties of Marxist Conceptions of Class Structure," *Politics & Society*, vol. 9, no. 3, 1980; Anthony Giddens, *The Class Structure of the Advanced Societies*; Frank Parkin, *Marxist Class Theory: a Bourgeois Critique*, New York 1979; Ralph Dahrendorf, *Class and Class Conflict in Industrial Societies*, Stanford 1959; Gerhard Lenski, *Power and Privilege*, New York 1966; Werner S. Landecker, *Class Crystallization*, New Brunswick 1981; John H. Goldthorpe, *Social Mobility and Class Structure in Modern Britain*, Oxford 1980; Dennis Gilbert and Joseph Kahl, *The American Class Structure*, Homewood, Ill. 1982; Nicos Poulantzas, *Classes in Contemporary Capitalism*, London 1975; Gordon Marshall, Howard Newby, David Rose and Carolyn Vogler, *Social Class in Modern Britain*, London 1988.

thus to identify that person's relationship to specific kinds of mechanisms which generate inequalities of income and power. In a relational class concept, capitalists and workers do not simply differ in the amount of income they acquire, but in the mechanism through which they acquire that income.

It is possible to deploy both gradational and relational concepts of class in the analysis of politics. Many people, for example, use a basically gradational concept of class to examine the different political attitudes and voting behaviors of the poor, the middle class, and the rich. However, most of the systematic work on class and politics has revolved around relational class concepts. There are two basic reasons for this. First, relational concepts are generally seen as designating more fundamental aspects of social structure than gradational concepts, since the relational concepts are anchored in the causal mechanisms which generate the gradational inequalities. To analyze the determinants of political phenomena in terms of relational class concepts is therefore to dig deeper into the causal process than simply to link politics to distributionally defined class categories. Second, relational class categories have the analytical advantage of generating categories of actors who live in real interactive social relations to each other. The "rich," "middle," and "poor" are arbitrary divisions on a continuum; the individuals defined by these categories may not systematically interact with each other in any particular way. Capitalists and workers, on the other hand, are inherently mutually interdependent. They are real categories whose respective interests are defined, at least in part, by the nature of the relations which bind them together. Building the concept of class around these relations, then, greatly facilitates the analysis of the formation of organized collectivities engaged in political conflict over material interests.

Adopting a relational perspective on class, of course, is only a point of departure. There are many ways of elaborating such a concept. In particular, much has been made of the distinction between the Marxian and Weberian traditions of class analysis. Weberians, as has often been noted, define classes primarily in terms of *market* relations, whereas Marxists define classes by the social relations of *production*.[3] Why is this contrast of theoretical importance? After all, both Marxists and Weber-

---

3. The concept of "market relations" is simpler than that of "production relations." Market relations are defined by the structured interactions of exchange that occur between actors who own different kinds of commodities. Production relations, on the other hand, also include the social relations into which actors enter inside the production process after such exchanges have occurred. Thus, when a worker sells labor-power to a capitalist in exchange for a wage, the market relation is confined to the interactions in which the right to use that labor-power is sold to the capitalist, whereas the production relation includes the social interactions that take place when that labor-power is actually deployed in production.

ians recognize capitalists and workers as the two fundamental classes of capitalist societies, and both define these classes in essentially the same way – capitalists are owners of the means of production who employ wage-earners; workers are non-owners of the means of production who sell their labor-power to capitalists. What difference does it make that Weberians define these classes by the exchange relation into which they enter, whereas Marxists emphasize the social relations of production?

First, the restriction of classes to market relations means, for Weberians, that classes only really exist in capitalist societies. The relationship between lords and serfs might be oppressive and the source of considerable conflict, but Weberians would not treat this as a class relation since it is structured around relations of personal dependence and domination, not market relations. Marxists, in contrast, see conflicts over the control of productive resources in both feudalism and capitalism as instances of class struggle. This is not simply a nominal shift in labels, for it is part of the effort within Marxism to construct a general theory of historical change built around class analysis. Aphorisms such as "class struggle is the motor of history" only make sense if the concept of "class" is built around the social relations of production rather than restricted to market relations.

Second, the elaboration of the concept of class in terms of production relations underwrites the linkage between class and exploitation that is central to Marxist theory. In the traditional Marxist account, exploitation occurs primarily within production itself, for it is in production that labor is actually performed and embodied in the social product. Exploitation, roughly, consists in the appropriation by one class of the "surplus labor" performed by another. While the exchange relation between workers and capitalists may create the *opportunity* for capitalists to exploit workers, it is only when the labor of workers is actually deployed in the labor process and the resulting products are appropriated by capitalists that exploitation actually occurs.[4] The characteristic lack of

---

4. In recent years there has been a very lively debate over the question of whether or not exploitation can be adequately theorized strictly in terms of exchange relations. John Roemer, in "New Directions in the Marxian Theory of Class and Exploitation," *Politics & Society*, vol. II, no. 3, 1981 and *A General Theory of Exploitation and Class*, Cambridge, Mass. 1982, has argued that the concept of exploitation does not require any analysis of the labor process or the "point of production." Exploitation can be generated strictly by the unequal exchange of commodity owners with different amounts of productive assets. His critics have insisted that while unequal exchange can generate exploitation, in the context of capitalism the unequal exchange between workers and capitalists would not generate exploitation unless surplus labor was actually performed in production, and this requires forms of domination inside of production itself. For the debate over Roemer's conception of exploitation and class, see chapter 3 above; Jon Elster, "Roemer vs. Roemer," *Politics & Society*, vol. 11, no. 3, 1981; Adam Przeworski, "Exploitation, Class Conflict and Socialism: the Ethical Materialism of John Roemer," *Politics & Society*, vol. 11, no. 3, 1981.

discussion of exploitation by Weberian class analysts thus, at least in part, reflects their restriction of the concept of class to the exchange relation.

While these differences between the Marxian and Weberian theoretical foundations of the concept of class are important for the broader theory of society within which these class concepts are used, in practical terms for the analysis of capitalist society the actual descriptive class maps generated by scholars in the two traditions may not be so divergent. As already noted, both traditions see the capital–labor relation as defining the principal axis of class relations in capitalism. Furthermore, scholars in both traditions acknowledge the importance of a variety of social categories, loosely labeled the "new middle class(es)" – professionals, managers and executives, bureaucratic officials, and perhaps highly educated white-collar employees – who do not fit neatly into the polarized class relation between capitalists and workers. There is little consensus either among Weberian or among Marxist scholars on precisely how these new middle classes should be conceptualized. As a result, particularly as Marxist accounts of these "middle class" categories have become more sophisticated, the line of demarcation between these two traditions has become somewhat less sharply drawn.[5]

While Marxist and Weberian pictures of the class structure of capitalist society may not differ dramatically, their use of the concept of class in the analysis of political phenomena is generally sharply different. Weberians typically regard class as one among a variety of salient determinants of politics. In specific problems this means that class might assume considerable importance, but there is no general presumption that class is a more pervasive or powerful determinant of political phenomena than other causal processes. Marxists, in contrast, characteristically give class a privileged status in the analysis. In the most orthodox treatments, class (and closely related concepts like "capitalism" or "mode of production") may become virtually the exclusive systematic explanatory principles, but in all Marxist accounts of politics class plays a central, if not necessarily all-encompassing, explanatory role. In the final section of this chapter we will examine the problem of explanatory primacy for class. Before we engage that issue, however, we will examine the various ways in which Marxist class analysts sees class shaping politics.

---

5. This partial convergence underlies Frank Parkin's well-known statement that: "The fact that these normally alien concepts of authority relations, life-chances, and market rewards have now been comfortably absorbed by contemporary Marxist theory is a handsome, if unacknowledged, tribute to the virtues of bourgeois sociology. Inside every neo-Marxist there seems to be a Weberian struggling to get out." Parkin, *Marxist Class Theory: A Bourgeois Critique*, p. 25.

How Class Shapes Politics

Robert Alford and Roger Friedland,[6] building on the analysis of Steven Lukes[7] and others, have elaborated a tripartite typology of "levels of power" that will be useful in examining the causal role of class on politics:

1. *Situational* power refers to power relations of direct command and obedience between actors, as in Weber's celebrated definition of power as the ability of one actor to get another to do something even in the face of resistance. This is the characteristic form of power analyzed in various behavioral studies of power.

2. *Institutional* power refers to the characteristics of different institutional settings which shape the decision-making agenda in ways which serve the interests of particular groups.[8] This is also referred to as "negative power," or the "second face of power" – power which excludes certain alternatives from a decision-making agenda, but not, as in situational power, which actually commands a specific behavior.[9]

3. *Systemic* power is perhaps the most difficult (and contentious) conceptually. It refers to the power to realize one's interests by virtue of the overall structure of a social system, rather than by virtue of commanding the behavior of others or of controlling the agendas of specific organizations.

Alford and Friedland discuss this typology of power in an interesting way, using a loose game-theory metaphor: systemic power is power embedded in the fundamental nature of the game itself; institutional power is power embodied by the specific rules of the game; and situational power is power deployed in specific moves within a given set of rules. When actors use specific resources strategically to accomplish their goals, they are exercising situational power. The procedural rules which govern how they use those resources reflects institutional power. And the nature of the social system which determines the range of possible rules and achievable goals reflects systemic power. There is thus a kind of

---

6. Alford and Friedland, *The Powers of Theory*.

7. Steven Lukes, *Power: A Radical View*, London 1974.

8. Alford and Friedland prefer the term "structural power" for this second "level." All three levels of power, however, are "structural" in the sense of being systematically structured by and through social practices. The distinctive characteristic of this second level of power is the way it is embodied in features of institutional design, and thus it seems more appropriate to call it simply institutional power.

9. The idea of the "second face of power" was introduced by Peter Bachrach and Morton S. Baratz in their analysis of "non-decision-making" in "Two Faces of Power," *American Political Science Review* 51, December 1962, pp. 947–52.

cybernetic relationship among these levels of power: the system level imposes limits on the institutional level which imposes limits on actors' strategies at the situational level. Conflicts at the situational level, in turn, can modify the rules at the institutional level which, cumulatively, can lead to the transformation of the system itself.[10]

The class analysis of politics is implicated in each of these domains of power and politics.[11] Although class theorists of politics do not explicitly frame their analyses in terms of these three levels of power, the distinctions are nevertheless implicit in many discussions.

Class and situational power

Much of the theoretical debate over the relative explanatory importance of class has occurred at the situational level of political analysis. Marxists (and non-Marxists heavily influenced by the Marxian tradition) typically argue that actors whose interests and resources are derived from their link to the class structure generally play the decisive role in actively shaping political conflicts and state policies. Sometimes the emphasis is on the strategic action of the dominant class, on the ability of capitalists to manipulate the state in their interests. Other times the emphasis is on the political effects of class struggle as such, in which case popular action as well as ruling-class machinations are seen as shaping state policies. In either case, class is seen as shaping politics via its effects on the behavioral interactions among political actors.

The theoretical reasoning behind such treatments of the class basis of situational power is fairly straightforward. Class structures, among other things, distribute resources which are useful in political struggles. In particular, in capitalist societies capitalists have two crucial resources available to them to be deployed politically: enormous financial resources and personal connections to people in positions of governmental authority. Through a wide variety of concrete mechanisms – financing politicians, political parties, and policy think tanks; financially controlling the main organs of the mass media; offering lucrative jobs to

---

10. Alford and Friedland also relate this typology to common political terms for the degree of polarization in political conflicts: liberal vs. conservative politics constitute conflicts restricted to the situational level; reformist vs. reactionary politics are political conflicts at the institutional level of power; and revolutionary vs. counter-revolutionary politics are located at the systemic level of power.

11. Alford and Friedland argue that the systemic level of power is the "home domaine" of class theory, especially in its Marxian variant. That is, they claim that class theory is most systematically elaborated at the systemic level of political analysis and has the strongest claim to being the most powerful causal process at this level. Nevertheless, class analysis is by no means restricted to the systemic level; indeed, some of the most interesting recent contributions in recent years have been located at the other levels of power.

high-level political officials after they leave state employment; extensive lobbying – capitalists are in a position to use their wealth to shape directly the direction of state policies.[12] When combined with the dense pattern of personal networks which give capitalists easy access to the sites of immediate political power, such use of financial resources gives the bourgeoisie vastly disproportionate direct leverage over politics.

Few theorists deny the empirical facts of the *use* of politically import-ant resources in this way by members of the capitalist class in pursuit of their interests. What is often questioned is the general efficacy and coherence of such actions in sustaining the class interests of the bour-geoisie. Since individual capitalists are frequently preoccupied by their immediate, particularistic interests (e.g. in specific markets, technol-ogies, or regulations) when they deploy their class-derived resources politically, some scholars argue that they are unlikely to do so in ways which place the class interests of the bourgeoisie as a whole above their own particularistic interests. As Fred Block among others has noted, the capitalist class is often very divided politically, lacking a coherent vision and sense of priorities.[13] Thus, even if capitalists try to manipulate politics in various ways, such manipulations often work against each other and do not generate a consistent set of policy outcomes.

The fact that capitalists have considerable power resources by virtue of their control over capital thus does not ensure a capacity to translate those resources into a coherent class direction of politics. What is more, in terms of situational power, capitalists are not the only actors with effective political resources. In particular, as Theda Skocpol,[14] Anthony Giddens,[15] and others have stressed, state managers – the top-level politicians and officials within state apparatuses – have direct control of considerable resources to pursue political objectives. While in many instances the interests and objectives of state managers may be congru-ent with the interests of the capitalist class, this is not universally the case, and when overt conflicts between state managers and the bourgeoisie occur there is no inherent reason why capitalists will always prevail. Even

---

12. The focus on these kinds of mechanisms which link the state to the bourgeoisie are by no means limited to scholars who explicitly see their work as Marxist. G. William Domhoff, in *The Powers that Be*, New York, 1979, *Who Rules America Now?*, Englewood Cliffs 1983, and *The Power Elite and the State*, Hawthorne, NY 1990, for example, specifically situates his work in opposition to "Marxism" (or, at least, to the main currents of neo-Marxism prevalent since the early 1970s) and yet places the networks and resources of capitalists at the center stage of his analysis of the "power elite."

13. Fred Block, *Revising State Theory*, Philadelphia 1987.

14. Theda Skocpol, "Political Response to Capitalist Crisis: Neo-Marxist Theories of the State and the Case of the New Deal," *Politics & Society*, vol. 10, no. 2, 1980.

15. Anthony Giddens, *The Class Structure of the Advanced Societies*, New York 1973; *A Contemporary Critique of Historical Materialism*, Berkeley 1981.

more to the point, in many situations, because of the disorganization, myopia, and apathy of the capitalist class, state managers will have considerable room to initiate state policies independently of pressures from the capitalist class.

These kinds of arguments do not discredit the claim that class structures do shape both the interests of actors and the political resources they can deploy in struggles over situational power. What is called into question is the blanket claim that class-derived interests and power resources are always the most salient.

Class and institutional power

It was at least in part because of a recognition that at the level of situational power capitalists are not always present as the predominant active political actors that much class analysis of politics has centered around the problem of the institutional dimensions of power. The argument is basically this: the state should be viewed not simply as a state *in* capitalist society, rather, as a *capitalist* state.[16] This implies that there are certain institutional properties of the very form of the state that can be treated as having a specific class character to them. The idea here is not simply that there are certain *policies* of the state which embody the interests of a specific class; rather, that the very structure of the apparatuses through which those policies are made embodies those class interests.[17]

Claims about the class character of the institutional level of power involve what is sometimes called "non-decision-making power" or

---

16. This linguistic turn of phrase – "the state in capitalist society" vs. "the capitalist state" – was, to my knowledge, first formulated by Nicos Poulantzas in "The Problem of the Capitalist State," *New Left Review*, no. 58, 1969, pp. 67–78, his well-known critique of Ralph Miliband's book, *The State in Capitalist Society*, New York 1969. The thesis itself, however, has a long Marxist pedigree, going back to Marx's own work, particularly his analysis of the class character of the state in his discussions of the Paris Commune. This theme was then forcefully taken up by Lenin in "The State and Revolution," where he argued that because the very form of the state in capitalism was stamped with a bourgeois character, it could not simply be captured; it had to be smashed. For a general discussion of the problem of capturing vs. smashing the state, see Erik Olin Wright, *Class, Crisis and the State*, London 1978, chapter 5.

17. Policies as such could embody particular class interests because actors external to the state with specific class interests were able to impose those policies on the state. That is, if capitalists were always actively present politically and always predominant in conflicts involving *situational* power, then, even if the state itself was a completely class-neutral apparatus, state policies could be uniformly pro-capitalist. The claim that the form of the state itself embodies certain class principles was meant to provide a way of explaining why state policies are broadly consistent with the interests of the bourgeoisie even when capitalists are not present as the ubiquitous, active initiators of state policies.

"negative power." The basic argument was crisply laid out in an early essay by Claus Offe.[18] Offe argued that the class character of the state was inscribed in a series of negative filter mechanisms which imparted a systematic class bias to state actions. "Class bias," in this context, means that the property in question tends to filter out state actions which would be inimical to the interests of the dominant class. The form of the state, in effect, systematically determines what does *not* happen rather than simply what does.[19]

An example, emphasized by Offe and Ronge[20] and Therborn,[21] would be the institutional rules by which the capitalist state acquires financial resources – through taxation and borrowing from the privately produced surplus rather than through the state's direct appropriation of the surplus generated by its own productive activity. By restricting the state's access to funds in this way the state is rendered dependent upon capitalist production, and this in turn acts as a mechanism which filters out state policies which would seriously undermine the profitability of private accumulation.[22] Or, to take another example, given considerable emphasis by Poulantzas,[23] the electoral rules of capitalist representative democracies (in which people cast votes as individual citizens within territorial units of representation rather than as members of functioning groups) has the effect of transforming people from members of a class into atomized individuals (the "juridical citizen"). This atomization, in turn, serves to filter out state policies that would only be viable if people were systematically organized into durable collectivities or associations. To the extent that this filter can be viewed as stabilizing capitalism and thus serving the basic interests of the capitalist class, then exclusive

---

18. Claus Offe, "Structural Problems of the Capitalist State: Class rule and the political system. On the selectiveness of political institutions," in Von Beyme, ed., *German Political Studies*, vol. I, 1974.

19. Offe emphasizes the extremely difficult methodological issues involved in empirically demonstrating such "negative selections." The basic issue is being able to distinguish between things which simply have not *yet* happened from things which have been systematically excluded as "non-events" and therefore *cannot* happen.

20. Claus Offe and Volker Ronge, "Theses on the Theory of the State," *New German Critique*, no. 6, Fall 1975.

21. Göran Therborn, *What Does The Ruling Class Do When It Rules?* London 1978.

22. Logically, one could have a capitalist system of production in which the state directly owns a significant number of enterprises and uses the profits from these businesses to finance its general budget, thus not needing to tax private capital and wages at all. The fact that with very few exceptions – such as the ownership of Statoil (the North Seal Oil Company in Norway) by the Norwegian State, or perhaps (if they are genuine capitalist states) the oil sheikdoms in the Persian Gulf – capitalist states do not acquire their principal revenues in this way is not a feature of capitalism as such, but of the way states have institutionally developed within capitalism.

23. Nicos Poulantzas, *Political Power and Social Classes*, London 1973.

reliance on purely territorial, individualized voting can be viewed as having a class character.[24]

This way of understanding the class character of an apparatus suggests a certain functionalist logic to the thesis that the state is a capitalist state: its form is capitalist in so far as these institutional features contribute to the reproduction of the interests of the capitalist class. This functional logic has been most systematically elaborated in Göran Therborn's remarkable (and rather neglected) book on the state.[25] Therborn stresses that the real analytical bite of the thesis that the state has a distinctive class character occurs when the state is analyzed comparatively, particularly across historical epochs. The class character of the state apparatus is a variable; state apparatuses corresponding to different class structures will have distinctively different properties which impart different class biases on state actions. If this "correspondence principle" is correct, then it should be possible to define the specific class properties of the feudal state, the capitalist state and – perhaps – the socialist state. Take the example already cited of the mechanism through which the state acquires resources. In the capitalist state this occurs primarily through taxation, thus ensuring the fiscal subordination of the state to private capital accumulation. In the feudal state, revenues are acquired through the direct appropriation of surplus from the personal vassals of the king. And in the socialist state, state revenues are acquired through the appropriation of the surplus product of state enterprises. In each case, the argument goes, these class forms of revenue acquisition selectively filter out political practices which might threaten the existing class structure. Developing a nuanced inventory of such variability in class properties of the state is the central task of Therborn's book.[26]

---

24. There is some ambiguity in many discussions of the class character of the state over the status of the claim that a particular formal property of the state – in this case atomized territorial representation – has a particular class character. Some writers – Therborn, for example – seem to suggest that the element in question inherently has a given class character. Others, for example, Chantal Mouffe, "Hegemony and Ideology in Gramsci," in Chantal Mouffe, ed., *Gramsci and Marxist Theory*, London 1979, or Norberto Bobbio, "Are There Alternatives to Representative Democracy?," *Telos*, no. 35, 1978, suggest that the class character comes from the gestalt in which a given element is embedded. Territorial representation thus has a capitalist character because it is not articulated to various forms of more functional representation and direct democracy, rather than because intrinsically territorial representation as such reproduces capitalism.

25. Therborn, *What Does The Ruling Class Do When It Rules?*

26. Therborn develops an elaborate schema for building this inventory, organized around the distinction between inputs, internal processing, and outputs of state apparatuses. In all he compares the various class forms of the state in terms of eleven different aspects of state institutions. While the arguments supporting his specific claims are sometimes not entirely convincing, the conceptual structure he has developed is a valuable first step towards a more comprehensive conceptual repertoire of epochal variability in state forms.

Many critics of the thesis that the state has a distinctive class character have argued that this claim implies a functionalist theory of the state. This accusation is certainly appropriate in some cases. In the early work on the state by Nicos Poulantzas,[27] for example, and even more in the work of Louis Althusser,[28] there was very little room for genuinely contradictory elements in the state. The class properties of the capitalist state were explained by the functions they served for reproducing capitalism. The functional correspondence principle for *identifying* the class character of aspects of the state slid into a principle for *explaining* the properties of the state.

This kind of functionalism, however, is not an inherent feature of the class analysis of the institutional level of political power. While the thesis that state apparatuses have a class character does follow a functional logic (i.e. what makes a given property have a given "class character" is its functional relation to the class structure), this does not necessarily imply a full-fledged functionalist theory of the state.[29] Therborn, for example, does not insist that states will invariably embody the requisite class features that are optimal for the reproduction of the class structure within which they exist. Feudal properties of the state can persist within capitalist societies, and it is even possible that prefigurative socialist properties can be constructed within capitalist states. In general, then, the state can have many contradictory elements. In Therborn's view it is to a large extent class struggle – the balance of power at the situational level of analysis – which determines the extent to which a given state will fully embody the properties which are indeed functional for reproducing the dominant class.

Class and systemic power

To say that capitalists have *situational* power is to say that they command a range of resources which they can deploy to get their way. To say that

---

27. Nicos Poulantzas, *Political Power and Social Classes*, London 1973.
28. Louis Althusser, "Ideology and Ideological State Apparatuses," in Althusser, *Lenin and Philosophy*, New York 1971.
29. It should be noted that a functional logic is not the only possible way of constructing a conceptual correspondence between class and aspects of the state. One might argue, for example, that there are homologies between class relations and state apparatuses which have nothing to do with the functional relation between the two. Capitalism could create atomized relations between individuals (via market competition) which are translated into atomized political relations in the state through some mechanism like imitation or diffusion, without political atomization in any way benefiting capitalism. Some strands of state theory in what is sometimes called the "capital logic" or "capital derivation" school seems to argue for this sort of non-functional, form-correspondence, in which formal relations within capital–labor relations are somehow copied within political relations without there being any implication that the latter reproduce the former.

they have *institutional* power is to argue that various institutions are designed in such a way as to selectively exclude alternatives which are antithetical to their interests from the political agenda. To say that they have *systemic* power is to say that the logic of the social system itself affirms their interests quite apart from their conscious strategies and the internal organization of political apparatuses.

The idea that capitalists have such systemic power has been forcefully argued by Adam Przeworski, building on the work of Antonio Gramsci. Przeworski writes:

> Capitalism is a form of social organization in which the entire society is dependent upon actions of capitalists. . . . First, capitalism is a system in which production is oriented toward the satisfaction of the needs of others, toward exchange, which implies that in this system the immediate producers cannot survive on their own. Second, capitalism is a system in which part of the total societal product is withheld from immediate producers in the form of profit which accrues to owners of the means of production. . . . If capitalists do not appropriate a profit, if they do not exploit, production falls, consumption decreases and no other group can satisfy its material interests. Current realization of material interests of capitalists is a necessary condition for the future realization of material interests of any group under capitalism. . . . Capitalists are thus in a unique position in capitalist system: they represent future universal interests while interests of all other groups appear as particularistic and hence inimical to future developments.[30]

So long as capitalism is intact as a social order, all actors in the system have an interest in capitalists making a profit. What this means is that unless a group has the capacity to overthrow the system completely, then at least in terms of material interests even groups opposed to capitalism have an interest in sustaining capitalist accumulation and profitability.

This kind of system-level power has been recognized by many scholars, not just those working firmly within the Marxist tradition. Charles Lindblom's well-known study, *Politics and Markets*, for example, is built around the problem of how the interests of capitalists are imposed on political institutions by the operation of markets even without any direct, instrumental manipulation of those institutions by individual capitalists.[31] Indeed, this essential point, wrapped in quite different rhetoric, is also at the core of neo-conservative supply-side economics arguments about the need to reduce government spending in order to spur economic growth.

There are two critical differences between Marxist treatments of this

---

30. Adam Przeworski, *Capitalism and Social Democracy*, Cambridge 1985, pp. 138–9.
31. Charles Lindblom, *Politics and Markets*, New York 1977.

systemic level of analysis and most mainstream treatments. First, Marxists characterize these system-level constraints on politics as having a
distinctive *class* character. Neo-conservatives do not regard the private
investment constraint on the state as an instance of "class power," since
they regard capitalist markets as the "natural" form of economic interaction. The constraint comes from the universal laws of economics rooted
in human nature. In contrast, the Marxist characterization of these
constraints in class terms rests on the general claim that capitalism is an
historically distinct form of economy. More specifically, the treatment of
capitalism as imparting systemic power to the capitalist class depends
upon the thesis that there is an historical alternative to capitalism –
usually identified as socialism – which embodies a different kind of class
logic and thus generates a different pattern of systemic power.

The second important difference between Marxist and mainstream
perspectives on the constraints capitalism imposes on the state is that
most liberal and neo-conservative analysts see this system-level logic as
much less closely tied to the institutional and situational levels of analysis
than do Marxists. Neo-conservatives, in particular, grant the state
considerably more autonomy to muck up the functioning of the capitalist
economy than do Marxists. For neo-conservatives, even though the
political system is clearly dependent upon the private economy for
resources and growth, politically motivated actors are nevertheless quite
capable of persisting in high levels of excessive state spending in spite of
the economic constraints. The state, being pushed by ideological agendas
of actors wielding situational power, can, through myopia, "kill the
goose that lays the golden egg." The reason Marxists tend to see state
spending and state policies as less likely to deviate persistently from the
functional requirements of capitalism is that they see the levels of
situational and institutional power as generally congruent with the level
of systemic power. The structure of state apparatuses and the strategies
of capitalists, therefore, generally prevent too much deviation from
occurring. Neo-conservatives, on the other hand, see the three levels of
politics as having much greater potential for divergence. They believe
that the democratic form of institutions and the excessive mobilization of
popular forces systematically generates dysfunctional levels of state
spending which are not necessarily corrected by the exercise of capitalist
situational power or the negative feedback.

Variability in the Effects of Class on Politics

We have reviewed three clusters of mechanisms through which class
shapes politics: the class-based access to resources which can be strategic-

ally deployed for political purposes; the institutionalization of certain
class-biases into the design of state apparatuses; and the way in which the
operation of the system as a whole universalizes certain class interests.
Frequently, in the more theoretical discussions of these mechanisms, the
class character of these mechanisms is treated as largely invariant within
a given kind of class society. Abstract discussions of "the capitalist
state," for example, emphasize what all capitalist states have in common
by virtue of being capitalist states. Relatively less attention has been
given to the problem of variability. In many empirical contexts, however,
the central issue is precisely the ways in which class effects concretely
vary across cases.[32] Let us look briefly at such variability in class effects at
the situational, institutional, and systemic levels of political analysis.

One of the central themes of much Marxist historical research is the
shifting "balance of class forces" between workers and capitalists (and
sometimes other classes) in various kinds of social and political conflicts.
Generally, expressions like "balance of forces" refer to the relative
situational power of the contending organized collectivities – i.e. their
relative capacity to actively pursue their interests in various political
arenas. The task of an analysis of variability in the class character of
situational power is thus to explain the social determinants of these
varying capacities. Generally this involves invoking mechanisms at the
institutional and systemic levels of analysis. Thus, for example, the
enduring weakness of the American working class within electoral
politics has been explained by such institutional factors as the existence
of a winner-take-all electoral system which undermines the viability of
small parties, the lack of public financing of elections which enhances the
political influence of financial contributors, and voter registration laws
which make voter mobilization difficult, as well as by such systemic
factors as the location of American capitalism in the world capitalist
system.[33] Each of these factors undermines the potential situational
power of the working class within electoral politics. This enduring
situational weakness, in turn, blocks the capacity of the popular forces to
alter the institutional properties of the state in ways which would
enhance their power. While in all capitalist societies it may be the case

---

32. One way of characterizing this issue is that Marxist discussions of the class character
of politics have tended to be framed at relatively high levels of abstraction, where the
central issue is variability across modes of production. Less attention has been given to
specifying the effects of class at more concrete levels of abstraction, where the central issue
is forms of variation within capitalism itself. For a methological discussion of the problem of
class analysis at different levels of abstraction, see Erik Olin Wright, *Classes*, London 1985,
chapter 1 and *The Debate on Classes*, London 1990, pp. 271–8.

33. For an extended discussion of the ways the US electoral system erodes working-
class political power, see Francis Fox Piven and Richard Cloward, *Why Americans Don't
Vote*, New York 1988.

that capitalists have disproportionate situational power, capitalist societies can vary considerably in power of different subordinate groups relative to the bourgeoisie.

The same kind of variation is possible in terms of power embodied in the institutional properties of the state. In various ways, non-capitalist elements can be embodied in the institutional structure of capitalist states. Consider the example of workplace safety regulations. A variety of institutional forms can be established for implementing safety regulations. The conventional device in most capitalist states is to have a hierarchical bureaucratic agency responsible for such regulations, with actual enforcement organized through official inspections, licensing requirements and various other aspects of bureaucratic due process. An alternative structure would be to establish workplace occupational safety committees within factories controlled by employees with powers to monitor compliance and enforce regulations. To build such administration procedures around principles of "associational democracy" violates the class logic of the capitalist state by encouraging the collective organization rather than atomization of the affected people.[34] To the extent that such non-capitalist elements can be incorporated into the institutional structure of the capitalist state, the class character of those apparatuses can vary *even within capitalism*.[35]

Finally, some theoretical work entertains the possibilities of variation in the class character of systemic power within capitalist societies. The essential issue here is whether the overall relationship between state and economy within capitalism can significantly modify the dynamics of the system itself. Do all instances of capitalism have fundamentally the same system-logic simply by virtue of the private ownership of the means of production, or can this logic be significantly modified in various ways? Most Marxists have insisted that there is relatively little variation in such system-logic across capitalisms, at least as it relates to the basic class character of system-level power. The transition from competitive to "monopoly capitalism," for example, may greatly affect the *situational* power of different classes and fractions of classes, and it might even be reflected in changes in the class character of the institutional form of the

---

34. The expression "associational democracy" is advanced by Joshua Cohen and Joel Rogers, "Secondary Associations and Democratic Governance," *Politics & Society*, vol. 20, no. 4, 1992, as a general way of understanding ways in which democratic institutions can institutionally articulate with organized collectivities rather than simply atomized citizenry.

35. Acknowledging such variation raises a host of complex conceptual issues. By virtue of what can the state still be considered a "capitalist" state if it can incorporate non-capitalist elements in its internal organization? What precisely does it mean to say that the capitalist logic remains *dominant* within a state that contains heterogeneous class elements, thus justifying the use of the adjective "capitalist"? Can a state apparatus which contains contradictory class principles in its internal organization be stably reproduced over time?

state (for example, petty bourgeois elements in state apparatuses might disappear as capitalism advances). But the basic system-level class logic, Marxists have traditionally argued, remains organized around the interests of capital in both cases.

There has been some challenge to this view by scholars generally sympathetic to Marxian perspectives. Gosta Esping-Andersen, for example, argues that differences in the forms of the welfare state (which he refers to as conservative, liberal and socialist welfare state regimes) can have a basic effect on the system-logic of capitalism, creating different developmental tendencies and different matrices of interests for various classes.[36]

Joel Rogers has forcefully argued a similar view with respect to the specific issue of industrial relations.[37] He argues that there is an "inverse-J" relationship between the interests of capital and the degree of unionization of the working class. Increasing unionization hurts the interests of capitalists up to a certain point. Beyond that point, however, further increase in unionization is beneficial to capitalists, because it makes possible higher levels of coordination and cooperation between labor and capital. What this means is that if, for example, the legal regime of industrial relations prevents unionization from passing the trough-threshold in the curve (as, he argues, is the case in the U.S.), then unions will be constantly on the defensive as they confront the interests of capital, whereas if the legal order facilitates unionization moving beyond the trough (as in Sweden), then the system-logic will sustain unionization. High unionization and low unionization capitalisms, therefore, embody qualitatively different system-patterns of class power within what remains an overall capitalist framework.

Class Primacy

Few scholars today would argue that class is irrelevant to the analysis of political phenomena, but there is much contention over how important class might be. The characteristic form of this debate is for the critic of class analysis to attack class *reductionism*, i.e. the thesis that political phenomena (state policies, institutional properties, political behavior, party strategies, etc.) can be fully explained by class-based causal processes. Defenders of class analysis, on the other hand, attack their critics

---

36. Gosta Esping-Andersen, *The Three Worlds of Welfare Capitalism*, Princeton 1990.
37. Joel Rogers, "Don't Worry, Be Happy: Institutional Dynamics of the Postwar Decline of Private Sector US Unionism," *University of Wisconsin Law Review*, 1990. See especially pp. 29–42.

for claiming that political phenomena are completely independent of class determinants. Both of these positions, when stated in this form, have no real defenders. Even relatively orthodox Marxists introduce many non-class factors in their explanations of any given example of state policy and thus are not guilty of class reductionism; and even the most state-centered critic of class analysis admits that class relations play some role in shaping political outcomes.

The issue, then, is not really explanatory reductionism versus absolute political autonomy, but rather the relative salience of different causal factors and how they fit together.[38] A good example is the recent discussions of the development of the welfare state sparked by the work of Theda Skocpol and others advocating a "state-centered" approach to the study of politics. In an influential paper published in the mid-1980s, Orloff and Skocpol argue that the specific temporal sequence of the introduction of social security laws in Great Britain, Canada and the United States cannot be explained by economic or class factors. Rather, they argue, this sequence is primarily the result of causal processes located within the political realm itself, specifically the bureaucratic capacities of the state and the legacies of prior state policies.[39]

The empirical arguments of Orloff and Skocpol are quite convincing, given the specific way they have defined their object of explanation. But suppose there was a slight shift in the question. Instead of asking, "why was social security introduced in Britain before the First World War, in Canada in the 1920s and the USA in the 1930s?" suppose the question was "why did no industrialized capitalist society have social security in the 1850s while all industrialized capitalist societies had such programs by the 1950s?" The nature of class relations and class conflicts in capitalism and the transformations of the capitalist economy would surely figure more prominently in the answer to this reformulated explanatory problem.

In general, then, the issue of causal primacy is sensitive to the precise formulation of the explananda. It is certainly implausible that class (or anything else) could be "the most important" cause of *all* political phenomena. For claims of causal primacy to have any force, therefore, it is essential that the domain of the explanations over which the claims are being made be well defined. Can we, then, specify the domain of

---

38. For an extended philosophical discussion of the problem of assessing the relative explanatory importance of different causes, see Erik Olin Wright, Andrew Levine and Elliott Sober, *Reconstructing Marxism*, London 1991, chapter 6.

39. Ann Orloff and Theda Skocpol, "Why Not Equal Protection? Explaining the Politics of Public Social Spending in Britain, 1900–1911, and the United States, 1880s–1920," *American Sociological Review*, vol. 49, no. 6, 1984, pp. 726–50.

explananda for which class is likely to be the most important causal factor?

Class analysts have not, in general, systematically explored this metatheoretical issue.[40] Nevertheless, implicit in most class analysis of politics are two very general hypotheses about the range of explanatory problems for which class analysis is likely to provide the most powerful explanations:

1. The more coarse-grained and abstract is the explanandum, the more likely it is that general systemic factors, such as class structure or the dynamics of capitalism, will play an important explanatory role. The more fine-grained and concrete the object of explanation, on the other hand, the more likely it is that relatively contingent causal processes – such as the specific legislative histories of different states or the detailed rules of electoral competition – will loom large in the explanation.[41] All things being equal, therefore, the decision to examine relatively nuanced concrete variations in political outcomes across cases with broadly similar class structures is likely to reduce the salience of class relative to other causal processes.

2. The more the reproduction of the class structure and the interests of dominant classes are directly implicated in the explanandum, the more likely it is that class factors – at the situational, institutional and systemic levels – will constitute important causes in the explanation. This is not a tautology, for there is no logical reason why class mechanisms must be causally important for explaining class-relevant outcomes. Such a hypothesis also does not reject the possibility that causal processes unconnected to class might play a decisive role in specific instances. But it does argue that one should be surprised if class-based causal processes do not play a significant role in explaining political phenomena closely connected to the reproduction of class structures and the interests of dominant classes.

---

40. An important exception is the innovative work of G.A. Cohen on the explanatory scope of Marxist theory. In particular, his analysis of "restricted" and "inclusive" historical materialism is an attempt to give precision to the explananda of historical materialism. See Cohen, *History, Labour and Freedom: Themes from Marx*, Oxford 1988, chapter 9.

41. Imagine, in the above example, that one state passed social security legislation in February and another in September of the same year and one wanted to explain this sequence. The specific details of legislative calendars is likely to figure very prominently in the explanation.

PART II

Socialism

Introduction

For well over a century, those who have dreamed of a world in which inequalities of material well-being have been drastically reduced or even eliminated have looked to socialism as a way of accomplishing this goal. The basic idea is pretty simple: if inequalities of material well-being are generated to a significant extent by inequalities of wealth, then eliminating such wealth inequality would go a long way toward reducing inequalities of welfare. "Eliminating inequalities of wealth," of course, can mean a variety of things: state ownership with central planning; workers' and consumers' cooperatives; and even schemes for equalized individual ownership of shares in firms. But underlying all of these is the idea that a basic change in capitalist property relations is an essential part of a serious attack on the inequalities generated by capitalism.

In Marxism this idea has been embodied in the attempt to build a social scientific theory of the historical tendencies of capitalist development, or what has traditionally been called "historical materialism." Within historical materialism, socialism is seen not simply as a moral ideal for accomplishing certain emancipatory goals, but also as a real historical alternative actively posed within capitalism by the contradictions of its own development. Socialism, the argument goes, is the future of capitalism not just because it is desirable, but because capitalism creates the conditions for its realization.

The two chapters in this section explore a number of basic issues in the concept of socialism. (Other discussions of socialism and the emancipatory goals of radical egalitarianism can be found in chapters 10 and 11.) Chapter 6, "Capitalism's Futures," engages a specific aspect of the classical Marxist view of socialism. In classical Marxism, socialism (as the first stage toward communism) was viewed as the only real alternative to capitalism. Sometimes the expression "socialism or barbarism" was used to describe the alternatives facing capitalism, but this was largely a rhetorical device to increase support for socialism rather than a systematic part of the theory of historical trajectory. In the chapter we explore the idea that capitalism can have multiple futures and that the theory of history must therefore become a theory of possible historical trajectories. Once this way of thinking about alternatives is accepted, then we face the conceptual task of defining the inventory of these alternative possibilities. Working with the traditional Marxist concept of mode of production, chapter 6 explores one strategy for elaborating such a typology of possible futures by defining two post-capitalist modes of production and then examining the various ways in which these modes of production can be combined with capitalism and with each other to constitute different social formations.

Chapter 7 explores a striking challenge to traditional Marxist defenses of socialism. Marxists have always argued that some form of public ownership of the means of production is an essential condition for the transition to "communism," where communism is understood as a radically egalitarian, classless society governed by the distributive principle "to each according to need, from each according to ability." While "public ownership" might be subject to very different interpretations – from centralized state ownership and planning to decentralized forms of economic democracy – socialism was always seen as the necessary first step toward classlessness.

Philippe Van Parijs and Robert Van der Veen challenge this claim in their provocative essay.[1] They argue that we can move a long way toward communism *within* a capitalist society through a radical, if simple, reform of capitalism. The reform consists of granting every individual in the society an unconditional grant of income sufficient to live at a morally acceptable, if non-luxurious, standard of living. Such unconditional grants have the immediate consequence of breaking the link between "separation from the means of production" and "separation from the means of subsistence," that is the hallmark of the condition of the working class ("proletarianization") in capitalist society. In effect, paid work becomes voluntary since people can withdraw from the paid labor force and still live decently. Van Parijs and Van der Veen then argue that this kind of reformed capitalism would have the effect of moving the society significantly toward communism, at least in the sense that a sphere of communist distribution would be created inside of capitalism.

In chapter 7 I endorse the normative principles that lie behind basic income grants, but argue that such reforms cannot plausibly be instituted inside of an economy dominated by the private ownership of the means of production, since capital flight and disinvestment would undermine

---

1. Philippe Van Parijs and Robert Van der Veen, "A Capitalist Road to Communism," *Theory and Society*, vol. 15, 1987.

the sustainability of adequate levels of the grants. Socialism, at least in the minimal sense of public control over significant aspects of property rights, is thus a necessary condition for sustainable unconditional income grants.

===========================6===========================

Capitalism's Futures:
A Reconceptualization of the Problem
of Post-capitalist Modes of Production

This chapter is an exercise in a particular kind of concept formation: the construction of theoretically grounded social taxonomies. Its point of departure is the claim that the repertoire of concepts available within the Marxist tradition for exploring the potential futures for capitalism is not up to the task. Specifically, the tradition lacks adequate concepts for thinking about multiple possible post-capitalist forms of society. The chapter then proposes a strategy for enriching this conceptual space: define a series of abstract concepts of pure modes of production and then specify the ways in which these concepts can be combined to generate more concrete categories of social forms. The rationale for this strategy is the view that the concrete variability of forms of society can be understood as complexity generated by variable combinations of simpler elements (in this case modes of production).

The credibility of the exercise rests on three things: the credibility of the strategy itself, the credibility of the specification of the simple elements, and the credibility of the ways in which such simple elements are combined to define more complex forms. When this chapter was originally written, in 1979, I felt no need to engage with the first of these issues. While there were many debates over how best to define the concepts of mode of production and relations of production, I had no doubt that these concepts were firm foundations for building analytically powerful typologies of social forms. I also felt no need to defend the claim that socialism was a feasible future for capitalism. The issue of the times on the left was how best to define socialism and differentiate it from other possible post-capitalist social forms, not whether it was itself a plausible possible future. Most of the effort in the chapter, therefore, is devoted to defending a particular way of specifying the distinctions among post-capitalist modes of production and elaborating the concrete social formations constituted by their possible combinations.[1]

One of the central theses of historical materialism is that capitalism has a non-capitalist future. Capitalism is a transient social form, it is argued, since the contradictions within that social form make its indefinite reproduction impossible. Just as there was a period in human history when capitalism existed nowhere on earth, so eventually there will come a time when capitalism will have completely disappeared.

Given this thesis, the critical question then becomes: what can we say theoretically about the future of capitalism – is capitalism as a social form a stage in a single historical trajectory with only one eventual outcome, or does capitalism have multiple, qualitatively divergent possible futures?

The classical Marxist answer to this question was simple: there is only one future to capitalism, communism, with socialism as the transitional phase (or, equivalently, the "lower stage" of communism). This claim is based on four general propositions:

PROPOSITION 1 *The contradictions inherent in the capitalist mode of production make the reproduction of capitalism as a social form progressively less viable.* Principal among these contradictions is the contradiction between the development of the forces of production and the capitalist relations of production. In its early phases capitalism was a progressive, indeed a revolutionary, mode of production. It stimulated the development of the forces of production, generating historically unprecedented advances in human productivity; it destroyed social and cultural barriers to human invention and creativity; and opened up, for the first time in history, the possibility of a basic human emancipation from the constraints of pervasive scarcity. But mature capitalism blocks that possibility. The forces of production become "fettered," both in the sense that their development stagnates and their use becomes increasingly irrational.[2] The capitalist relations of production thus progressively come

---

1. All writing is stamped by the intellectual and political context in which it is written, but rarely has that context shifted as rapidly as it has for left-wing intellectuals in the fifteen years since this paper was originally written. In the late 1970s the radical critique of capitalism was nearly always posed from the vantage point of some kind of socialism as a practical (rather than simply a normative) alternative. While there was much interesting discussion about precisely what one meant by socialism and what kinds of institutional arrangements were necessary for socialism to function effectively, there was relatively little skepticism on the left about socialism *per se*. The tone and preoccupations of this chapter, and to a somewhat lesser extent, the next, reflect these presuppositions.

2. The thesis that capitalist relations lead to the stagnation of the forces of production is usually based on arguments about the systematic tendency for the rate of profit to fall with capitalist development, and thus for the driving force of technological innovation in

to contradict the forces of production, and this in turn makes the ideological and political reproduction of capitalist society more and more precarious.

PROPOSITION 2   *These contradictions simultaneously create the essential preconditions for socialism.* Productivity increases enormously and thus the social surplus expands, the forces of production become ever more social in nature, the population becomes more literate and mobile, etc. Thus, just as capitalism becomes less and less viable, socialism becomes more and more *possible.*

PROPOSITION 3   *The contradictions of capitalist development also produce the class capable of realizing that possibility in practice.* Capitalism, to use the classic expression, produces its own "grave-digger," the proletariat. Thus, not only does socialism become more possible as capitalism develops but it becomes progressively more *likely,* and eventually becomes *inevitable.*

PROPOSITION 4   *No other alternative principle of social organization besides socialism is generated by the inherent logic of capitalist contradictions.* The only preconditions for an alternative social form are socialist preconditions, and the only class capable of destroying capitalism and transforming it into a non-capitalist future is the working class. As a result, socialism – and eventually communism – constitutes the only possible resolution of the contradictions of capitalism. Thus, the practical question of socialist revolutionary politics becomes how to speed up the process, how to avoid strategies that might delay this single possible outcome. But there is no question about what that outcome will eventually be.[3]

Many Marxists continue to accept the essential arguments of this classical position. The classical position, however, has three important implications which have led others to question some of its assumptions. First, if socialism as the transition to communism is the only future to capitalism, then to be steadfastly anti-capitalist is necessarily to be pro-socialist. This implies that in the aftermath of a revolutionary break with capitalism,

---

capitalism to be undermined. Recent Marxists have tended to de-emphasize this formula because of a variety of problems with the law of the tendency for the rate of profit to fall, and instead stress the deepening irrationality of the way capitalism uses the mighty forces of production it has generated. For a particularly cogent argument to this effect, see G.A. Cohen, *Karl Marx's Theory of History: A Defense,* Princeton, N.J. 1978, chapter 11.

3. For a sophisticated discussion of the logic of the historical trajectory of capitalism, see ibid. For a fairly strong statement that socialism is the only conceivable future to capitalism, see John McMurtry, *The Structure of Marx's World View,* Princeton, N.J. 1978, especially chapter 8.

revolutionaries really have only one counter-revolutionary fear: the possibility of the restoration of capitalism. If that can be prevented (typically by repressive means), then the socialist future is secured automatically. Second, the classical position implies that countries such as the Soviet Union which have experienced anti-capitalist revolutions must either be socialist or capitalist. No other possibility exists. This has led to the elaboration of various theories of state capitalism on the one hand, and theories of "deformed" or "bureaucratic" socialism on the other.[4] Third, the working class is the only "bearer" of a future within capitalist society, since the only future to capitalism is one within which the working class is the ruling class. This means that all classes and social groups within a capitalist society must ultimately become aligned along a capitalist–socialist political axis. All other political stances are "utopian" or masks for what really amount to pro-capitalist orientations.

The dissatisfaction with these implications in light of the historical development of both Western capitalist societies and Eastern "actually existing" socialist societies has led to a variety of attempts at reconstructing elements in the original theory. In particular, propositions 3 and 4 have been modified in crucial ways:

PROPOSITION 3A   *While the proletariat is formed as a class in the course of capitalist development, its capacity to assume leadership of the society and reorganize the relations of production may be blocked, perhaps indefinitely.* Many different mechanisms may have the effect of blocking the capacity of the proletariat to become a ruling class: forms of ideological domination by the bourgeoisie may saturate the working class with capitalist values, needs, and subjective interests;[5] forms of political domination may incorporate the workers as citizens into the state and undermine their capacity to become formed as a class;[6] forms of economic domination may fragment the working class into hostile occupational

---

4. The state capitalism thesis is most closely associated with theorists in the Maoist tradition. For the best-known proponent of this view, see Charles Bettelheim's various works, e.g., *Class Struggles in the USSR*, New York 1976, *Economic Calculation and Forms of Property*, New York 1975. For a Trotskyist argument defending a version of the state capitalism thesis, see Tony Cliffe, *State Capitalism in Russia*, London 1974. The second formulation – the Soviet Union as a deformed socialism – is most typically associated with the Trotskyist tradition. See, for example, Ernest Mandel's writings on the subject, e.g., "Ten Theses on the Social and Economic Laws Governing the Society Transitional between Capitalism and Socialism," *Critique*, no. 3, Autumn 1974.

5. See, for example, Herbert Marcuse, *One-Dimensional Man*, Boston 1964 for a classical statement of this position.

6. See Adam Przeworski, "The Material Bases of Consent: Economics and Politics in a Hegemonic System," *Political Power and Social Theory*, vol. 1 (JAI Press, 1979), and "Material Interests, Class Compromise and the Transition to Socialism," *Politics and Society*, vol. 10, no. 2, 1980.

strata, incapable of struggling collectively for economic goals, let alone more radical political and ideological objectives; and social divisions within the working class based on race, ethnicity, religion, etc., may replace class as the central forms of identification and consciousness, thus undermining class formation altogether. Capitalism may become less viable as a social system, its contradictions and crises may deepen, and yet the working class remain incapable of acting decisively to seize power and become a ruling class.

PROPOSITION 4A *Capitalism contains within itself the potential for non-socialist, post-capitalist alternative principles of social organization.* Not only is the working class potentially immobilized as a revolutionary subject, it is not the sole bearer of a future to capitalism. At least two other, overlapping social categories are sometimes seen as bearers of a *potential* alternative to capitalism: bureaucrats or managers, particularly within the state, and professionals and technical experts. Sometimes these two categories are combined as a "professional-managerial class" or a "technocratic stratum." In any event, these social groupings are seen as posing a new form of exploitation and domination as an alternative to capitalism, one in which experts/bureaucrats appropriate the surplus product and dominate the direct producers not by virtue of their owner-ship of private property in the means of production, but by virtue of their incumbency in bureaucratic positions and their possession of technical expertise. The fate of capitalism, therefore, cannot be reduced to the simple polarization of bourgeoisie vs. proletariat, but involves the much more complex matrix of conflicts among workers, capitalists, state bureaucrats and experts, the possible outcomes of which include radically non-socialist yet post-capitalist forms of social organization.

Many of the analyses that defend some version of proposition 4a are decidedly non-Marxist, even anti-Marxist, in their theoretical commit-ments (although frequently the theorists involved passed through a Marxist phase in their intellectual development).[7] Typically the concept of mode of production drops out of the discussion, and if the concept of exploitation is used at all it is as an evaluative label for privilege rather than a technical term describing a form of appropriation of surplus labor. Furthermore, the political-ideological thrust of most theories of a state-centered bureaucratic-technocratic transcendence of capitalism is to demonstrate the impossibility of socialism, and the general desirability of the pluralistic character of capitalist society. For these reasons Marxists have generally rejected out of hand the claims in proposition 4a.

---

7. In this regard see, in particular, James Burnham, *The Managerial Revolution*, Bloomington, Indiana 1960; and Milovan Djilas, *The New Class*, New York 1957.

This rejection, I will argue in this chapter, is unwarranted. While it is true that positing the possibility (let alone the actual existence) of post-capitalist class modes of production does require certain changes in classical historical materialism, it is possible to develop a concept of such modes of production that is consistent with the core concepts of Marxist theory: relations of production, exploitation, mode of production, and classes.

The central objective of this chapter is to elaborate a conceptual framework for specifying possible forms of non-socialist futures to capitalism. I will assume throughout the chapter the essential adequacy of propositions 1 and 2, and will treat only in passing the problems raised in propositions 3 and 3a. The focus, then, will be on the problem of understanding the logic and structure of the multiple alternative social forms of production to the capitalist mode of production, the alternatives that constitute the potential futures of capitalism

As a result of this agenda, the discussion will be theoretical and conceptual rather than historical, although I will use historical examples by way of illustration for specific conceptual points. While the conceptual points themselves come out of an attempt to grapple with historical experience, I will not attempt to chart a proper historical analysis. In particular, I will not try to solve systematically the riddle of "What is the class nature of the Soviet Union?" or other countries that claim to be socialist. Although toward the end of the chapter there will be some discussion of "actually existing socialism," the preoccupation of the chapter will be more with clarifying the conceptual terrain for such an analysis than in developing a sustained empirical assessment of the Soviet Union in light of these concepts. My feeling is that the debates on the Soviet Union are so charged with polemical fervor and conceptual confusion that the most important immediate task is to clarify the conceptual parameters of the debate.

Modes of Production

General conceptual clarifications

Like most concepts in historical materialism, there is relatively little consensus over how to define the concept "mode of production." In the current debates over the concept, four different positions can be discerned:

1. *The mode of production consists of a specific articulation of the social relations of production and forces of production.* This is probably the most conventional usage. The concept "mode of production" is seen

as designating abstractly the essential structure of the "economic base." The contradiction between the forces and relations of production, then, is seen as a contradiction *within* the mode of production.[8]

2. *The mode of production consists of the relations of production alone.* This usage is not defended explicitly, but in practice it is often the effective meaning of the term. Discussions of the salient differences between capitalism and socialism or communism, for example, rarely mention systematic differences in the nature of their forces of production, but rather emphasize the salient differences in the relations of production.

3. *The mode of production consists of the totality of social dimensions of the productive process.* G.A. Cohen, for example, defines the social mode of production as "the social properties of the production process. Three dimensions of production are relevant here: its purpose, the form of the producers' surplus labor, and the means of exploiting producers (or mode of exploitation)."[9] Relations of production as such are not included in this definition, although they are clearly implicated in all three of the social properties specified.

4. *The mode of production consists of the totality of economic, political and ideological determinations associated with a given set of production relations.* The concept of production relations remains at the core of the concept of mode of production, but that concept loses its character as primarily an economic concept. Rather, it is a concept for grasping the interconnection and interpenetration of all aspects of social relations as they are bound up with the social relations of production. This concept is most closely associated with the work of Nicos Poulantzas.

I do not wish to enter into the debate over the appropriateness of one or another of these usages. This debate is important, if only because substantive discussions are often confused by an inadequate specification of the concepts involved, but it would take us too far afield to deal with it rigorously here. What I propose to do is adopt a usage basically in keeping with the third definition above, but which understands the term

---

8. This position is argued with some rigor by Barry Hindess and Paul Hirst in their book *Pre-Capitalist Modes of Production*, London 1976, where they argue that the concept of an "Asiatic Mode of Production" is theoretically incoherent because it is impossible to specify a set of forces of production that correspond to the relations of production identified with this mode of production. In later works, especially *Marx's Capital and Capitalism Today*, London 1977, 1978, they abandon the concept of mode of production altogether and restrict their discussion to "relations of production."

9. Cohen, *Marx's Theory of History*, p. 80.

"social" in a way in keeping with the fourth definition. That is, the mode of production will be defined as *the totality of the social dimensions of the productive process, where "social" includes economic, political and ideological aspects.*[10] Understood in this way, the mode of production clearly has as its object, *production*, but it does not comprehend production as purely "economic" in character.

Defining the mode of production as the totality of social dimensions of production is obviously too vague to be of much use for the specific analysis of capitalism and post-capitalist mode of production. What we need to do is specify the content of those social dimensions that are most critical for differentiating modes of production. In this analysis, I will emphasize four critical issues:

1. *The mechanisms of appropriation of surplus labor*, that is, how it comes to pass that the surplus products embodying surplus labor are appropriated from the direct producers.[11]

2. *The logic of the allocation of resources and disposition of the surplus labor*, that is, what processes constrain the ways in which the surplus product is used once it is appropriated from direct producers.

3. *The form of the political dimension of the production relations*, that is, the specific ways in which domination/coercion are organized within the total process of production.

4. *The nature of the classes determined by the relations of production.* This chapter is about capitalism's futures. Which of these futures will actually occur will depend upon the practices of classes pursuing different, and often antagonistic, projects of social change and social reproduction. It is of great importance, therefore, not only to decode the structural properties that differentiate one mode of production from another, but to specify some of the salient consequences of these properties for class structure, class formation, and class struggle.

---

10. A terminological distinction must be made between the structure *of* something and that same thing *as a* structure. When we talk about the structure *of* the mode of production it is essential to recognize that this structure has political and ideological as well as economic aspects, and as a result the mode of production cannot be analyzed as purely economic reality. On the other hand, when we refer to the mode of production *as a* structure, it is appropriate to call it an "economic structure" because its organizing principle is economic and its most fundamental effects are economic.

11. The term "appropriation" rather than "exploitation" is being used here since in some modes of production surplus labor may be appropriated without exploitation occurring (e.g. in communism). Exploitation always implies through one mechanism or another a process of appropriation which (*a*) involves coercion, based on (*b*) different relationships to the means of production of producers and non-producers.

These four aspects of the analysis of modes of production are obviously not independent criteria. For example, as we shall see, it is impossible to specify the mechanism of appropriation in a mode of production without talking about the relations of domination (form of the political dimension of production). Each of these aspects presupposes the others, and thus the modes of production they define are fully distinguished only by the gestalt of all four criteria taken together.

Specifying capitalist and post-capitalist modes of production

The next step in our analysis is to use the four criteria presented above to specify three modes of production: the Capitalist Mode of Production, the Communist Mode of Production, and what, for want of a better name, I will call the Statist Mode of Production. Several preliminary remarks may help to avoid some unnecessary contestation.

First, the two post-capitalist modes of production we will be examining – communism and statism – are not meant to be logically exhaustive of all possible post-capitalist modes. With a little ingenuity one could construct other conceivable forms of post-capitalist systems of production. I am limiting the analysis to these two because, first of all, they are the two images of post-capitalist alternatives that have received the most attention in the Marxist literature, and second, they have the clearest empirical basis in the immanent tendencies of capitalism itself. They thus constitute not simply logical alternatives to capitalism, but historically possible alternatives.

Second, the term "statist mode of production" or "statism" does not imply that every instance of state involvement in economic activity is necessarily a form of this mode of production. I will be using the term in a theoretical and technical sense, not simply a descriptive one, and thus it is only in the course of elaborating the concept and differentiating it from other concepts that its content will become specified. Various writers have proposed other labels for this system of production – bureaucratic collectivist mode of production, state bureaucratic mode of production, rational redistributive system of production, and so forth – and each of these has specific advantages and disadvantages. Since "statism" is the most succinct term and captures a critical part of the essential logic of the mode of production – that the state as such is the direct organizer of the entire system of production and appropriation – I will use the shorter term throughout this discussion.

Third, in the traditional Marxist lexicon "socialism" itself is not a mode of production, but rather the transitional phase between capitalist and communist modes of production. The status of such transitional phases will be discussed in detail below. Our discussion in this section will deal only with modes of production and thus will analyze communism rather than socialism.

Fourth, in a number of places in the discussion that follows, it will be useful for purposes of exposition to make contrasts between the modes of production being discussed and both feudalism and simple commodity production (i.e., production for the market in which no labor-power is employed). No attempt will be made, however, to provide a full discussion of these forms of production.

Finally, two points need to be made about the methodology of concept formation employed in this analysis. First, concepts should be viewed as the core theoretical tools employed in empirical investigations and theory construction. They are not, however, directly given by the "facts" or "data" of those investigations. To be sure, obstacles to understanding encountered in the course of research may suggest the need for new concepts; and the ability (or inability) of a new concept to penetrate those obstacles may demonstrate the success (or failure) of the attempt at concept formation. But concepts are never simply given by the data alone; they are always produced through a theoretical process. This leads to the second point: in one way or another the process of concept formation involves drawing lines of demarcation between different concepts and establishing the structure of interdependencies among concepts. The full meaning of a concept, of course, can only be established contextually within the theories in which the concept figures. But the parameters of its content can be established by elaborating the multiple dimensions in terms of which the concept differs from various kindred concepts. This will be the essential strategy of the exposition that follows.

The discussion that follows will be organized around the four aspects of modes of production listed earlier. Since the specification of capitalism in terms of these criteria is quite familiar, most of the analysis will revolve around the statist and communist modes of production.

Mechanisms of appropriation of surplus labor

Surplus labor represents the difference between the amount of time (labor) it takes to produce the total social product and the amount of labor it takes to produce those products consumed by the direct producers (the producers of the social product). In different modes of production this surplus labor is appropriated through different mechanisms. The contrast between feudalism and capitalism in these terms is a familiar one: in feudalism producers (serfs) are forced to work a certain number of days on the land of the feudal lord. The surplus product (and thus surplus labor) is thus directly appropriated through what is usually termed "extra-economic coercion." In capitalism, on the other hand, surplus labor in the form of surplus value is appropriated by capitalists by virtue of the difference between the total value of the commodities produced by workers and the value of the commodities they consume (i.e., purchase with their wage).

For purposes of drawing lines of conceptual demarcation between capitalism, statism, and communism, two dimensions underlying the process of appropriation are particularly salient:

1. *Forms of property*. Here the critical distinction is between forms of property in which the means of production are *privately* owned and forms in which they are *publicly* owned. "Private property" implies that the decisions to invest or disinvest, to buy and sell means of production are made by autonomous groups of individuals in control of the resources of specific enterprises; "public property" implies that all such decisions are made within some kind of state apparatus. As we shall see, there are intermediate cases such as "public utilities" in capitalism which are regulated by the state (and thus complete freedom to disinvest is blocked), and "semi-autonomous enterprises" in statism, in which enterprise directors have some possibilities of trading means of production.

2. *Relation of direct producers to means of production*. Here the critical distinction is between modes of production in which the direct producers own their own means of production and can therefore produce their own means of subsistence (or at least the equivalent of their means of subsistence), and modes of production in which workers are separated from the means of production and therefore must seek employment in order to obtain subsistence.

These two dimensions taken together generate the fourfold table presented as Table 6.1. *Capitalist exploitation* is defined by the combination of private ownership of the means of production (means of production can be bought and sold) and the separation of direct producers from the means of production (they must sell their labor-power to capitalists to obtain subsistence). Where they are not dispossessed of the means of production, we have *simple commodity production* rather than capitalism. If a surplus is produced in such a system, it is appropriated by the direct producers themselves and thus does not constitute "exploitation."

In contrast to both capitalism and simple commodity production, the means of production are publicly owned in both statism and communism. Where these modes of production differ is in the relation of direct producers to the means of production: in *communism* the direct producers collectively own and control the means of production. Whatever surplus is produced, therefore, is appropriated through some kind of

Table 6.1 Typology of Forms of Appropriation of Surplus Labor

		Forms of Property Relations	
		Public	*Private*
Relation of the direct producers to means of production	*Separated from means of production (non-owners)*	Statism	Capitalism
	Not separated from means of production (owners)	Communism	Simple Commodity Production

collective process.[12] The mechanism of appropriation can thus be designated "social-collective self-appropriation" (the rationale for the adjective "social" appended to "collective" will become clear when we discuss workers' self-management below). The central idea is that the direct producers decide through a collective social process how much labor will be performed in excess of simple social reproduction, and the obligation to perform such labor is collectively imposed on individual workers.[13] "Collectively" in this context implies necessarily that the process is participatory and democratic, but it leaves open the precise institutional form through which this would be accomplished and of course does not imply that there is necessarily universal consensus on every decision.

In *statism*, on the other hand, direct producers are fully dispossessed

12. The argument is sometimes made, if only implicitly, that the distinction between surplus labor and necessary labor becomes meaningless in a communist society. If all labor is freely chosen and scarcity has been totally abolished so that accumulation in either value or physical terms is unnecessary, then all labor is simply creative labor, a free expression of human individuality, and cannot be broken down into a surplus labor component. Such a final state of affairs may or may not be a real possibility in some future historical epoch. But it seems to me unnecessary to restrict the concept of communism as a mode of production to such an eventuality. I will use the term "communist mode of production" to designate a set of production relations within which necessary labor still exists and surplus labor is performed, but in which the social process for its appropriation and disposition is organized collectively by the direct producers.

13. Unless one takes a rather utopian view of the nature of a communist society, it is unlikely that the performance of surplus labor (or even necessary labor for that matter) will be universally voluntary at the individual level. In any event, there is no need to build such an assumption into the definition of such production relations. The key issue is that where obligations are generated they are done so through a participatory collective process rather than through either an impersonal market or a bureaucratic-hierarchical state.

of the means of production and thus must seek employment if they are to obtain subsistence. To be sure, in communism people may have to *work* (produce) but they will not have to seek *employment* in the sense of working for someone else who owns and controls the means of production as is the case in statism. However, since all means of production are publicly owned in statism, there is no market mechanism to adjust prices to values of commodities, and thus exploitation does not occur through an impersonal, market-mediated value mechanism. Rather, the form and magnitude of surplus product is determined politically through some kind of bureaucratic planning mechanism. That is, the surplus product is physically appropriated through technical plans which specify the amounts of different products to be produced, levels of consumption, investment, etc. (of course, subject to political constraints, class struggle, etc.).

Dynamics of resource allocation and disposition of the surplus
Modes of production are characterized not only by specific mechanisms for the appropriation of the surplus from direct producers, but by different dynamics for the disposition of that surplus. Two dimensions of the production system bear particularly heavily on the problem of resource allocation and surplus disposition:

1. *The immediate purpose of production: exchange versus use.* Marxist political economics distinguishes between two central characteristics of commodities: their *exchange value* and their *use value*. The former designates the quantitative differences among commodities in terms of how much of one commodity is the equivalent of another; the latter designates the qualitative differences among commodities in terms of what uses or needs the commodity helps satisfy. The hallmark of capitalism, it is often noted, is that exchange value dominates use value: only those commodities are produced that can be exchanged on the market, and the quantities of production of different commodities are determined by exchange criteria rather than by how much the commodity might be needed.

2. *Dynamic of disposition of the surplus: accumulation versus consumption.* Surpluses can be used for two basically different purposes: they can be accumulated as additional means of production to produce greater surpluses in the future which are accumulated as additional means of production, etc., *or* they can be used for various kinds of final consumption of either an individual or collective variety. This does not imply that investments would not occur, or even that growth could not occur, but that the purposes and direction of such growth would be strictly subordinated to the needs it would help satisfy. There is no pressure for accumulation for the sake of accumulation.

Table 6.2 Typology of the Logic of Resource Allocation

		Immediate Purpose of Production: Use vs. Exchange	
		Use Value	*Exchange Value*
Dynamic for the disposition of the social surplus	*Accumulation*	Statism	Capitalism
	Consumption	Communism	Simple Commodity Production

Taking these two criteria together, we have the fourfold possibilities presented in Table 6.2. In the capitalist mode of production, capitalists are not free to dispose just as they please of the surplus they appropriate, at least if they wish to remain capitalists. They are systematically constrained by the pressures of class struggle and competition to convert much of the surplus value they control into new capital, i.e., to accumulate. The logic of production, therefore, is not simply production for exchange – this is true for all commodity production, including simple commodity production – but production of exchange value to be used to produce more exchange value.

In communist production, things are produced because they satisfy needs. Use value guides the production decisions of each individual production process, and consumption is the organizing principle for production as a whole. Where growth in productive capacity is planned it is with the specific aim of increasing the possibilities of consumption.

Statist production can be thought of as system of accumulation of use values rather than exchange values. Production is planned in physical terms, and the decision to produce a given quantity of a given product is because of the specific uses to which those products will be put within such a plan rather than because of the abstract exchange value represented in those products. If exchange value exists at all, it is strictly subordinated to use-value criteria in production decisions. But the dynamic of resource allocation and surplus disposition remains centered around accumulation and growth of productive capacity.

It might be asked, where does the pressure for accumulation come from? What mechanisms produce an abstract growth dynamic? In capitalism two complementary answers are usually given to this question:

on the one hand, *competition* among capitalists means that each capitalist will potentially face bankruptcy if he or she refrains from using profits to expand production; on the other hand, *class struggle* between capitalists and workers means that in the absence of growth, all distributive conflicts between workers and capitalists become zero-sum. This makes the task of containing the class struggle much more difficult, both for the capitalist class as a whole and for individual capitalists.

But why should accumulation be a central dynamic in statist production, in which property is publicly owned and thus bankruptcy precluded (at least in the normal sense)? The reasons are somewhat parallel to the capitalist case. First, the power of different segments of the state bureaucratic-productive apparatus depends upon the amount of social resources at their disposal, and this largely hinges on the priorities established in the central plan. In the absence of general growth, therefore, all struggles over resources in the planning process – which are essentially power struggles – become zero-sum conflicts. One sector's gain is necessarily another sector's loss. There will thus be systemic pressures on the planning process itself to pursue a growth policy, since this makes the management of conflict much easier.

This dynamic might be termed "bureaucratic competition" since it involves competition over resources by different segments of the bureaucracy, but it is a qualitatively different sort of competition from capitalist competition. The mechanism that translates the individual competitive pursuit of interests into a social outcome – accumulation – in capitalism is an impersonal market, an essentially economic mechanism. In statism, the mechanism is primarily political. The process by which conflicting interests are aggregated into a growth agenda is a conscious one, requiring action, communication, and negotiation, not a spontaneous, unconscious process.

The second reason why systemic pressures for accumulation exist in the statist mode of production centers on the problem of the reproduction of the class power of the statist ruling class as a whole. The material basis of the power of any ruling class is the amount of surplus product/labor it is able to appropriate. This power base can be increased either by raising the rate of exploitation or by a strategy of general growth which increases productivity and expands production.[14] While both strategies are pursued, there are clearly much greater limits on the former, both

---

14. There is an assumption here that ruling classes will attempt to expand their power, or at a very minimum, reproduce their power. The motivational assumption underlying this thesis is that the privileges and prerogatives of members of the ruling class are contingent upon such power and that people generally attempt to reproduce or expand their privileges if they have the opportunity to do so. The sociological assumption underlying the thesis is

because of physical constraints of subsistence levels and because of resistance by exploited classes. The reproduction and expansion of the class power of the statist ruling class thus tends systematically to require growth.

Both capitalism and statism are thus characterized by a systemic process of accumulation. But these are quite different kinds of accumulation. Capitalist accumulation is accumulation of value structured by the impersonal forces of the market. Statist accumulation is accumulation of concrete productive capacity structured by the political forces of the state bureaucracy. This leads us to the next important element in our discussion: the form of the political within the system of production.

The form of the political dimension of production relations

The third aspect of modes of production we will discuss is somewhat less familiar than the previous two and therefore requires some additional preliminary discussion.

Many Marxists would argue that it is illegitimate to talk about the political dimension of production relations. Production relations are economic; political relations are the domain of the state. While political relations may be important in maintaining the outer parameters of the system of production, at least in capitalism they are not a constitutive dimension of production itself.

Such an argument implies that exploitation can be understood as strictly an economic process. The systematic use of coercive force might be needed to reproduce the system of exploitation (the "outer parameters"), but such force is not part of the functioning of exploitation as such, at least in capitalism. Such arguments usually are supported by a contrast between feudal exploitation and capitalist exploitation: in feudalism, it is argued, exploitation itself does require the exercise of political power – usually referred to as extra-economic coercion – since without such coercion serfs would not work the land of the feudal lord. In capitalism, on the other hand, exploitation occurs through a purely economic mechanism centered in the wage–labor exchange. Extra-economic coercion is unnecessary. Thus, in feudalism there is supposedly a fusion of the economic and the political, whereas in capitalism there is

---

that the power of ruling classes is always under challenge in one way or another, either from subordinate classes or from competing ruling classes (in other societies). The need to attempt to expand the base of power is thus imposed on a ruling class by the threats to its power, even if they have little personal incentive to do so to increase privileges. In the statist mode of production it might be expected that conflicts between states as such might be a particularly significant pressure in this direction since the ruling class is so intimately tied to the state.

an institutional differentiation between the political (the state) and the economic (the market and factory).

Such an account of the difference between feudalism and capitalism is quite misleading. Exploitation in capitalism cannot be considered a simple consequence of the sale of labor-power, as a purely economic transaction. For surplus labor (value) to be appropriated workers must also perform actual labor within the labor process in excess of the labor they consume in the commodities they buy. And for this to occur some kind of coercion is needed within the labor process itself. Without such coercion, why would workers perform unpleasant tasks within production processes at a rate or intensity sufficient to produce profits for the employer? Capitalist exploitation thus implies the exercise of political power within the factory combined with the economic exchange in the labor market.

This way of understanding the status of the political within capitalist exploitation implies that the general relationship between the political and the economic in capitalism and feudalism – and indeed in modes of production in general – has to be rethought. As Ellen Meiksins Wood has argued, capitalism should not be understood as a production system in which the political and the economic are totally institutionally differentiated.[15] In capitalism the political dimension of production is differentiated institutionally from the political dimension of the state (i.e., the factory is differentiated from the state), but economic transactions and production are still immediately connected with the exercise of political power.

This problem of the status of the political within production relations becomes particularly crucial when we discuss the proposed concept of statism as a mode of production. Like feudalism, statism is a mode of production in which the political dimension of production relations is institutionally organized within the state apparatus. It thus becomes impossible to specify such a mode of production unless political dimensions can enter the discussion.

As a first cut into this dimension of modes of production, we can distinguish between political relations *within the labor process* itself, and the political dimension of production relations *outside the labor process*. Within each of these aspects of the production process the critical distinction is between two forms of political relations: relations of *domination* and relations of *self-determination* (either individual or collective self-determination). Taking these dimensions together we have the typology presented in Table 6.3.

---

15. Ellen Meiksins Wood, "The Separation of the Economic and the Political in Capitalism," *New Left Review*, no. 127, May–June 1981, pp. 66–95.

Table 6.3 The Form of the Political Dimension of Production Relations in Different Modes of Production

| | | Form of the Political Dimension of Production Relations *within* the Labour Process | |
		Self-determination	*Domination*
Form of the political dimension of production relations *outside* of the labor process	*Self-determination*	Communism	Capitalism
	Domination	Feudalism	Statism

Capitalism and feudalism represent polar opposites in this typology: in feudalism, the actual organization of the labor process is done primarily in a cooperative, self-determined way by peasant communities, but they are coerced into engaging in production on the lands of the feudal lord; in capitalism, workers are free to sell their labor-power to any employer, to move to seek better employment, etc. In advanced capitalism this freedom in the exchange relations has been further enhanced by unionization, welfare, and unemployment insurance, all of which give workers greater capacity to self-determine the sale of their labor-power. But once they enter the labor process they enter the coercive domain of the political domination of capital.

In statism, political domination is exercised in both domains: the allocation across sectors of means of production and possibly even individual laborers is decided bureaucratically within the state economic apparatus; and within production the performance of labor is coercively organized.[16] The "politics of production," to use Michael Burawoy's apt phrase, are thus much more transparent in statism than in capitalism, because coercive processes operate in all phases of the production process. As we shall see in the next section, this has important implications for the character of class struggles in such societies.

The presence of domination relations in the allocation of means of production and labor power across sectors (i.e., centralized, bureaucratic planning) does not necessarily imply that the political apparatuses

---

16. There is no logical requirement in a statist mode of production that individual workers be coercively assigned to jobs. Wage rates would be administratively established through a central plan, as would the job offerings in different sectors, but individuals could still be given choices in applying for jobs.

of the state will take a despotic form. It is important to distinguish the nature of *state economic apparatuses* – those directly engaged in organizing and planning social production – and the *state political apparatuses* – institutions of representation and conflict management (legislatures, courts, police, etc.). While the relationship between these two is not random, there is no reason to suppose that there is a one-to-one correspondence between them either. As I will argue in the following section, there are probably systemic pressures within a statist mode of production for the political apparatuses of the state to take relatively despotic forms, but such outcomes are conditioned by class struggles, institutional traditions, and other factors.[17]

Class structure and class struggle

In this section I will focus almost exclusively on the problem of class structure of the statist mode of production, since this is clearly the most problematic issue. Since in communism there is by definition no exploitation, there can be no classes as such. The class structure of capitalism is well theorized – if still hotly debated – so I won't discuss it in any detail here except by way of contrast with statism.[18]

I will explore two central issues in the problem of classes in a statist mode of production: first, how should the ruling class be conceptualized? What defines the central principle of its relationship to the subordinate class? And second, what are the central principles of class struggle within this relationship?

Theorists who either explicitly or implicitly hypothesize the existence of something akin to a statist mode of production have conceptualized the ruling class of that mode in one of two ways: either as a class of technical experts (or intelligentsia) who monopolize scientific-technical knowledge, or as a class of bureaucrats who monopolize positions of bureaucratic power. While discussions of these alternatives typically revolve around empirical assessments of the Soviet Union, and are thus at a lower level of abstraction than the present analysis, nevertheless it

---

17. As in the discussion of the capitalist state, the analysis of the "statist state" requires a distinction between the form of the state and the form of regime. All statist states would have some common basic traits: the institutional boundary between political and economic activities would be permeable; revenues of the state would come primarily from state-produced surplus, not taxation; the stability of the state would depend upon the stability of the economic planning process; and so on. Given such general characteristics, it is quite possible to imagine forms of democratic representation, perhaps of a corporatist nature, as well as more strictly despotic forms of regimes.

18. For a general review of the current debates on class structure among Marxists, see Erik Olin Wright, "Varieties of Marxist Conceptions of Class Structure," *Politics & Society*, vol. 9, no. 3, 1981.

will be instructive to examine briefly the logic underlying each of these two positions.

The claim that the technical intelligentsia constitutes the ruling class in a statist society typically revolves around three complementary arguments. First, technical experts are portrayed as having a common relationship to a special means of production – technical knowledge, or what is sometimes called "cultural capital" – which they monopolize. Second, because of the nature of production in advanced industrial (or "post-industrial") societies, the monopoly of technical knowledge becomes a material basis of power since such knowledge is the pivot of technologically sophisticated production. Third, where market principles are suppressed and rational planning becomes the central mechanism for distributive decisions, the technical expertise of the planners becomes the central basis for legitimating their control of the system of production. Control of technical knowledge thus confers both economic power and legitimacy on technical experts, and this constitutes the essential basis for technical experts becoming a ruling class in a statist society. The fundamental class relation of such a society in these terms is between experts and non-experts (or between credentialed and noncredentialed, or mental and manual, etc.). Arguments of this sort, with various modifications, can be found in the work of Gouldner, Konrad and Szelenyi, and many others.[19]

The alternative position argues that while credentials or expertise may be one criterion for recruitment into ruling-class positions in a statist society, the monopoly of technical knowledge as such cannot be considered the core of the class relation. The pivot of the class relation must be located in the relation of bureaucratic domination itself. Exploitation – the appropriation of surplus labor from direct producers – occurs in a statist society not because non-experts relinquish a portion of their product to experts on the basis of the technical superiority of experts, but because they are forced to do so by coercively enforced bureaucratic edicts.

For knowledge *qua* knowledge to constitute the mechanism of exploitation (and thus the axis of the class relation), it would have to be the case that knowledge possession per se conferred the capacity to appropriate surplus, rather than that knowledge possession facilitates personal recruitment into positions that confer the capacity to appropriate surplus. The contrast with capitalism is instructive in this regard: an owner of capital is, by virtue of that ownership, able to exploit and

19. For recent discussions of these issues, see especially Alvin Gouldner, *The Future of Intellectuals and the Rise of the New Class*, New York 1980 and George Konrad and Ivan Szelenyi, *Intellectuals on the Road to Class Power*, New York 1979.

dominate workers. Owning capital may also give people access to other kinds of positions – for example, political positions – but this is not essential to the specification of the basic class relation itself. For the case of the possession of knowledge the question then becomes: can we imagine a system of production in which the possession of "cultural capital" or technical knowledge by itself conferred the capacity to appropriate surplus?

For this to be the case two things would have to hold: first, the more cultural capital a person possessed, the more surplus that person would be able to appropriate. This would imply that it was the cultural capital as such and not the bureaucratic position into which the possessor of such capital was recruited that conferred the capacity to appropriate. Second, it would imply that orders given by technical experts would be followed primarily because they were seen as technically "rational," either because of past performance of the person giving the order or because of technical argument. But they would not be followed primarily because of legally sanctioned lines of command rooted in the hierarchical organization of the bureaucratic structure. If orders are followed because of formal sanctions for non-obedience rather than because of rational persuasion on technical grounds, then the social relation involved must be considered primarily a bureaucratic-authoritative one rather than one based on differences in technical knowledge.[20]

If the above account is correct, then it seems to me to be implausible that a technical intelligentsia could ever be a ruling class simply *in its role as possessor of technical knowledge*. Once in power it would consolidate its position by becoming either a statist-bureaucratic ruling class or some kind of new bourgeoisie, since it is very hard to see how it could reproduce its dominance and capacity to appropriate the social surplus solely, or even primarily, on the basis of the persuasive capacity of its technical competence. Thus, while it may well be the case that credentials or technical competence are important criteria for recruitment into ruling-class positions in a statist society, the defining criterion of the class relation itself is the system of bureaucratic domination that determines relations to the means of production and defines the central mechanism of surplus labor appropriation.

The ruling class in a statist society is thus defined by those positions within the relations of bureaucratic domination that control the basic allocation of means of production and distribution of the social surplus. This implies that vast numbers of positions within the bureaucratic structure of the state economic apparatuses are *not* in the ruling class.

---

20. Gouldner, *Future of Intellectuals*, stresses this distinction between bureaucratic and expert rule.

Rather, they must be considered "contradictory locations within the class relations" of the statist mode of production: positions simultaneously dominated by the bureaucratic ruling class and dominating direct producers. As in the case of managerial-supervisory positions within capitalism, they are objectively torn between the basic poles of the class relation in that society.[21]

Given this class structure, what can we say about the nature of class struggle structured by a statist mode of production, and what are the most salient differences from class struggle in capitalism? One feature above all is striking: in capitalism the institutional separation of the "politics of production" from the state means that there are built-in mechanisms tending to contain economic class struggle at the economic level. One of the pervasive dilemmas the working-class movement has always faced in capitalism has thus been the systemic pressures toward a depoliticization of class conflict. Furthermore, the forms of representative democracy that have developed in capitalist society have, if anything, tended to deepen this depoliticization by transforming workers into citizens, by transforming leaders of mobilized social movements into representatives of atomized electorates, by placing a premium on short-run demands over long-term reforms, and so on.[22]

In statism, on the other hand, economic class struggle – struggle over the size and distribution of the surplus product – is immediately a political conflict. The politics of production become a form of political struggle involving the state. There is thus no tendency for struggles by direct producers to be purely economistic; they are always politicized by virtue of the social relations they confront. This implies that democratic forms of regime are likely to have very different effects in such societies than in capitalist societies. Rather than contributing to depolicitization of demands, democratic forms are likely to contribute to the focusing and intensifying of the process of politicization. In capitalism, the institutional separation of economic apparatuses from state political apparatuses means that even when popular demands are registered in representative institutions there are severe institutional barriers to their threatening the bases of class power. In statism, the basic institutional unity of state political and economic apparatuses means that such barriers are likely to be much weaker. Challenges to the class power of

21. For an extended discussion and defense of the concept of "contradictory locations," see Erik Olin Wright, *Class, Crisis and the State*, chapter 2. It should be noted that many of the incumbents of such contradictory locations in a statist mode of production will be precisely those technical experts who are sometimes seen as the "new class" in such a society.

22. For a penetrating analysis of these mechanisms, see Adam Przeworski's studies of capitalist democracy cited in note 6 above.

the bureaucratic ruling class are thus much more likely to be expressed in representative bodies and when expressed, to pose a more serious threat to the basis of that power in the state economic apparatuses.

There are thus systematic pressures generated by the basic structure of a statist mode of production for the state political apparatuses to take relatively despotic forms. Where elected representative bodies exist, they are likely to be either largely symbolic in character, or to be elected under arrangements that foreclose the possibility of their expressing popular demands in a serious way. If a more democratic form were to exist it is likely that it would be highly "corporatist" in character. That is, instead of representing individual citizens, elected bodies would represent hierarchically organized "interest groups" of various sorts, whose own bureaucratic structures would serve to diffuse and fragment popular protests. Even then such corporatist forms would probably be relatively precarious mechanisms of representation and would probably become largely symbolic in character.

The class struggles in societies dominated by the capitalist mode of production and the statist mode of production are thus likely to have very different characters. In the former, class struggles will tend to revolve around narrowly "economic" issues and only under exceptional circumstances become highly politicized. While in a statist society workers would still engage in demands for higher wages, better living and working conditions, and so on, such demands would immediately lose their economistic character because of the institutional setting in which they were raised. The pivot of class struggles is thus likely to be the "struggle for democracy," for relatively free and open forms of political representation, for such struggles potentially call into question the class power of the bureaucratic ruling class itself.

Articulation and Interpenetration of Modes of Production

General conceptual clarifications

So far this discussion has remained at the highest level of abstraction: the analysis of modes of production as such. But as many recent discussions of this concept have emphasized, no concrete society is ever characterized exclusively by a single mode of production. Real societies always involve complex combinations of modes of production, coexisting with each other in various ways. Early capitalism, for example, involved the coexistence of capitalist, feudal, and simple commodity production, and perhaps other relations of production as well. The term "social formation" has been used to designate the specific forms of combination of different modes of production within concrete societies. The investigation of the future of capitalist society, therefore, must involve an examination of capitalist social formations and not simply modes of production.

This distinction between mode of production and social formation has been an important clarification in the theory of capitalist society. However, the use of expressions like "articulation," "coexist," "combination," and the like, do little to clarify this issue, since these terms themselves need specification.

A beginning at elaborating the interconnections among modes of production within a social formation can be made by distinguishing between the "articulation" and "interpenetration" of modes of production. The following discussion will begin by explicating this distinction and explaining its importance. Once this is accomplished we will examine the significant forms of interpenetration between capitalist and post-capitalist modes of production.

Articulation

Articulation occurs when two modes of production exist side by side and have systematic *external* relations to each other. Typically, this implies that they exist on different turfs, and that the relations between them are largely relations of exchange. The simplest example is a situation in which capitalist factories purchase on the market at least some of their raw materials from simple commodity producers, or perhaps even from feudal (or semi-feudal) agricultural production. Such an articulation of capitalist and pre-capitalist modes of production often implies that they exist in some kind of symbiotic relation, where the capitalist production process contributes to the reproduction of the pre-capitalist relations of production through the exchange relations that bind them together. But articulation does not necessarily imply perfect functional complementarity between the articulated modes of production, and it is quite possible for the capitalist mode simultaneously to engage in such articulated exchange with simple commodity production and systematically to attack and destroy simple commodity producers.[23]

---

23. The concept of articulation of modes of production is not restricted to articulation within the political boundaries of a particular country. Some of the most important forms of articulation in fact occur internationally. Such international articulation is a salient feature of imperialism, where the transfer of value from the periphery to the center exploits certain opportunities provided by the persistence of pre-capitalist modes of production in the Third World. International articulation of modes of production is also involved in the economic relations between the Eastern countries and the West (however one wants to define the dominant mode of production within those countries).

Interpenetration

Interpenetration occurs when two modes of production coexist within a single concrete organization of production. Elements of each mode of production are present simultaneously within a single production process. The two modes of production therefore have systematic *internal* relations with each other rather than external ones. A good example of such interpenetration is the form of artisanal labor within early capitalist factories. In many cases, artisanal wage laborers hired their own subordinates and paid them wages out of their own wages in a complex system of subcontracting.[24] The social relations of guild-artisan production were thus interpenetrated with the social relations of capitalist production. The result was a structure of production relations that combined aspects of each basic system.

The interpenetration of modes of production is obviously a much more complicated affair than the simple articulation of modes of production. In the case of articulation one can locate spatially distinct organizations of production and directly observe and analyze their interconnections. In the case of interpenetration, the two modes of production are internally fused and empirically appear distinct from both modes of production. The deciphering of the texture of their combination thus requires a much more enegetic theoretical effort.

A given social formation will be characterized by complex patterns of articulation and interpenetration of modes of production. In many situations, in fact, there will occur what could be termed "articulated interpenetration": that is, not only can two modes of production be articulated, but a mode of production and an interpenetrated form of production can be articulated, existing side by side in different units of production engaged in exchange relations with each other. As we shall see, all of these forms of the coexistence of different modes of production are important for understanding the problem of transitional societies and post-capitalist futures.

The importance of the distinction between interpenetration and articulation

An analogy with chemistry may help to explain the importance of the concept of interpenetrated modes of production (although such analogies are always a bit dangerous). Articulation corresponds to a situation in which two basic elements coexist, for example in a solution, without ever chemically combining to form a compound. The properties of the solution are different than would be the case if only one of the

---

24. For a discussion of artisanal subcontracting in early stages of capitalist development, see Dan Clawson, *Bureaucracy and the Labor Process*, New York 1980.

elements was present (e.g., a difference in taste or feel), but those properties are in a sense the simple sum of the properties of each element. As a result it is a fairly straightforward task to determine which elements are in the solution. When two elements combine to form a compound, on the other hand, the situation is quite different. Here the properties of the solution must be considered "emergent" rather than simply additive, and it is no longer easy to determine which elements make up the compound in the solution. Indeed, it is because this is so difficult that the heart of chemistry as a science consists of decoding compounds, understanding the principles of the "internal relations" among elements as they combine, and the "emergent properties" of the compounds so produced.

Interpenetrated forms of production are analogous to chemical compounds. Modes of production are analogous to basic elements. To make the claim that the compound is indeed a compound and not itself a basic element – i.e. that the interpenetrated form is not itself a special mode of production – is to argue that it is made up of components that are themselves stable, with their own conditions of existence and mechanisms of reproduction. (It could happen that in nature a given element may only concretely exist in various compounds. Free-floating hydrogen, for example, might not exist in nature but is always combined with some other elements, such as oxygen to form water, and yet water could properly be described as a compound, and hydrogen as an element, if hydrogen could be stably produced as an entity with specific properties, dynamics, etc.)

Typically, then, modes of production exist in concrete societies in interpenetrated forms. While it could happen that a pure form existed, more frequently it will be "contaminated" with various residual elements of other production relations. The precise effects of the concrete relations of production "on the ground" depend upon the significance of these residual elements.

The example of artisanal subcontracting mentioned earlier might help to clarify this argument about the emergent properties of interpenetrated modes of production. Compare the following two situations of artisanal production, one characterized primarily by an articulation of modes of production and one by an interpenetration. In the first situation, artisans own their own shops, hire apprentices who eventually become master craftsmen, and sell for a market. They purchase some of their inputs from capitalist producers and sell some of their outputs to capitalist factories, and thus through the market they are articulated to capitalist production. In the second situation, artisans are partially incorporated into factory production itself, but they still own their own tools, hire their own subordinates, and in a guild-like manner control their own labor process. Here we have the interpenetration of two different production relations. As Ron Aminzade has shown, the effects on the actors involved are dramatically different in these two situations. Where artisans are inserted in interpenetrated forms of production, they typically become among the most militant participants in the working-class movement, often assuming leadership positions; when they are simply articulated with capitalist production they are more likely to play a much more marginal role within class struggles.[25]

The distinction between interpenetrated and articulated modes of production is thus important for understanding the dynamics and contradictions of class formation. When articulated modes of production are significant, the central problem of class formation revolves around building durable class alliances between classes determined within the different modes of production. Different concrete people live their lives within the different relations of production. Thus, for example, in the articulation of simple commodity production and capitalist production, one of the important tasks for revolutionary movements may be to forge a class alliance between the petty bourgeoisie and the working class, each of which is constituted by distinct (although articulated) relations of production. Where interpenetration of modes of production is the decisive reality, on the other hand, the different relations of production bear directly on the lives and experiences of each individual. The ideological problem ceases to be how to form alliances between different groups of individuals, but how to resolve the competing principles of class determination within each individual. Depending upon the modes of production involved and the relative weight that each plays in the interpenetrated form, such situations may either facilitate or impede the practical tasks of class formation.[26]

The interpenetration of capitalist and post-capitalist modes of production

Having defined the central features of capitalist, statist and communist modes of production, and introduced the problem of interpenetration of

---

25. See Ron Aminzade, *Class, Politics and Early Industrial Capitalism*, Binghamton, N.Y. 1981.

26. The distinction between articulation and interpenetration of modes of production may be of great importance politically. For example, in the Third World today, it may make a great deal of difference whether peasants are stable smallholders articulated with capitalist production, or whether they are semi-proletarianized producers in an interpenetrated form of production. In both cases the system of production combines simple commodity production, subsistence production (production for one's own immediate consumption) and capitalist production, but the effects on the actors involved may be radically different.

modes of production, our next task is to specify various forms of interpenetration involving these modes of production. Since any given mode of production has several aspects, more than one form of interpenetration is possible even between two modes of production. When we consider possible combinations involving all three modes, the interpenetrated forms become potentially very complex.

In this analysis I will not attempt to map out all the logically possible interpenetrated forms of capitalist/post-capitalist modes of production. Even if I were capable of doing so, the result would be a tedious catalogue of hypothetical forms of production. What I will try to do is specify the content of five basic forms of such interpenetration that have particularly salient historical or political significance, and which therefore are especially relevant to the problem of specifying the futures of capitalist society:

1. State capitalist production;
2. Workers' self-management production;
3. Socialist production;
4. Party-bureaucratic socialist production;
5. Market socialism.

Before looking at each of these forms of interpenetration in detail, it will be helpful to examine their overall interconnection with the three modes of production we have been discussing. These interconnections can be visualized through a spatial metaphor, as illustrated in Figure 6.1. In this Venn diagram, each of the modes of production is represented by a circular space on a plane, and the intersections of these circles represent the interpenetrations of modes of production. Thus: state capitalist production is the interpenetration of capitalist and statist production; party-bureaucratic socialist production is the interpenetration of statist and communist production; socialist production is the interpenetration of communist and capitalist production, with the communist mode of production dominant; workers' self-managed production is the interpenetration of the same two modes of production with capitalism dominant; and market socialist production is the interpenetration of all three modes of production.

In order to keep the discussion of these five interpenetrated forms of production to a reasonable length, the analysis will be restricted to the first two aspects of modes of production discussed earlier: the mechanisms of appropriation of the surplus and the dynamics of the allocation of resources. The question of the form of the political within production and the nature of class struggles will be discussed only where it is of particular importance in clarifying the nature of a specific interpenetrated form. The analysis that follows is summarized in Table 6.4.

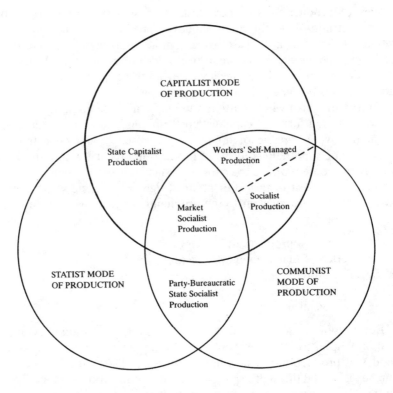

Figure 6.1 Interpenetrated Forms of Production

State capitalist production

State capitalist production constitutes an interpenetration of capitalist and statist modes of production.[27] Certain means of production are owned by the state, but there remains a generally free market for labor-power and for commodities. The result is that the mode of exploitation remains substantially capitalist, revolving around the difference between the value of labor-power and the value of commodities produced in the state capitalist enterprises. But this principle is modified in one critical respect: because the enterprise is owned by the state and is thus partially free from imperatives of market competition, the direct exploitation of workers in state capitalist enterprises is systematically supplemented by

---

27. As in our earlier discussion of statism as such, state capitalist production should not be conflated with the capitalist state. Here we are referring strictly to productive enterprises organized by the state – the state economic apparatuses – and not to the political apparatuses of the state (courts, police, foreign policy apparatuses, legislatures, etc.).

Table 6.4   Interpenetrated Forms of Production

Interpenetrated Forms of Production	Constituent Modes of Production	Mechanisms of Appropriation of Surplus Labor	Dynamics of Resource Allocation
state capitalist production	capitalism + statism	free wage labor + tax-exploitation	bureaucratic planning under market constraints
workers' self-management production	capitalism + communism (capitalism dominant)	private-collective self-appropriation	competition + accumulation (exchange value dominates use value)
socialist production	capitalism + communism (communism dominant)	wage labor + collective appropriation	collective planning with market constraints (use value dominates exchange value)
party-bureaucratic socialist production	statism + communism	party-mediated bureaucratic appropriation	party-mediated bureaucratic planning
market socialist production	capitalism + statism + communism	free wage labor + partial bureaucratic appropriation + private collective appropriation	bureaucratic planning for competition and accumulation (exchange value dominates use value)

tax-exploitation.[28] State enterprises need not produce a profit, and thus it is possible for the value of the commodities they produce to be equal to or even less than the value of the labor-power employed, with tax-exploitation providing the necessary compensation. In this sense the amount of exploitation within state capitalist production is directly affected by bureaucratic-political planning and, in this respect, is similar to statist production.

The dynamics of resource allocation also represent a combination of capitalist and statist elements. Production decisions involve specific combinations of bureaucratically planned use-value criteria and market-

28. For a defense of the view that taxation can constitute exploitation, see Wright, *Class, Crisis, and the State*, pp. 154–5.

determined exchange-value criteria. The precise balance between these two, and indeed which is the dominant element, depends upon the precise form of interpenetration of the two modes of production. Where the capitalist mode of production plays the dominant role, as in situations where unprofitable but essential capitalist enterprises are nationalized to prevent them from going bankrupt but continue to be run largely on capitalist principles, then the bureaucratic planning is likely to be systematically subordinate to general market imperatives. When, on the other hand, state capitalist enterprises are created out of bureaucratic and political initiatives, then politically and/or bureaucratically defined use-value criteria may dominate the planning process. What is produced and how much is produced in such cases may be dictated by the requirements of bureaucratic reproduction and expansion more than by the requirements of the market.

Workers' self-management production
Workers' self-management constitutes production in which the workers in a particular enterprise own the means of production and control the production process, and thus exercise rights over the disposition of the surplus produced by themselves within that enterprise. The mechanism of appropriation of the surplus labor can thus be designated "private-collective self-appropriation." The direct producers appropriate their own surplus labor, and they do so through a collective process of management and control over the production process. But this collective process remains essentially private in that the means of production are fully alienable and thus the surplus is appropriated by the workers in individual enterprises rather than by the working class as a whole. The mechanism of appropriation thus contains within itself both capitalist and communist elements: it is communist in that it is collective self-appropriation rather than exploitation; it is capitalist in that it is private rather than social.

The result of the private character of the system of appropriation is that the logic of the disposition of the surplus and the allocation of resources within a workers' self-management system of production remain essentially capitalist in character. Individual enterprises are still compelled to accumulate by a logic of competition, since they produce for an impersonal market and since the means of production remain private property. Because of the dominance of exchange value over use value in this form of production, and because of the private character of appropriation (albeit, a private-collective form of appropriation), in general the capitalist mode of production can be said to be dominant within this interpenetrated form of production.

Socialist production

In order to undermine the dominance of the logic of capitalist production within a system of workers' self-management, two things would have to happen: first, some mechanism would have to be created to constrain, if not block altogether, the imperative to accumulate by individual enterprises, and second, some process for making basic production decisions on the basis of socially defined use-value criteria would have to be created. These modifications would imply that property was no longer primarily private, but assumed at least a partially public character. In short, it would imply that the communist aspects of the interpenetrated modes of production had become dominant. This defines the essential character of socialist production.

The mechanism of appropriation in socialist production can be described as wage labor combined with collective self-appropriation. There is a market for labor-power, but it is not an entirely free market since the structure of wages in the market is determined by collectively defined priorities. Workers produce commodities that are sold on a market, but the free market price of those commodities is modified through collective decisions on price subsidies of basic necessities and surcharges for luxuries. Furthermore, the length and intensity of the working day, two critical ingredients in determining the amount of surplus available for appropriation, are determined through a collective decision-making process, in part located within individual units of production and in part located in a broader political arena. Thus, while surplus appropriation does involve market-mediated wage relations as in capitalism, those relations are systematically constrained by a collective process of self-appropriation, as in communist production.

The logic of the allocation of resources is also a combination of capitalist and communist elements, with communist principles dominating. Production is both for use and exchange (a market continues to exist), but use value dominates exchange values. And the content of that use-value production is determined by a collective planning process, modified by market conditions. Such dynamics of resource allocation differ from pure communist dynamics since exchange relations continue to impinge upon the process, but they differ from workers' self-management and capitalism in that exchange value is subordinated to collectively defined use-value criteria for production.

The specific combination of elements that constitutes socialist production is impossible to imagine without a political apparatus providing some degree of centralized coordination to the system of production. Furthermore, since socialist production implies the continuation of capitalist elements, although in a subordinate form, such political apparatuses would have to do more than merely coordinate; they would have to prevent the development and reassertion of capitalist relations. That is, they would have to engage in repressive activities as well (activities which actively intervene to prohibit the development of certain practices). It is for this reason that Marxists have traditionally insisted that socialism requires a specific form of the *state*,[29] a state in which the principles of the communist relations of production were systematically defended and deepened. While the traditional term for such a state – the "dictatorship of the proletariat" – may no longer be appropriate, the concept behind that term is still important: for a socialist form of production (the interpenetration of capitalist and communist modes within which communism is dominant) to be reproduced over time and to develop towards communism, a state apparatus dominated by direct producers and oriented towards coordinating production and preventing the resurgence of capitalism is essential.[30]

Party-bureaucratic socialist production
Socialist production, as just described, requires a strong state apparatus, with at least some significant centralized functions. If, for whatever historical/structural reasons, such a state develops strong bureaucratic-hierarchical forms of organization and ceases to coordinate but actually begins to direct production, then elements of the statist mode of production would become significant. As capitalist elements in the production relations disappeared or were weakened, they could be replaced by statist elements rather than by a strengthening of the communist elements.

Such a trajectory of development, however, need not imply the full consolidation of statism (although this may happen). What it might produce is a new form of interpenetrated modes of production, which I will refer to as "party-bureaucratic socialism," one form of interpenetration of communism and statism. As in statist production, the means of

---

29. Political apparatuses need not be "states." To be a state a political apparatus must have as one of its central organizing principles the monopoly of the use of force. Traditionally Marxists have argued that in a communist society the state "withers" away. Coordination functions would of course still have to be performed, but the distinctively repressive function of the political apparatuses would disappear. This claim, it seems to me, has a strong utopian element in it. I doubt very much if a society with literally no state is possible under conditions of advanced social production. But what may be possible is a state in which the repressive functions are highly attenuated, democratically organized and executed (rather than bureaucratically structured) and no longer the defining principle of political coordination. In any event, in a *socialist* society, a state would seem to be essential.

30. The term "dictatorship of the proletariat" was introduced in a time when dictatorship did not have the connotations it does today. It was meant to define a form of the state – one that dictates the interests of the working class – not a form of regime. Indeed, all of the classical writers of Marxist theory stressed that a dictatorship of the proletariat had to have a profoundly democratic form of regime, one that guaranteed much higher levels of participation and debate than was the case in capitalist democracies.

production are owned by the state and effective control is organized through centralized, hierarchical bureaucratic planning. The difference from statism is that mechanisms exist through which the bureaucracy itself is systematically tied to and subordinated to the working class. Since this mechanism is most likely to involve the role of a political party, the interpenetrated form is referred to as party-bureaucratic socialist production. The use-value criteria that guide the bureaucratic planning and appropriation process, therefore, are themselves determined simultaneously by a principle of bureaucratic domination and by a principle of working-class needs as mediated through the party. The mechanism of appropriation and the dynamics of resource allocation can thus be respectively designated party-mediated bureaucratic appropriation and party-mediated bureaucratic planning.

The claim that this form of production in fact constitutes an interpenetration of statist and communist production itself rests heavily on the argument that the party both genuinely represents the working class and effectively dominates the bureaucracy in the state economic apparatuses. If the bureaucracy becomes structurally autonomous from the party, or if the party becomes more a representative of the bureaucracy itself than of the working class, then the statist mode of production would dominate this particular form of interpenetration. If, on the other hand, the party is organically linked to the working class in communities and workplaces, if party militants are responsive to working-class demands and are effectively held accountable by workers, and if the party retains the capacity to substantially dictate priorities in the process of appropriation and disposition of surplus, then the communist mode would be the dominant one within this form of interpenetrated production.

Market socialist production
Market socialist production contains elements from all three modes of production we have been discussing, and will take different forms depending upon the relative weight of the different elements and the specific ways in which they are combined. Some forms could look very much like party-bureaucratic socialist production with marginal market principles governing certain aspects of production; others could look like state capitalism, with workers having a certain degree of effective power within the production process; and still others could look like socialist production, with the state bureaucracy partially blocking the democratic control of appropriation and resource dispositions by workers. The designation "market socialism" thus encompasses a wide range of concrete possibilities, and it is only through a rigorous assessment of the actual form of interpenetration that the real nature of this form of production can be decoded.

Social Formations and the Futures of Capitalism

The analysis presented above has attempted to decode the modes of production and their interpenetrated forms which constitute the elements of the production structure of present and future social formations. The potential futures of capitalist society can be mapped as specific combinations of these modes of production and interpenetrated forms, with different specific modes of production being dominant. In order to shift the analysis to the level of social formation, therefore, we need to give more content to what it means to claim a specific mode of production is "dominant" within a complex articulation and interpenetration of modes of production. Once we have done this we will address two important questions about social formations: first, within social formations in which the capitalist mode of production is dominant, what are the immanent tendencies of development of alternative modes of production, and, second, within social formations existing today in which the capitalist mode of production is not dominant, how can we best describe the dominant relations of production?

Dominance of modes of production in social formations

Except for relatively short periods of time it is unlikely that two modes of production can have equal weight, either within interpenetrated forms of production or in the articulation of modes of production. Since the different modes of production represent competing principles or logics of social practice, often implying contradictory dynamics or purposes, situations in which two or more modes of production have equal weight are likely to prove unstable. In state capitalist production, for example, either the logic of the market and accumulation will be the central principle with bureaucratic planning and politically defined use-value criteria operating within capitalistically determined limits, or the reverse will be true; it is hard to see how both principles (exchange value dominates use value, and use value dominates exchange value) could exert equal weight for an extended period. There will thus be systematic tendencies in any social formation for one mode of production to become dominant. What we need, then, is a criterion for identifying which mode of production is dominant.

There are two complementary criteria in terms of which we can talk about a mode of production being "dominant." First, we can identify the dominant mode of production by the ruling class within a social formation: a specific mode of production is dominant if the ruling class in the society is the dominant class within that mode of production. This, of course, simply displaces the problem, since we need some sort of criterion for identifying the ruling class at a societal level. As a first approximation, Göran Therborn's conceptualization seems particularly useful: the ruling class is that class whose position of domination – that is, whose capacity to appropriate and dispose of the social surplus – is most systematically reproduced by the effects of the state on social relations. To say that the capitalist class is the ruling class is thus to argue that its position of privilege and domination is systematically reproduced by the activities of the state.[31]

This first strategy for defining dominance of a mode of production may be useful in analyzing the articulation of modes of production, where the classes of each mode are distinctly constituted and the only issue is which is dominant. But it is less useful for cases of complex interpenetrations of modes of production where the classes constituted by the interpenetrations themselves contain effects of different modes of production. In this situation, the dominance of a mode of production must be defined by the nature of the structural constraints and the dynamics of social change in the society. A mode of production can be said to be dominant when the structural constraints and limits specific to that mode of production characterize the most basic constraints/contradictions of the social formation as a whole, that is, when the basic limits on and dynamics of the process of social change are those derived from that mode of production. This again merely displaces the problem, since we need a way of identifying dominant constraints and dynamics. This is done by first theoretically specifying those constraints and dynamics for the pure mode of production (as Marx did for capitalism in *Capital*), and then observing empirical patterns of dynamics and constraints in a given society. To the extent that those empirical patterns can be adequately characterized in terms of the theoretically posed dynamics and constraints of a given mode of production, that mode of production can be said to be dominant. The theoretical preconditions for this task have been well specified for the capitalist mode of production, but the specification of such constraints and dynamics has hardly begun for statist production or for communist production.

These two definitions of dominance thus take two different vantage points on the effects of modes of production on societies: the first centers on the processes of *reproduction* of class relations, the second on the processes of *dynamic social change*. It can happen, of course, that these two definitions produce contradictory results. In the transition from feudalism to capitalism, for example, it is usually argued by Marxists that capitalism had become the dominant mode of production in terms of the

31. See Göran Therborn, *What Does the Ruling Class Do When It Rules?* London 1978, pp. 144–61.

logic and limits on social change long before the bourgeoisie was reproduced systematically by the state as the ruling class. This is precisely why,
it is usually argued, bourgeois revolutions were needed. On the other
hand, in the transition between capitalism and communism it is often
argued that the proletariat becomes the ruling class – seizes state power –
before communism is structurally the dominant mode of production.

Dominance, understood in this way, applies both to situations of
articulated modes of production and to situations of interpenetrated
modes of production. In the case of articulated modes of production,
dominance implies that the terms of exchange between the two modes of
production are dictated by the dominant mode of production; in the case
of interpenetrated modes of production, it implies that the dominant
mode of production has greater weight within the structural determination of the interpenetrated form. Thus, for example, when we analyze
situations of state capitalist production, we need to ask questions about
both of these form of dominance. First, within a state capitalist enterprise itself, are the capitalist elements or the statist elements dominant?
Some state enterprises are run almost exactly like their purely capitalist
analogues; others are run much more like state apparatuses, organized
around political and bureaucratic objectives rather than market principles. Second, in the relationship between the state enterprise and
capitalist production, which is dominant? Are the possibilities of action
and direction of development of state capitalist enterprises fundamentally constrained by capitalist production proper, or not? Very complex
patterns are thus potentially possible. It could happen that within state
enterprises, capitalist elements are not dominant, and yet in the articulation with capitalist production itself, the capitalist mode of production is
dominant. Such situations are likely to produce particularly sharp
contradictions.[32]

Immanent tendencies of "actually existing capitalism"

Capitalist societies are societies within which the capitalist mode of
production is dominant in the sense described above. Within such

---

32. The integration of various national economies into the world system poses particularly clear forms of this contradiction between dominance within interpenetrated forms and
dominance between articulated modes of production. In certain Third World countries one
might argue that statist relations of productions are dominant within interpenetrated forms
of state capitalist production, yet because of their articulation with capitalism in the world
system, capitalist relations become the effectively dominant relations in the social formation. This is one way of re-posing the thesis of "world systems theory" that all societies
within the world system are capitalist.

societies, however, there are systematic tendencies that prefigure two future forms of society: a trajectory towards statism via state capitalism, and a trajectory towards communism via socialism.

The statist trajectory is perhaps the more obvious. The massive growth of the state apparatus and its increasingly direct role in organizing pieces of social production represent emergent forms of state capitalism. To be sure, such bureaucratically organized, state-owned production processes are systematically subordinated to the needs of accumulation and face basic limits to their development imposed by the capitalist mode of production – this is in fact why we say that the capitalist mode of production remains unquestionably dominant within such interpenetrated forms – but nevertheless they constitute embryonic forms of genuinely non-capitalist relations of production.

The communist trajectory is somewhat less striking, but nonetheless important. As Marxists have always argued, the increasingly interconnected "social character" of the production process, when combined with increasing literacy, education, and forms of communication among workers, makes socialized production increasingly more viable as an alternative to privatized property relations. In such a structural context, the tentative movements toward limited forms of workers' participation, especially when they involve real elements of self-management and the struggles for democratization of state bureaucratic institutions, represent the development of embryonic elements of communist relations of production. Particularly when the demands for workers' self-management are extended to include the effective capacity to veto important investment decisions – such as plant closings – as has been discussed in Sweden, such changes can be viewed as augmenting non-capitalist elements within the dominant capitalist relations of production. Again, as in the case of state capitalism, the form and possibilities of such workers' self-management are heavily shaped and limited by the imperatives of accumulation and competition. Thus, in the foreseeable future, such tendencies are unlikely, in any spontaneous way, to threaten the actual dominance of the capitalist mode of production and inaugurate the consolidation of a post-capitalist society.

The critical proviso is, of course, "in a spontaneous way." Capitalism will not be replaced spontaneously, but through the organized, collective struggle of classes. The question then becomes: which of these tendencies in advanced capitalist societies is more likely to be seized by organized class forces? Historically, revolutionary movements in backward capitalist societies have tended to produce either some form of state capitalism or party-bureaucratic socialism. This does not imply that such revolutions were launched (necessarily) by an organized, state bureaucratic class, but the consolidation of such a class in one form or another has often been the ultimate result of such revolutions.[33] Whatever might have been the intentions of the revolutionaries themselves, the creation of important aspects of statist production has become an important reality in post-revolutionary societies, even though statism may not be the dominant mode of production in those societies. Is the outcome likely to be the same in advanced capitalist societies?

At first glance, the statist tendencies would appear to be the most powerful and likely trajectory of capitalism's futures. First, the proportion of the total social product that passes through the state has increased considerably, reaching 50 per cent or more in some capitalist countries. This means that even though this has not yet developed into systematic anti-capitalist principles of allocation, a material basis for such a development is being laid.

Second, the substantial growth of professional, technical and managerial occupations in both the state and private sectors could be viewed as creating a broad social base for the kind of technical bureaucratic rationality that the emergence of statist production would represent. It certainly is the case that the expansion of such occupational groups in recent decades has been closely linked to the expansion of the state. It has been shown that if the state had not grown in terms of relative employment in the decade of the 1960s, for example, there would have actually been a decline of "semi-autonomous employees" in the United States during that decade.[34]

Third, at the ideological level, there has been a gradual shift within capitalism from a system of legitimation based largely on rights to private property and claims that socialism is immoral, to a system based on claims of the technical rationality of capitalism compared to other alternatives. Such claims, however, are a double-edged sword, for they suggest that decisions should be made by experts rather than by property-holders. Such technocratic principles of legitimation can also serve, under conditions of prolonged capitalist stagnation, to support the strengthening of statist relations of production. To some extent, there-

---

33. Such a consolidation may have been historically unavoidable in many cases. Statism as a mode of production is oriented around accumulation rather than consumption, and given the economic backwardness of these countries, a growth-centered system of production was probably necessary. In any event, nothing in the present analysis should be taken as implying that a revolutionary break with capitalism in a Third World country that leads to a strengthening of statism is not progressive. It could well be that a socialist transition in such societies under the given historical conditions was "utopian," and that the most progressive real alternative to capitalism – progressive in the sense of opening up the maximum possibilities for social and human development – was some form of statism.

34. These data are reported in Erik Olin Wright and Joachim Singlemann, "Proletarianization in American Class Structure," *American Journal of Sociology*, vol. 88, supplement, 1982.

fore, the ideological basis for a statist trajectory has been partially laid within capitalism itself.

Finally, virtually all politically significant oppositions to capitalism have traditionally sought solutions to capitalist contradictions that center on the strengthening and development of various forms of state intervention and control. This is true of traditional social democracy, liberal reformists, and parliamentary communist parties. The political parties committed to a socialist future have, wittingly or unwittingly, adopted strategies and objectives that are more consistent with building a statist future.

With this array of factors tending to strengthen statism as a future to capitalism, it is hard to be exuberantly optimistic about the prospects for socialism as a transition to communism. Yet, I think that there are important counter-tendencies, factors that can be strengthened as part of the strategic agenda of the left. First of all, I think that it is very easy to overstate the potential class basis for the consolidation of statism. The top leadership of the state productive apparatuses within state capitalist enterprises is extremely well integrated into the bourgeoisie socially and ideologically, and in many ways economically as well. The people in such positions are very unlikely to function as a vanguard for the advent of a statist mode of production within capitalist societies. For statism to become the real future of capitalism, therefore, it will need to be generated by social movements opposed to the elites within the state economic apparatuses themselves.

Secondly, while it is true that the expansion of the state has contributed greatly to the expansion of "middle strata," it is equally true that within the state sector itself there has been a process of proletarianization of state employees, of reductions of autonomy and control.[35] This implies that at least potentially there is considerable room for organizing a working-class movement that transcends the boundary between public and private employment as the conditions of work become similar in both institutional settings. Thus, while the social basis for statism may be growing, the social basis for socialism is expanding as well.

Thirdly, even though socialist and communist parties continue to orient the heart of their programs around demands that are either compatible with the reproduction of capitalism or supportive of statist alternatives to capitalism, there is increasing discussion on the left of the problem of democratization of all spheres of social life, of the problem of workers' control and quality of life, and so on. To the extent that such

---

35. See ibid.

demands move closer to the core of practical left politics, then the struggle within capitalism will itself begin to forge elements of the socialist alternative to capitalism. And if embryonic communist relations – interpenetrations between communism and capitalism – are forged by struggles within capitalist society, then it is more likely that the struggle against capitalism will itself generate a socialist transition.[36]

The dominant mode of production in "actually existing non-capitalism"

The analysis of this chapter will hopefully contribute to a clarification of the debates on "actually existing socialism." If we accept the categories developed in this chapter, then in purely descriptive terms such societies can be characterized as social formations structured by an interpenetration of the statist mode of production with the communist mode of production and at least some elements of capitalist production as well. Such societies could thus generally be described as party-bureaucratic socialist societies with limited forms of market relations.

The question then becomes: within this complex interpenetrated form of production, which mode of production is dominant? Can we argue that at least in the Soviet Union the non-statist elements are of such residual importance that we have a fully developed example of a statist society? Or is it the case that communist relations, or possibly even capitalist relations, are sufficiently central to the system of production that even in the Soviet Union statism is not yet the dominant mode?

If our discussion of the party-bureaucratic socialist form of production is theoretically satisfactory, then the answers to these questions ultimately boil down to a question of the precise nature of the party, of its links to the working class and to the bureaucratic apparatus of production. At least some theorists are prepared to argue that these relations are such that communist relations are either an important aspect of Soviet production relations or even the dominant aspect. For example, Göran Therborn suggests in his analysis of the character of the party in the Soviet Union that the form of leadership in the Soviet Communist Party – what he calls cadre leadership – is deeply non-bureaucratic in

---

36. This does not imply, one way or another, that the transition to socialism can be accomplished as a smooth, incremental, or peaceful process. In fact, I believe that for *both* statism and socialism, at some point a revolutionary rupture with capitalism would be necessary, although it seems implausible that such a rupture would take the form of an armed assault on the state.

character, and by virtue of its role in mobilizing the working class, it sustains real and effective ties to that class.[37] If this account is correct, then in spite of the authoritarian form of the regime in the USSR, the communist mode of production could be said to dominate the interpenetrated form of production in that society. Al Szymanski takes an even more radical position and argues not only that the party remains a genuinely proletarian instrument, but that the political apparatuses of the state are fundamentally democratic in ways that ensure that the bureaucracy is effectively subordinated to the working class.[38] The effect of this, Szymanski argues, is that social and economic inequalities in the Soviet Union (measured both in terms of outcomes and opportunities) have steadily declined over the past several decades, a decline which would probably be inconsistent with the dominance of any class-exploitative mode of production.

Other writers have argued that the links to the working class by the party are weak and that in any event they are not of a form that allows the working class to hold the party accountable to its interests in any serious way. If anything, it is claimed, the party is an instrument of the bureaucracy (or, alternatively, that the two are so intertwined that they form a single apparatus). If this account is correct, then the statist mode of production would be the dominant one, and any claim to being socialist would be of a purely propagandistic character.

I do not have a sufficiently deep knowledge of the social reality in the Soviet Union to make a rigorous judgment on this issue. The weight of the evidence is such, however, that it is difficult to see the Soviet Union and similar societies as having dominant communist relations of production within a party-bureaucratic socialist form. However, I do not think that accounts that simply reduce such societies to a statist mode of production (or any other mode of production) are satisfactory either. If for no other reason, the contradictory character of the international role of the Soviet Union, sometimes very progressive, other times undermining progressive social movements, suggests that the class relations within the Soviet Union cannot be considered exclusively statist. In any event, the important point in the present context is that an adequate assessment of the relations of production and class structure of the Soviet Union and other similar societies must rest on a careful empirical decoding of the forms of interpenetration and articulation of modes of production. Within such an investigation, the possibility of the existence of a statist mode of production must be entertained.

---

37. Therborn, *What Does the Ruling Class Do?*
38. Al Szymanski, *Is the Red Flag Flying?* London 1979.

Implications for Historical Materialism and
Socialist Practice

If the arguments advanced in this chapter are sound, certain features of historical materialism will have to be changed. One of the central thrusts of historical materialism has always been that historical development occurred along a single developmental trajectory. While there are ambiguities about the character of this trajectory in precapitalist societies, the overall trajectory is clear: primitive communalism to precapitalist class societies to capitalism to communism (with socialism as the transitional phase). There may be reversals, and possibly under certain circumstances stages can be skipped, but there is only one road. It is for this reason that historical materialism is often considered a teleological philosophy of history with one final state inexorably pulling social change towards it.

We have now suggested that there are branches in the road, alternative destinations for capitalist society. Of course it is possible that the fork is just a detour: communism may be the only future to statism, and thus ultimately the different paths rejoin. But introducing the possibility of radically different paths also brings into question the inevitability of a single final destination.

Such qualitatively different structural alternatives as futures to existing social structures implies a different relationship between social structural determination of outcomes and conscious social practices. Marxists committed to the traditional theses of historical materialism have usually argued that structural determination and contradictions must be given primacy over conscious class practices in understanding historical development. How much primacy, of course, is a frequently debated matter. Few Marxists argue any more for a purely mechanical unfolding of structurally given outcomes. But typically it is argued that social structural factors are of the greatest importance. This is what Marx implied when he stated that "history is the judge, the proletariat the executioner" in describing the role of class struggle in destroying capitalism.[39] And it is what G. A. Cohen means when he states that in Marxist theory class struggle is of "immediately secondary" importance.[40]

If the strategic choices of class actors influence not only the rate of social change, the delays on the road, the possibilities of reversals, and so on, but the actual destinations, then this traditional conception has to be modified. At a minimum a distinction would have to be made between

39. Cited in Cohen, *Marx's Theory of History*, p. 150.
40. G. A. Cohen, "Reply to Elster on Marxism, Functionalism, and Game Theory," *Theory and Society*, vol. 11, no. 4, 1982.

two kinds of situations of class struggle: situations in which strategic moves have effects on trajectories of future change and situations in which class struggles only affect the secondary processes within a given trajectory. This implies that the relationship between structural determinations and practices is historically variable rather than constant. A central task of Marxist theory would then be to try to analyze the conditions of such variability.

This is not to suggest, of course, that the critical strategic choices that have systemic effects on future structural changes are themselves undetermined, that they are unexplainable or somehow acts of pure will. The alternative to the teleological structuralism of the evolutionary theory of successions of modes of production is not voluntarism. Rather, the argument is that such strategic choices cannot in any way be themselves derived from the dynamics, properties, limits, contradictions, etc. of modes of production themselves. (If they were so derivable we would be back to a teleological account and the strategic choice would have been an illusion.) To understand the process of their determination we must examine other kinds of relations which are themselves irreducible to modes of production: cultural determinations, psychological processes, etc. The analysis of modes of production remains essential to this enterprise, since the decisive alternatives that are historically possible revolve around the system of production and appropriation. Class structure remains the key *stake* in projects of fundamental social change, since class power defines the ways in which resources are made available for social use and development. But, if the arguments of this chapter are accepted, then the theory of modes of production can no longer be considered an adequate guide to the actual patterns of social change.

These consequences for historical materialism also have important implications for socialist practice. If socialism were the only alternative to capitalism, then being steadfastly anti-capitalist would be equivalent to working for socialism. After a revolutionary rupture this implies that the central preoccupation of revolutionaries would be vigilantly to prevent the restoration of capitalism. If they succeeded in that endeavor, then socialism would necessarily be assured. Before a revolutionary rupture it implies that relatively little attention has to be given to forging positive preconditions for socialism. The important thing is to mobilize sufficient power to challenge capitalist power.

The basic political message of this chapter is that socialists must be much more self-conscious about the character of the alternative they are struggling for, both within capitalist societies themselves and after revolutionary breaks with capitalism. In advanced capitalist countries this means that projects for socialist transformation should be militantly democratic. Demands should center not simply on the provision of various services by the state and various state regulations of capital, but also on the active democratization of the forms of delivery of such services and the forms of administration of such regulations. To take just one example, in the area of occupational safety and health, the socialist demand should be not simply for tougher state regulations, but for direct worker participation (and ultimately control) over the setting of standards, the investigation of abuses, and the adjudication of violations. This does not imply that the gradual institutionalization of such demands would itself constitute a socialist revolution. The problem of the political form of a socialist rupture with capitalism has not been addressed at all in this chapter. But it does imply that however such a rupture occurs, if the outcome is to produce a transition to communism rather than a consolidation of a statist mode of production, anti-capitalist struggles must be self-consciously anti-statist as well.[41]

---

41. This is not a call for anarchism or for a reliance on "self-help" strategies. The state will play an essential role in any conceivable socialist transition, both because of the need for repression and because of the need for an institutional apparatus of centralized coordination. And in capitalism itself, the state plays an important redistributive role. If popular social movements attempt to entirely side-step the state through self-help projects they inevitably end up with meager resources. The bourgeois democratic form of the capitalist state allows for certain margins of real redistribution to occur, and the goal of popular movements should be to create a sufficiently strong political base to be able to win redistributive victories and to control the use of redistributed resources.

7

Why Something like Socialism is Necessary for the Transition to Something like Communism

One of the hallmarks of much contemporary Marxist theory has been the dedicated attack on dogmatism. Theoretical positions are expected to be defended by systematic arguments and evidence, not by their unreflective faithfulness to some orthodoxy or classical text. Virtually all concepts and theses in Marxism have thus been subjected to intense scrutiny and reconstruction.

It is notable in these terms that one thesis has remained virtually untouched by this broadly self-critical stance, namely the thesis that socialism, understood as a society within which workers collectively own the means of production, is the necessary condition for human liberation. To be sure, there has been an intense Marxist reevaluation of "actually existing socialism" both in terms of the historical record of post-capitalist societies and in terms of the theoretical logic of the concept of socialism. But to the extent that these reevaluations continue to see themselves as Marxist, they have not questioned systematically the necessity for some kind of socialism. Indeed, a good case can be made that the only thesis that in practice unites all theorists who consider themselves Marxist is the claim that socialism of one sort or another is necessary and desirable.

Robert Van der Veen and Philippe Van Parijs (hereafter VP) challenge this thesis in "A Capitalist Road to Communism."[1] What is more, they do so in the name of the classical Marxian vision of communism: true communism as defined by Marx, they argue, can develop within the institutional structure of capitalist property relations without requiring any form of state or social ownership of society's productive capacity. Whether or not in the end one finds their arguments and proposals compelling, their article is an important contribution to the agenda of rethinking basic Marxist concepts.

---

1. Robert Van der Veen and Philippe Van Parijs, "A Capitalist Road to Communism," *Theory and Society*, vol. 15, no. 5, 1986.

In this chapter, I argue that some form of social ownership of the principal means of production is essential for the development and reproduction of communist social practices. Indeed, I show that, in spite of their own arguments, the models that VP propose implicitly assume the existence of significant elements of public or collective ownership.

A Capitalist Road to Communism: the Basic Argument

The core of the VP argument is as follows: communism, following Marx, is defined by the distribution principle "From each according to his/her abilities, to each according to his/her needs." This implies, VP argue, "that the social product is distributed in such a way (1) that everyone's basic needs are adequately met, and (2) that each individual's share is independent of his or her (freely provided) labor contribution" (p. 636; *A Capitalist Road*). In contrast, socialism is defined by VP as:

> a society in which workers collectively own the means of production – and in which therefore they collectively decide what these should be used for and how the resulting product should be distributed, namely according to the principle "To each according to his labor." (p. 636)

Stated in somewhat different terms, they write:

> socialism, as defined, implies that exploitation is abolished – workers appropriate the whole of the social product – while communism, as defined, implies that "alienation" is abolished – productive activities need no longer be prompted by external rewards. (p. 636)

This definition of communism is a considerably thinner one than is usually found in Marxist discussions. Typically when Marxists talk about "communism," the concept also entails collective ownership of the means of production and some kind of associated collective planning of social and economic life. VP wish to separate such institutional specifications from the distributive principle of communism in order to see if the latter requires the former. They believe – I think correctly – that the normative ideal represented in Marx's concept of communism (the abolition of alienation) is captured by the distributive principle; collective institutional arrangements are to be defended to the extent that they facilitate this ideal, not for their own sake.[2]

---

2. Although VP state that communism as they will use the term does not entail collective ownership of the means of production, they do say in note 3 that it "does entail collective ownership of the social product by society as a whole." It should be noted that this statement, in contrast to the characterization in the main body of the text, also implies the elimination of capitalist exploitation in communism. Communism thus implies the abolition of both exploitation and alienation.

The basic issue that VP address is whether communism understood in this way can develop within capitalist society without passing through the "stage" of socialism. Is a "capitalist road" to communism possible? It is important to be clear on precisely what question they are attempting to answer: they are not asking the question of whether socialism is the optimal route for accomplishing communism, nor are they addressing the question of whether socialism is superior to capitalism for reasons other than its instrumental value in furthering communism. While these are important issues, VP are investigating the more restricted problem of the necessity of socialism for communism and the possibility of communism developing within capitalism.

To demonstrate this possibility, they face two tasks. First, they must examine the typical arguments advanced by Marxists for why socialism is necessary for communism, and second they must propose an institutional mechanism through which communism could develop within capitalism.

VP examine two basic arguments that are frequently advanced for why socialism might be a necessary means for the emergence and development of communism. First, Marxists often argue that mature capitalism blocks the development of social productivity whereas socialism enhances productivity; second, they sometimes argue that socialism is necessary for the formation of altruistic personalities that are themselves necessary for a viable communist society. Although VP agree that a continual rise in social productivity is essential for the advent of communism, they demonstrate that the conventional arguments that capitalism inevitably fetters the development of the productive forces are flawed.[3] They criticize the altruism argument by arguing that altruism is not in fact an essential cultural norm for the viability of communism (as defined above) and thus, even if it were true that socialism fosters altruism (which they doubt), this would not be a persuasive argument for the necessity of socialism.

If it is correct that socialism is not a *necessary* means to communism, the question then becomes whether institutional innovations within capitalism can be introduced that allow for the development of communism within capitalist society itself. The heart of the VP proposal to accomplish this is very simple: every person in a capitalist society is given an *unconditional* grant of income, referred to as a "universal grant," that is sufficiently high to allow each individual to live at a socially acceptable

---

3. Even if social productivity would indefinitely increase under capitalism, it could still be that it would develop more rapidly and be deployed less wastefully under socialism. Although this might mean that socialism was a more efficient vehicle for creating this precondition for communism (relative abundance), it would still not be an essential vehicle, and this is all that VP try to demonstrate.

standard of living (i.e., a standard of living that covers basic needs). Such
a universal grant implies that it is basically a free choice on the part of
each individual whether or not to work for additional income. This
choice would depend upon each individual's preferences for additional
consumption, work, and leisure.

If the universal grant is sufficiently high to cover basic needs, then
immediately one of the central goals of communism is achieved: work is
no longer a necessity for survival of individuals, but becomes a free
choice, and distribution is at least partially geared toward needs. In a
sense, then, the VP model implies that a given society would be divided
into two distinct segments: a communist segment of unalienated activity
freely chosen by each individual, and a capitalist segment of wage labor
and capitalist investment. Labor is recruited from the communist sector
to the capitalist sector for productive purposes, and part of the surplus
generated within the capitalist sector is redistributed to the communist
sector to sustain the "realm of freedom." If the dynamics of a capitalist
society with an unconditional universal grant are such that over time the
level of the universal grant can rise, then it will also be true that over time
the degree to which the society is communist could also increase.[4]
Although VP do not believe that it is likely that a society could ever be
one hundred percent communist – i.e., all distribution could not be
according to need – they do believe that communism can function as a
regulative ideal, and that communist practices can become unequivocally
predominant within a society.

One of the obvious issues with this model is how the universal grant is
to be financed. VP explore a variety of taxation schemes and criteria, and
they demonstrate, *given certain assumptions*, that the economy will
continue to grow even with the redistributive taxes needed for the
scheme.[5] What is more, they show that there will be considerable
pressures on the economy to grow in a particular manner: to favor
selectively innovations that eliminate unpleasant work. As they put it,
"workers' unconditional entitlement to a substantial universal grant will
simultaneously push up the wage rate for unattractive, unrewarding
work (which no one is forced to accept in order to survive) and bring
down the wage rate for attractive, intrinsically rewarding work . . . "
(pp. 645–6). This kind of technological bias, in turn, creates the possi-

---

4. VP do not actually argue that the "communistness" of the society will necessarily
increase under such circumstances, but just that it could increase. It would remain a
political issue, rather than an issue of economic feasibility, whether people would opt to
expand the realm of communist activities or not.

5. The technical details of the argument are presented elsewhere, in Robert J. Van der
Veen and Philippe Van Parijs, "Capitalism, Communism and the Realm of Freedom. A
Formal Presentation," Louvain-la-Neuve Working Paper no. 8501, 1985.

bility for a smooth, continual development in the direction of communism. While the extent to which rises in productivity will be translated into higher levels of the universal grant would still be a fundamentally political question, the material preconditions for such increasing redistribution are generated within capitalism itself.

A Capitalist Road to Communism: a Critique

Is this scenario for the emergence of communism within capitalist society a plausible one? Can capitalism and communism be made compatible principles of economic organization and social life? We will first look at the problem of the economic plausibility of a communism-inducing universal grant system and then briefly turn to the issue of political plausibility.[6] Of course, it is crucial whether the proposal for a communism-inducing universal grant is politically feasible – that is, whether such a proposal could ever gain sufficient mass support to be legislated or whether the bourgeoisie would mount such intensive political opposition, including perhaps a violent counter-revolution, to make it impossible. However, unless the proposal is economically viable, there is little point in exploring the problem of political feasibility, and thus the economic plausibility has a certain logical priority.[7]

Economic feasibility

The analysis of the universal grant presented by VP is based on one critical assumption. "Let us suppose," they write, " . . . that technology, stocks and preferences are such, in advanced capitalist countries, that it is possible to provide everyone with universal grant sufficient to cover his or her 'fundamental needs' without this involving the economy in a downward spiral" (p. 645). There are three elements in this assumption: claims about technology, stocks, and preferences. The first two of these pose no serious difficulties: it is indeed likely that the existing technical level of production combined with the accumulated means of production

---

6. I will use the term "communism-inducing universal grant" to indicate a system of unconditional universal grants sufficiently generous to set in motion the dynamics outlined by VP.

7. In any event, it is important to keep in mind that the point of the present analysis is to assess the plausibility of the VP proposal for a "capitalist road to communism" relative to the classical Marxist argument for a "socialist road to communism." Because it must be recognized that scenarios for socialist revolutions also do not have a great deal of political plausibility in the advanced capitalist countries, it is not a very compelling criticism of the VP model that it is politically infeasible.

are quite sufficient to provide a sufficiently high universal grant to set in motion the development logic of the model.

But what about "preferences"? The preferences of two categories of actors are essential for the model to work: those of wage-earners (workers) and those of capitalists.[8] If, for example, all wage-earners would prefer leisure over labor at the level of the universal grant and could not be induced to work at any wage, then the system would collapse. This, however, is an implausible assumption. It is not unreasonable to assume that preferences of workers would be sufficiently varied that some would opt for zero-paid work and some would opt for differing amounts of paid work at any level of the universal grant.

In the case of capitalists, on the other hand, it is much more problematic to imagine a set of preferences compatible with the logic of the model. VP really only consider one aspect of capitalist preferences: the preferences for savings versus consumption. If this were the only preference that mattered, then VP would be on relatively safe ground, for there is no obvious reason why the desire to save and invest should necessarily decline as the social dividend rises. Of course, investments might decline for this reason – capitalists might prefer to consume a higher proportion of their total income if the expected returns on their "abstention" declined due to taxation; but this is not logically entailed by the sheer fact of their being capitalists.

Capitalists, however, have other preferences. In particular, they want to get the highest possible return on their "savings" from current income (investments). If their preferences are such that they prefer future higher consumption over present lower consumption and thus choose to save, they would also want to maximize their returns to that abstention. VP certainly assume that capitalists are rational maximizers in this sense.

There are basically two ways in which we might expect the high level of taxation implied by the VP model to affect investments of profit-maximizing capitalists: first, it could affect the propensity of capitalists to save versus consume, and second, it could affect the geographical location of their investments. While there is no logically necessary reason why high taxes (depending upon the form of taxation) would reduce savings, is it plausible that they would have no substantial effect on the location of investments? In other words, is the preference for profit-maximization really compatible with the VP model?

---

8. At the level of abstraction at which the VP model is elaborated, the only classes are workers – understood as all wage-earners – and capitalists. While for some purposes, particularly the analysis of the political feasibility, we will have to introduce class-like distinctions within the wage-earner category, in general I will assess their arguments at this "mode of production" level of abstraction.

There are some conditions, in fact, in which profit-maximizing prefer-ences of capitalists would be compatible with the model. If, for example, the proposal for a universal social dividend were enacted everywhere in the world simultaneously, then the behavior of a profit-maximizing capitalist would be unaffected by the scheme.[9] Or, alternatively, if there were substantial obstacles to capitalist investment in areas without the universal grant – because of such things as political instability, or inadequacy of skilled labor, or some other factor – then again the introduction of a universal grant would not necessarily dramatically affect decisions about investment locations.

However, if these conditions were not present, why would capitalists continue to invest in the regions with universal grants and high taxation? Imagine for a moment that the proposal for a universal grant were enacted in a single city: all residents of the city are given an unconditional annual income sufficient to live a decent, respectable life. At the time of enactment of this proposal, the level of production within the jurisdiction of the municipal government is sufficient to provide for such a standard of living. What would happen? Two movements are likely: first, one would expect a dramatic migration of people from outside the city into the city; second, one would expect a dramatic migration of capital (and of high-paid managers and capitalists) out of the political jurisdiction of the city's taxation authority. At the level of the nation state, the first of these problems is solved by citizenship laws and border controls. But given the transnational organization of capitalist investment in the world today, it would be very difficult to imagine a feasible solution to the exodus of capital.

For the sake of argument, however, let us imagine that a political regime is able to solve this problem. That is, the state establishes effective "citizenship" status and border controls on capital, thus pre-venting its flight. What does this imply for the VP model? Above all, it implies that we no longer have, properly speaking, a "capitalist road" to communism: the private character of the ownership of capital would be severely compromised if a public authority prohibited capital flight. One critical aspect of the property rights of capitalists – the right to invest and disinvest where they please – would have been nationalized. To be sure, on historical standards this would be a very weak form of "socialism": enterprises would be able to retain their profits and choose between investments and consumption, private owners would continue to receive a private return on their investments, etc. But the mobility of capital would be highly restricted and publicly controlled.

---

9. That is, the tax structure that accompanies the universal grant would not affect decisions about where to invest.

Our first general conclusion, then, is that even with the most benevolent economic assumptions (especially the assumption that the propensity of capitalists to save or invest is unaffected by the universal grant), "weak socialism" is required for the VP model to work. This, however, might not be considered too damaging to the spirit of the VP argument, because weak socialism retains many of the central features of capitalism. While effective restrictions on the mobility of capital would require a fairly strong, centralized administrative apparatus, it would not require central planning, centralized allocation of investment funds, and other attributes of socialized ownership of the means of production. What we have so far, therefore, is perhaps an argument for a "quasi-capitalist road to communism," but not an argument for the classical Marxist view of the necessity of a "socialist road."

When we examine the problem of political feasibility, however, the arguments for the necessity for socialism become considerably stronger.

Political feasibility

The problem of political feasibility can be decomposed into two issues: the political feasibility of establishing a system of communism-inducing universal grants in the first place, and the political feasibility of reproducing such a system of grants over time.

In terms of the problem of initially establishing a system of communism-inducing universal grants. I think that it is difficult to argue that socialism is politically more feasible. The political obstacles to both visions of social change are considerable.

The political obstacles to socialism are obvious and familiar: on the one hand, capitalists would mobilize considerable political force to oppose any serious move to socialize the principal means of production; on the other hand, given the record of bureaucratically centralized state socialist economies, workers in advanced industrial capitalism are very suspicious about the desirability of socialism and unwilling to engage in the necessary struggles for its realization.

The political obstacles to a proposal for sufficiently generous universal grants to make work a free choice are also substantial. Although capitalists might not be as militantly opposed to a universal grant scheme as they would be to socialism (because private profits would be retained), nevertheless they would generally oppose such proposals strenuously, particularly if the scheme were coupled with the necessary restrictions on capital mobility to make the proposals viable. Workers, on the other hand, are likely to support such proposals even less than they do socialism. In the case of socialism, the predominant belief of workers is probably skepticism: socialism is a good thing in theory, it just doesn't work very well in practice. In the case of a communism-inducing universal grant system, on the other hand, workers are likely to oppose it as being intrinsically undesirable. Given how vulnerable even modest welfare state proposals are to the accusations that people on welfare "live off of the backs of working people," it is hard to see how a universal grant system would not be viewed as exploitative by workers. It is difficult to imagine a program of generous universal grants gaining sufficient mass support to be enacted over the opposition of capitalists.

Given that socialism does not particularly fare better than the universal grant proposal in terms of the political feasibility of initial establishment, let us assume that these obstacles can be overcome in both cases. What about the political feasibility of reproducing over time a system of universal grants? In this case it seems to me that socialism is clearly more viable.

Once established, a system of communism-inducing universal grants within capitalism would be extremely vulnerable politically. Above all, because under the assumptions of the VP model, the decision to invest or not to invest (consume or hoard) would remain privately controlled, capitalists would always have the possibility of using an investment strike as a *political* weapon against the system. In our discussion of economic feasibility, I argued that on the basis of economic rationality alone there would be no necessary reason to assume that capitalists would reduce their propensity to save or invest in the face of a program of universal grants. On political grounds, however, they would have good reason to do so. Of course, it would remain a political problem for capitalists whether sufficient class solidarity within the capitalist class could be achieved to make an investment strike politically effective. However, given the stakes in the conflict and the potential benefits to capitalists if the universal grant system were eliminated, it seems likely that a serious investment strike would occur and that it would quickly destroy the viability of the program. Even if we are willing to assume that the bourgeoisie could not use its economic resources as a lever for some kind of military counter-revolution against a system of communism-inducing grants, they would be in a position to sabotage sufficiently the functioning of the system as to render it unviable.[10]

How could this be avoided in a system of universal grants? One possibility is that state controls over investments would be sufficiently

---

10. Marxists have also argued, of course, that socialism is needed to block the possibility of military counter-revolution as well. Socializing the principal means of production is the essential condition for the "dictatorship of the proletariat" without which the bourgeoisie will eventually attempt to restore its power through violent means. In the present discussion I will not explore this side of the problem.

strong and the working class would have sufficiently strong political control over the state that such economic sabotage could be effectively blocked by state intervention. We have already noted that the state must be strong enough to control effectively international flows of capital if the VP model is to be economically feasible. Perhaps the state could also be strong enough to block investment strikes. For example, the state could impose a tax rate of one hundred percent on incomes above a certain amount unless those incomes were productively invested.[11] The threshold could be set high enough to insure an incentive to invest (i.e., there would still be personal income returns on investments), but low enough to guarantee an adequate volume of investments. What would this imply for the VP model? It would imply, I suggest, that ownership of capital was no longer really private. Capitalists would have lost not only the right to move their investments where they like but also the right to choose between investment and consumption. To be sure, they would still have rights to some private income returns on investments and rights to choose in what to invest, but this begins to look much more like a compensation system for nationalized property with high levels of enterprise autonomy than the maintenance of genuine capitalist property itself.

The Necessity of Socialism for the Development of Communism

In this discussion we have distinguished four aspects of ownership of the means of production: the right to decide *where* to invest, the right to decide *whether* to invest, the right to decide *in what* to invest, and the right to a *personal income* from those investments. In a purely capitalist society, all four of these aspects of ownership are private; in a socialist society as traditionally conceived in Marxism, all four would be collectively controlled. What I have argued so far is that for economic reasons, the first of these four aspects would have to be controlled collectively for the VP model to work, and that for political reasons the second would have to be socially controlled as well. In effect, therefore, I have argued that even if we accept that a system of unconditional universal grants could form the basis for the development of communism, the viability of such a system is incompatible with capitalism and requires at least two of the basic elements of socialist property relations.

It is one thing to demonstrate that a "capitalist" road to communism is not viable, and another to argue for the necessity of a full-fledged

---

11. Of course, the tax rate would not necessarily have to be confiscatory to induce investments. Precisely what rate of taxation would be needed to block the potential for an investment strike would be as much a political as an economic question.

socialist road. Does the development of communism as defined by VP require that the third and fourth aspects of ownership of the means of production also be collectivized? Is it plausible that communism could grow and flourish in an economic system within which there was systematic public control over capital mobility and the amount of investment, but there continued to be substantial private income returns from investments and private control over what to invest in? As in our earlier discussion, the issue here is not whether socialization of these two aspects of ownership would be a good thing in and of itself, or whether it would provide a more efficient vehicle for developing communism, but whether it is necessary for the development of communism.

From a strictly economic point of view, I do not see why such a system of mixed property relations would be inconsistent with the growth of a communist sphere of social life based on a universal grant.[12] *Assuming the political stability* of the system, individuals with sufficient incomes would still have incentives to make investments, they would experience the kinds of pressures for labor saving and work quality enhancing innovations as described by VP, and they would be prevented from sabotaging the reproducibility of the system through capital flight and disinvestment.

Politically, on the other hand, it is much less clear that this kind of mixed system would in fact have the necessary stability. Classical Marxism frequently used the term "socialism" and "dictatorship of the proletariat" almost interchangeably. What this identity expressed was the critical importance for the working class to become the "ruling class" politically if capitalism was to be eliminated in a socialist society. What does this mean? The expression "ruling class" is fraught with ambiguities. Classes as such do not "rule"; organizations – typically parties and states – that represent the interests of classes through one mechanism or another actually do the ruling. The issue, then, is whether under the conditions outlined above the structural basis for working-class power could be such that parties representing the working class could effectively and stably control the state.[13] For a system of communism-inducing

---

12. The concept of a "mixed economy" usually refers to an economy that combines a capitalist sector and a state sector. In this case we are talking about an economy within which aspects of capitalist and socialist property relations are fused within each enterprise. This corresponds to what I have elsewhere referred to as an "interpenetration of modes of production." See chapter 6 above.

13. The analysis of "ruling classes," therefore, implies a distinction between their *structural power* – the power derived from their position within the economy – and their *instrumental power* – the power exercised by organizations that attempt to represent the interests of the class. The general Marxist claim is that structural power, in this sense, constitutes the basis for instrumental power (although instrumental power may have contingent properties that give it some autonomy from structural power).

universal grants to be reproduced over time, the working class (defined broadly as all people whose income does not come from the ownership of capital) would have to have sufficient political power to block both capital flight and disinvestment. For all practical intents and purposes this would have to be a "dictatorship" of the working class (wage-earners) – the working class would have to be able to dictate basic investment policy to the capitalist class.[14]

The question thus becomes: could the working class in a system of mixed property relations as described above be a ruling class politically? It is possible, I think, to give arguments to both sides of this issue. On the one hand, the fact that the subsistence of wage-earners is no longer contingent upon the sale of labor-power would give workers considerably greater structural power vis-à-vis capital than they have in capitalism. In capitalist societies, the link between income and employment acts as a powerful constraint on workers: the "reserve army of labor" puts a downward pressure on wages and the threat to jobs of capital mobility and disinvestment puts a damper on militancy. This structural vulnerability of workers is translated into political weakness of working-class parties.[15] A system of universal unconditional income grants combined with effective restrictions on capital mobility and disinvestment would structurally shift the balance of power between capitalists and workers in the direction of the working class. This structural shift in the balance of power, in turn, would give working-class political parties considerably more room to maneuver than in capitalist societies and thus might provide the basis for more stable and consistent political rule.

This, however, is only one side of the story. That capitalists would continue to control important aspects of basic investment decisions (in particular, what to produce and where to produce within the political jurisdiction of the universal grant) and would continue to appropriate significant amounts of the social surplus (through privately appropriated returns on investments), would still leave the capitalist class with considerable structural power. The continued existence of a capitalist class

---

14. Obviously, there is no necessity for such a state to be dictatorial in the sense of undemocratic and authoritarian, but it would have to be a strong state capable of pervasive economic monitoring and interventions, and it would have to have a strong political control by working-class parties for such interventions to reproduce effectively the "road to communism."

15. Of course there are considerable variations across capitalist societies in the strength of working-class parties, but all working-class parties in capitalism suffer from this fundamental vulnerability of workers rooted in the structural power of capital. The result is that all working-class parties face unavoidable strategic dilemmas, to use Adam Przeworski's formulation ("Social Democracy as a Historical Phenomenon," New Left Review, no. 122, 1980, pp. 27–58), which push them in the direction of supporting reforms that strengthen capitalism.

would also pose a constant ideological challenge to the rationale for the universal grants and the rationality of the system of coercive controls on investments necessary for the reproducibility of the system. Furthermore, the differentiation of the population between those living in the "communist sphere" and those working for a wage would potentially produce deep political divisions among noncapitalists. It is easy to imagine coalitions forming between skilled employed workers – workers who opt for employment even given the universal grant because the demand for their skills gives them a high wage component to their income – and capitalists against the communist sector in the name of economic rationality and justice. Given that the capitalist class would, because of its structural position, have considerable resources available for the task of coalition building, this could jeopardize the political stability of the system.

I do not know what the net effect on class power of these tendencies would be. While it is conceivable that the working class under these conditions might have sufficient political strength to maintain effective rule in spite of continual capitalist opposition, it seems more likely that the political conflicts generated by this combination of capitalist, socialist, and communist elements within the system of production would ultimately undermine the viability of the universal grant system itself. A full socialization of the means of production – socializing controls over what to produce and eliminating significant private income returns to investments – would stabilize the structural basis of working-class political rule and thus enhance the possibility for the growth in communist practices.[16]

Universal Grants as a Socialism-inducing Reform

VP introduce the concept of unconditional universal income grants in order to argue that it is possible to build communism within a capitalist society. My basic argument is that the dynamics of such a combination of social forms would quickly undermine the viability of the universal grant system itself, and thus communism would not in fact develop significantly within the interstices of capitalism as projected by the VP model.

The question still remains, however, whether the proposal for unconditional universal grants is a progressive reform in and of itself. In

_____

16. It should be noted, as VP emphasize, that even in socialism there is no inevitability for a development of the communist sphere; it would still be a political choice on the part of the population the extent to which the universal grant would grow relative to earned income.

particular, even if it is illusory that communism could directly be built within capitalism through the mechanism of such a system, it could be, contrary to the vision of VP, that an unconditional universal grant system might facilitate the emergence of socialism.

The progressiveness of reforms in capitalism can be assessed in terms of three principal criteria:

1. Does the reform in and of itself improve the lives of those people who suffer most under capitalism?
2. Does the reform increase the power of workers relative to capitalists?
3. Does the reform increase the likelihood of more progressive transformations in the future?

In terms of all three of these, a serious program for unconditional universal grants would be desirable. In particular, on the basis of each of these criteria, such grants are a progressive reform of redistributive programs based on means tests.[17]

Unconditional universal grants undermine the stigma associated with income-test based public welfare programs, and this in and of itself is a significant benefit to the poor. In the United States a majority of people eligible for welfare do not even apply for it because welfare is viewed as degrading. Furthermore, because everyone receives the grants in a universal system, they are less likely than income-tested programs to polarize people between a welfare underclass and a working class, and this means that in all likelihood the level of real redistribution in a universal system will be higher than in a targeted means-tested system. The fact that the "welfare backlash" of recent times has generally been sharper in countries like the United States in which universal programs are minimal compared to countries like Sweden within which many redistributive programs are universal reflects the fact that means-tested redistribution is more divisive than universal programs.

The implications for power relations also favor universal grants schemes. As already indicated, universal grants are likely to increase the degree of unity within the working class (relative to means-tested programs), and in and of itself this would increase working-class power relative to capital. Beyond this indirect effect, universal grant programs of even modest proportions would also tend to directly increase the power of workers relative to capital. By giving all workers a steady flow of income independent of their wages, individual workers would become

_____

17. "Means-tested" systems of redistribution are based on programs within which benefits are contingent upon satisfying some economic criterion, typically an income criterion.

less vulnerable to the wage contract and thus, all things being equal, be in a better position to engage in collective struggles.

Whether a program of unconditional universal grants would contribute to a trajectory of progressive reform is less clear than its immediate effects on general welfare and class power. However, if the arguments of this chapter are correct, then it would be expected that a program of universal grants might help to reveal the necessity for increasing the level of public constraint on capital mobility and private investments. At a minimum, therefore, the introduction of universal grants within capitalism would probably contribute over time to the development of a strategy for the kind of "mixed road" discussed above, where public controls on investment are combined with private incentives to invest. Such a strategy, in turn, by clarifying the limits of reform within capitalist property relations, could itself contribute to putting socialism more centrally on the agenda of politics.

The basic conclusion of the analysis of this chapter is that for a combination of economic and political reasons, a capitalist road to communism is implausible, and for political reasons a socialist road is more likely to succeed than the mixed road. The pure capitalist road is impossible because capital flight would immediately undermine the economic base of the communism-inducing universal grant proposal, and because even if this problem were solved, the political use of disinvestment would make the system unreproducible. The mixed road, combining elements of capitalist and socialist property relations, is economically feasible, but would be politically precarious. Only in a socialist society would the political conditions for a stable growth of the universal grants be secure enough to make movement along the road to communism likely.

This general conclusion is based on what is a largely unargued assumption present throughout this chapter, namely that socialism itself is unambiguously compatible with the emergence and development of communism – that collective ownership of the means of production by workers is compatible with a gradual growth in the "realm of freedom," in the predominance of distribution according to need. Following VP, I acted as if the only issue were the extent to which capitalism might also be so compatible, and if not, the extent to which certain aspects of capitalism might be compatible in what I have called the mixed road.

The assumption that socialism is compatible with the growth of communism rests on two more basic claims: first, that eliminating capitalist property relations does not necessarily produce authoritarian-bureaucratic forms of the state and politics, and, second, that in democratic socialism productivity will continue to increase (for without increasing productivity, expanding the sphere of distribution according to need becomes very problematic). While I will not attempt to defend them here, I believe both of these claims to be true. If either of these assumptions is false, however, then the only feasible road to communism, no matter how precarious it might be politically, may be the quasi-capitalist/quasi-socialist mixed road described above, a road that combines elements of substantial state control over investments with capitalist economic rationality.

PART III
Marxism

Introduction

For a very long time in much of the world, Marxism provided the theoretical coordinates for work by left-wing intellectuals and the ideological coordinates for popular struggles against capitalism. While there were always intense, and sometimes bitter, debates among people who shared these coordinates, Marxism provided a common language and set of basic understandings within which these debates could take place.

That common set of theoretical understandings has been seriously eroded in recent years and this has led to what many commentators, on both the left and the right, call the "crisis of Marxism." The evidence for this is simple enough to find.

First, there are the extraordinary changes in societies formerly ruled by communist parties under the ideological banner of Marxism. A decade ago it seemed that Marxist orthodoxy in one form or another was firmly in place as the ruling ideology of these societies. Now, with the complete collapse of those regimes and parties in Eastern Europe and the former USSR, and the emergence of widespread private enterprise in China, it is no longer clear what set of ideological principles actually guides the development of these societies.

Second, when we look at the policies and practices of communist, socialist and social democratic parties in the advanced capitalist world, it is often difficult to discern coherent programs for progressive social reform, let alone for revolutionary transformation. And it is certainly unclear whether or not the politics of most of these parties have even vestigial linkages to Marxism as a social theory.

Finally, when one looks more narrowly at Marxist theory itself, one is struck both by the rapid exit of many radical intellectuals from Marxism in recent years towards something that is often called post-Marxism, as well as by the decline in consensus among the remaining Marxist intellectuals over the core theoretical postulates of Marxism itself.

The four chapters in this section are all attempts to contribute to this

175

reconstruction of Marxism as a theoretical framework for radical social science. Chapter 8, "What is Analytical Marxism?," lays out the core principles of one general strategy for this task of reconstruction. Analytical Marxism is based on a rejection of claims that Marxism should try to have distinctive methodological and epistemological foundations. Instead, Analytical Marxists argue that any effective emancipatory social theory must embrace many of the principles of what Marxists often call "bourgeois social science." Just as a socialist society should embrace the "bourgeois" values of civil liberties and enhance their meaning by a redistribution of power and wealth, so socialist theory should embrace the analytical tools of "bourgeois" social science and philosophy and enhance their relevance by using them to answer emancipatory questions.

Chapter 9, "Marxism as Social Science," defends the idea that Marxism should be seen as a social science against two kinds of criticisms. First, it defends the project of a Marxist *social science* against those who feel that science is inevitably an ideology of oppression. While it is true that historically what went under the name of "scientific Marxism" was often guilty of the worst violations of free exchange of ideas, this was not due to the adherence of "scientific" Marxism to the canons of science, but rather to its subordination to political and ideological authority. Second, the chapter defends the project of a social science that is distinctively *Marxist* against critics who would like to see Marxism dissolve into a more eclectic intellectual field.

Chapter 10, "Explanation and Emancipation in Marxism and Feminism," explores the relationship between the distinctive emancipatory projects of the Marxist and feminist traditions and the kinds of social theory that have tended to develop within each. In a perhaps oversimplified way, the emancipatory project of Marxism is taken to be an end to class inequality and domination, and the emancipatory project of feminism, the end of gender inequality and domination. The chapter then makes the observation that Marxists have spent a considerable amount of time and energy worrying about the feasibility of a society that would embody these emancipatory goals, whereas feminists do not spend much time discussing the feasibility of a society without gender domination and inequality. Marxists debate the feasibility of socialism and communism and discuss a range of institutional designs that would make socialism work; a parallel set of debates among feminists about gender emancipation has not really occurred. The basic objective of the chapter is to explain this contrast between Marxism and feminism and explore some of its ramifications for the kinds of theories that characterize these two traditions of thought.

Finally, chapter 11, "Marxism After Communism," attempts to chart out the broad contours of the overall task of reconstructing Marxism. I argue that Marxist theory can be seen as built around three conceptual "nodes" – Marxism as class analysis, Marxism as a theory of historical trajectory, and Marxism as a theory of class emancipation. The problem of reconstructing Marxism, then, can be broken down into the tasks of reconstructing each of these nodes and their interconnections. After briefly describing some of the possible directions for such reconstruction for the theory of class emancipation and the theory of historical trajectory, the chapter turns to a somewhat more extended discussion of the reconstruction of class analysis, thus bringing us back to the themes outlined at the beginning of the book.

8

What is Analytical Marxism?

In recent years there has been an unmistakable decline in consensus among those people who see themselves as working within the Marxist tradition over the core theoretical postulates of Marxism itself. Of course, there has always been deep and often bitter debate within the Marxist tradition. Such divisions in the past, however, generally revolved around a common core of theoretical, if not political, agreement – the labor theory of value as the basis for analyzing capitalism; historical materialism as the basis for analyzing epochal historical development; class structure and class struggle as the basis for understanding the state and ideology. At present this core itself is much harder to discern, and there is certainly sharp disagreement over every one of its elements. There are now many theorists who consider themselves to be Marxists who nevertheless reject the labor theory of value as a satisfactory way of understanding capitalism, who are skeptical about the idea that historical materialism constitutes a plausible theory of history, and who see classes as only one of a variety of determinants of the state and ideology.

Now, one might argue that anyone who rejects these classical core elements of Marxist theory should not rightfully call themselves Marxists. There is, after all, a venerable tradition in the history of Marxism to draw lines of demarcation between true Marxists and phoney Marxists. The latter might use Marxist rhetoric, but they have abandoned Marxism itself. Alternatively, and I think more constructively, it could simply be recognized that Marxism is not a unified theory with well-defined boundaries, but a family of theories united by a common terrain of debate and questions. There has always been a plurality of Marxisms; what is new, perhaps, is the degree of theoretical and methodological heterogeneity that exists on this intellectual terrain.

Given this decline in intellectual consensus among Marxists over many of the core elements of their own theoretical tradition, it is certainly easy to see why many commentators consider this a period of profound theoretical crisis within Marxism, if not necessarily the mortal crisis proclaimed by the Right. However, it is equally a period of considerable theoretical vitality and innovation in which significant progress is being made in clarifying a whole set of problems. While it may at times be difficult to distinguish "crisis" from "dynamic change," I believe that the Marxism which will emerge from the present period of theoretical transformation will not only be more powerful theoretically than the Marxism of the heyday of the New Left, but will also be of more political relevance.

In this chapter I want to look at one particular strand of new theoretical development that has emerged rather forcefully as a tendency in the context of this internal turmoil in the Marxist tradition, particularly in the United States and Great Britain. This is a tendency that has come to be known as "Analytical Marxism." While Analytical Marxism is by no means the only vibrant intellectual current in contemporary Marxism, it does offer, in my judgment, the most promising general strategy for reconstructing Marxism.

The Emergence of Analytical Marxism

In the aftermath of the student movement and radical politics of the 1960s and early 1970s, Marxism entered the university in the developed capitalist democracies in an unprecedented way. Although, with few exceptions, Marxism never became a dominant perspective in academic departments, it nevertheless gained intellectual influence and even a measure of respectability in a wide variety of academic fields – history, sociology, education, political science, and economics, among others.

Analytical Marxism emerged in the late 1970s as one intellectual tendency within this newly influential academic Marxism.[1] It grew out of a belief that Marxism continued to constitute a productive intellectual tradition within which to ask questions and formulate answers, but that this tradition was frequently burdened with a range of methodological and metatheoretical commitments that seriously undermined its explanatory potential. The motivation for trying to rid Marxism of this burden

---

1. The term "academic Marxism" is often used pejoratively, suggesting politically disengaged careerism and intellectual opportunism. While the expression does embody a certain irony, since Marxism is above all a social theory committed to transforming the world rather than simply reflecting on it from the ivory tower, I do not mean to impugn the motives of Marxists who work in the university by referring to them as "academic Marxists." Rather, this expression reflects the historical reality that in the present period, Marxism is most rigorously articulated and elaborated within academic disciplines rather than within revolutionary movements as such.

was the conviction that the core ideas of Marxism, embodied in concepts like class, exploitation, the theory of history, capitalism, socialism, and so on, remained essential for any emancipatory political project.

As a self-conscious school of thought, Analytical Marxism began in 1979 when G.A. Cohen, a Canadian philosopher working in Britain, Jon Elster, a Norwegian political scientist, and a number of other scholars from several countries organized a meeting in London to discuss a range of theoretical issues in contemporary Marxism. This gathering subsequently became an annual event. After the third or fourth year, basically the same people have attended each year, with occasional additions and subtractions (Jon Elster and Adam Przeworski left the group in the early 1990s), to discuss each other's work. After fifteen years, in 1994, the group consists of G.A. Cohen, John Roemer, Robert Brenner, Philippe Van Parijs, Robert Van der Veen, Pranab Bardhan, Hillel Steiner, Sam Bowles, and myself.[2] The term "Analytical Marxism" was first publicly used by the group in 1986 with the publication under that title of an anthology of essays written largely by members of the group.[3]

The substantive concerns of this collection of people are quite wide-ranging – including such things as class structure, the theory of history, the problem of ideology, normative political theory, basic concepts of Marxian economics, social democracy and electoral politics, economic crisis, trade unions and the state. Theoretically, there is considerable internal disagreement over virtually all issues within this group. In the course of the group's first fifteen years of meetings, there have been debates over such things as the relevance of the concept of exploitation, methodological individualism, the nature of economic crisis in advanced capitalism, the ethical critique of "capitalism between consenting adults," the centrality of class struggle to historical transitions, Marxism

---

2. Some of the most important works published by the people affiliated to the group include: G.A. Cohen, *Karl Marx's Theory of History: a defense*, Princeton 1978; John Roemer, *A General Theory of Exploitation and Class*, Cambridge, Mass. 1982; Adam Przeworski, *Capitalism and Social Democracy*, Cambridge 1985; Erik Olin Wright, *Classes*, London 1985; Bob Brenner, "The Agrarian Roots of European Capitalism," in *The Brenner Debate*, T.H. Aston and C.H.E. Philpon, Cambridge 1985, pp. 213–327; Jon Elster, *Making Sense of Marx*, Cambridge 1985; Phillippe Van Parijs, *Evolutionary Explanation in the Social Sciences: an emerging paradigm*, Totowa, N.J. 1981; Sam Bowles and Herbert Gintis, *Democracy and Capitalism*, New York 1986. Analytical Marxism is by no means restricted to the people who participate in the annual London meeting. Work by other scholars in the Analytical Marxist mode would include Andrew Levine, *Arguing for Socialism*, London 1984 and *The End of the State*, London 1987; Richard W. Miller, *Analyzing Marx: morality, power and history*, Princeton 1984; Joshua Cohen and Joel Rogers, *On Democracy*, Harmondsworth 1983.

3. *Analytical Marxism*, ed. John Roemer, Cambridge 1986. The term itself seems to have been coined by Jon Elster in a seminar around 1980.

and feminism, and the economic feasibility of reforming the welfare state through a system of unconditional grants of income to all citizens. On none of these theoretical problems was there thorough consensus in the group. And, equally, the political positions are quite diverse – from fairly traditional commitments to revolutionary democratic socialism to the Greens to what might be termed left-wing libertarianism.[4] Given such substantive, theoretical and political diversity, what is it that unites this group of theorists and defines the essential core of Analytical Marxism?

What is "Analytical" about Analytical Marxism?

There are four specific commitments that I think characterize Analytical Marxism and justify considering it a distinct "school" of contemporary Marxist thought:

1. A commitment to *conventional scientific norms* in the elaboration of theory and the conduct of research.

2. An emphasis on the importance of *systematic conceptualization*, particularly of concepts that are at the core of Marxist theory. This involves both careful attention to definitions of concepts and to the logical coherence of repertoires of interconnected concepts.

3. A concern with a relatively *fine-grained specification of the steps in the theoretical arguments linking concepts*, whether the arguments be about causal processes in the construction of explanatory theories or about logical connections in the construction of normative theories. This commitment to elaborating the details of arguments is reflected in one of the hallmarks of Analytical Marxism: the use of explicit, systematic models of the processes being studied. The nature of these models may vary quite a bit, from formal mathematical models to less formal causal models. But in each case there is a belief that the possibility of theoretical advance is enhanced when we are able to generate systematic explicit models of the processes under study.

---

4. At one point in the history of the annual London meeting there was a serious disagreement, sparked by tensions generated by this political diversity, over whether or not there should be any political-ideological criteria for "membership" in the annual meeting. After considerable discussion of the matter it was decided that the essential principle of the group's cohesion was the possibility of constructive dialogue among the participants rather than actual adherence to a set of political positions.

4. The importance accorded to *the intentional action of individuals* within both explanatory and normative theories.

It would be arrogant to suggest that Marxism entirely lacked these elements prior to the emergence of Analytical Marxism as a self-conscious school. There have certainly been Marxists attentive to each of these issues, and there are Marxists attentive to them today who for one reason or another distance themselves from Analytical Marxism. What makes Analytical Marxism distinctive, then, is the extent to which these principles are brought to the forefront and systematically applied to the construction and reconstruction of theory.

In what follows, we will look at each of these points in turn, illustrating them with examples of specific work by Analytical Marxists. This will help to clarify what is analytical about Analytical Marxism. After this, we will briefly turn to the problem of what remains Marxist about it.

The commitment to conventional scientific norms

Marxism as a theoretical tradition has always had a rather peculiar relation to "science." On the one hand, there has always been a strong current within Marxism which is quite hostile to the canons of conventional science. Particularly in the strand of Marxism associated with the tradition of Critical Theory, positivism and claims to scientificity are often looked upon as instruments of ideological domination rather than emancipatory knowledge. On the other hand, the type of Marxism that has enthusiastically embraced the label "scientific socialism" and claimed the status of a full-fledged "science of society" has often been guilty of the most serious abuses of scientific norms. Self-styled "scientific Marxism" has often taken the form of a rigid ideology with pre-given answers to all questions, functioning more like a secular theology than a scientific discipline: Marxism became Marxology; classical texts were canonized; and the central arguments of the "science" were impervious to transformation. Instead of constituting a theoretical apparatus capable of learning new things about the world – the hallmark of a scientific theory – scientific Marxism has often been a closed system of thought continually reaffirming itself through its own selective observations and interpretations. Marxism has thus either been hostile to science or adopted a particularly distorted and unscientific identification with science.

Analytical Marxists are committed to the view that Marxism should, without embarrassment, aspire to the status of a genuine social science. Marxism should not be absolved from the standards of science even if it accepts other standards of evaluation and relevance in addition to strictly scientific ones.

Such a commitment to scientificity leaves unspecified exactly what is meant by "science," and this is, of course, a hotly contested issue in philosophy. Generally speaking, I think, most Analytical Marxists adopt what can be loosely described as a *realist* view of science.[5] This involves the following basic view of the scientific enterprise: science attempts to identify the *mechanisms* which generate the empirical phenomena we experience in the world. Our observations of those phenomena are simultaneously shaped by two kinds of mechanisms: mechanisms internal to the process of observation, and mechanisms which directly generate the phenomenon in question. Because of this duality, it is in general impossible inductively to discover truths about mechanisms simply from raw empirical "facts," since those facts are necessarily selected by the observation process itself. This implies a rejection of what might be called the naïve empiricist view that we can gather facts about the world and use them to generate scientific knowledge without theoretically informed principles of selecting the objects of our observation. In this specific sense, observations cannot be theory-neutral, and therefore our theories cannot simply be inductive generalizations from raw "facts."[6] But Analytical Marxists would also reject the anti-realist view that our observations are wholly constituted by the categories of thought, by the discourses we use in describing the world. Scientific theories attempt to construct explanations based on real mechanisms that exist in the world independently of our theories even though the selection of observations of those mechanisms and their effects depend in part upon the theories themselves.

There are three important implications of the general acceptance of conventional scientific norms by Analytical Marxists: first, Analytical Marxists tend to be quite skeptical of traditional Marxist claims to a distinctive "Marxist Methodology"; second, they tend to emphasize the importance of empirical research joined to systematic theoretical models

---

5. The issue of scientific realism, particularly of the sort advanced here, has not been explicitly discussed within the Analytical Marxist group. While I think that this general perspective on the philosophy of science is quite consistent with the general strategies of analysis one finds among Analytical Marxists, the arguments advanced here should not be viewed as generally held by Analytical Marxists. The account of realism which I discuss here is based on the work of Roy Bhaskar, *A Realist Theory of Science*, Sussex 1978 and *The Possibility of Naturalism*, Atlantic Highlands, New Jersey 1979.

6. The argument that our theories shape what we choose to look at – by framing our questions and the choice of which facts to observe – does not imply that the actual observations we make *given these principles of selection* are necessarily "biased" or distorted by our theories. "Facts" can be "objective" in the sense that anyone who used the same principles of selection would come up with the same facts.

for the advance of scientific knowledge; and third, they try to be open to continual reassessment of their own theoretical positions, acknowledging their theoretical failures as well as arguing for their successes.

There is a long tradition among Marxists which claims that Marxism has a distinctive method which differentiates it radically from "bourgeois social science." Such claims involve a familiar list of contrasts: Marxism is dialectical, historical, materialist, antipositivist, holist, while bourgeois social theory is undialectical, ahistorical, idealist, positivist and individualist. Analytical Marxists are quite skeptical of the value of such claims.[7] This is not to say that all of the specific elements that are traditionally subsumed under the expression "Marxist method" are rejected out of hand. Analytical Marxists, for example, have found ways of including notions of contradiction and even dialectics in their arguments. But when they do so they are generally quite careful to show how these complex ideas can be translated into a language of causes, mechanisms, and effects.

Take the notion of "contradiction." One way of explicating this concept is to treat it as a situation in which there are multiple conditions for the reproduction of a system which cannot all be simultaneously satisfied. Or, alternatively, a contradiction can be viewed as a situation in which the unintended consequences of a strategy subvert the accomplishment of its intended goals.[8] In either case, "contradiction" is not treated as a philosophically driven way of interpreting the essence of a process, but as a way of explicating the interactions among a set of causal mechanisms. This kind of translation of an element of Marxist method into a language of causal mechanisms would be characteristic of Analytical Marxism.

The second implication of the embrace of conventional scientific norms is a commitment to the importance of systematic empirical research. This is not to say that all Analytical Marxists are themselves directly engaged in empirical research. Some are primarily concerned with normative political theory, and do not engage in empirical research at all. Others are concerned with explanatory models, but are primarily preoccupied with the elaboration of the logic of the models themselves. Nevertheless, most Analytical Marxists feel that an essential element in the elaboration of theories is the systematic confrontation with empirical

---

7. Perhaps the strongest statement of this skepticism was made by Jon Elster in the first chapter of *Making Sense of Marx*, where he categorically denounces all such claims to a distinctive Marxian method, which he identifies with the unfortunate influence of Hegelian philosophy on Marx's work.

8. This is the meaning of contradiction preferred by Jon Elster. See *Logic and Society*, New York 1978, as well as *Making Sense of Marx*, for discussions of this view of contradiction.

research. This has led to the development of a number of substantial research projects by Analytical Marxists. My own research, for example, has involved conducting closely replicated social surveys on class structure, class biography and class consciousness in fifteen countries: the United States, Sweden, Norway, Finland, Denmark, Britain, West Germany, Canada, Australia, New Zealand, Japan, Spain, South Korea, Taiwan and Russia. The central objective of this research has been to develop strictly comparable micro-level data on class and its effects in this set of countries so that we could systematically explore variations in the causal interconnections among class-related variables across different macro-historical contexts.[9] Other empirical research projects by Analytical Marxists include Robert Brenner's research on the transition from feudalism to capitalism, Adam Przeworski's project on social democratic party politics, and Joel Rogers' research on the interaction of the state and the labor movement in American history. While none of these projects is based on a belief in simple empirical "tests" of complex theoretical ideas, they all affirm the conventional scientific view that theoretical advances depend in part on their engagement with relevant data from empirical research.

Finally, one of the striking properties of the work of Analytical Marxists is the extent to which they take seriously the problem of revising their own theoretical positions in the light of debate and criticism. Cohen's work on the Marxist theory of history has gone through a number of significant transformations in the light of issues raised in discussions of his original formulations. Roemer first developed a comprehensive concept of exploitation and then, in the context of critical discussions of his framework, moved on to question the very relevance of exploitation so defined for understanding and criticizing capitalism. And in my own work, my treatment of class structure has gone through at least two significant reconstructions in response to debates within class analysis.[10] The commitment to science, therefore, means that Analytical Marxists treat their arguments as needing to be continually subjected to criticism and revision rather than as constituting definitive embodiments of "truth."

---

9. The scope and initial results of this project are briefly reviewed in my essay, "The Comparative Project on Class Structure and Class Consciousness: an overview," *Acta Sociologica*, vol. 32, no. 1, 1989, pp. 3–22.

10. For the revisions of Cohen's views on the theory of history, see *History, Labor and Freedom*, Oxford 1989. Roemer's questioning of the relevance of exploitation can be found in his essay "Should Marxists be Interested in Exploitation?" *Philosophy and Public Affairs*, no. 14, 1985. The trajectory of my views on class structure is reviewed in my essay, "Rethinking, Once Again, the Concept of Class Structure," the concluding chapter of *The Debate on Classes*, London 1989.

Conceptualization

One of the distinctive signatures of work by Analytical Marxists is the amount of energy devoted to the elaboration of basic concepts. A great deal of time is spent defending specific definitions, discussing alternative criteria, examining the logical interconnections of concepts, puzzling over inconsistencies, and so on. Let me give you an example from my own work, the definition of the "middle class," to illustrate this concern with conceptualization.

Here is the problem: Marxian class concepts are built around a polarized notion of class relations. There are capitalists and workers, lords and serfs. What does it mean to occupy a middle-class location within such polarized relations? Traditionally, Marxists have dealt with this problem by treating the "middle" class as a residual – any location that cannot be firmly situated within the bourgeoisie or the proletariat is, by default, in the "middle class." I wanted a positive specification of this kind of class location. In my work, I proposed two basic solutions. The first was to treat the middle class as those locations in the class structure which were simultaneously in two or more classes. Managers, for example, could be thought of as being simultaneously in the bourgeosie and in the proletariat. I referred to such positions as "contradictory class locations." The second solution argued that capitalist societies consisted of multiple forms of exploitation, not simply capitalist exploitation proper. For example, following the work of John Roemer, I argued that the control over certain kinds of skills could constitute a mechanism of exploitation. The middle class, then, was defined as locations which were exploited capitalistically but were exploiters through some subordinate mechanism of exploitation.[11]

Many other examples of this kind of intensive work on concept formation could be given: John Roemer's work on exploitation; G.A. Cohen's analysis of forces of production or the meaning of "proletarian unfreedom"; John Elster's discussion of the concept of "solidarity"; Joel Rogers and Joshua Cohen's analysis of "democracy"; Andrew Levine's analysis of "freedom."[12] In each case there is the assumption that a necessary condition for the development of powerful theories is the

---

11. The logical structure of these two conceptualizations and the problems which each encounter are extensively discussed in my essay, "Rethinking, Once Again, the Concept of Class Structure," the concluding chapter in Erik Olin Wright and others, *The Debate on Classes*, London 1989.

12. See Roemer, *A General Theory of Class and Exploitation*; Cohen, *Karl Marx's Theory of History*, chapter 2, and "The Structure of Proletarian Unfreedom," in Roemer (ed.), *Analytical Marxism*; Elster, *Making Sense of Marx*, chapter 6.2; Cohen and Rogers, *On Democracy*; Levine, *Arguing for Socialism*.

elaboration of logically coherent concepts. It is in part from this preoccupation that Analytical Marxism gets its name: the analytical coherence of concepts is essential for the explanatory power of theories.

Elaboration of explicit models

One of the striking characteristics of Analytical Marxism has been the use of explicit abstract models, sometimes highly formalized as in game theory, other times somewhat less formalized as causal models. Many Marxists (as well as non-Marxist radicals) find such models objectionable on the grounds that they involve such dramatic simplifications of the complexity of real world situations that they cannot possibly deepen our knowledge of the world. Analytical Marxists counter such objections on several grounds.

First, the fact that models constitute simplifications of complexity is not in and of itself a failing, but a virtue. This is precisely what we want a good theory to do: to get to the heart of a complex problem by identifying the central mechanisms involved.

Second, the essential structure of a formal model is to create a thought experiment of some process. That is, one is forced to specify the underlying assumptions of the model, the conditions which are treated as parameters, and the ways in which the mechanisms work. The clarity forced upon a theorist by making explicit such assumptions and arguments is desirable. Furthermore, since in real-life social situations it is generally hard to construct real experimental conditions for revealing the operation of causal mechanisms (or even, through comparative methods, quasi-experimental designs), thought-experiments are essential to give plausibility to the causal claims we actually make about any concrete problem.

Finally, it is generally the case that lurking in the weeds behind every informal causal explanation is a tacit formal model. All explanatory theories contain assumptions, claims about the conditions under which the explanations hold, claims about how the various mechanisms fit together. The difference between what Analytical Marxists do and what many historical and empirical Marxist researchers do, then, may be basically a question of the extent to which they are prepared to put their cards on the table and articulate the causal models in their theories.

To get a sense of how Analytical Marxists actually use these kinds of models to engage Marxist questions, it will be useful to look in some detail at two prominent examples: Adam Przeworski's analysis of social democracy, which relies on elements of rational choice theory, and G.A.

Cohen's reconstruction of Marx's theory of history, which is built around functional explanations.[13]

Adam Przeworski develops a general theoretical model of the historical trajectory of social democratic politics in capitalist societies. He argues that once bourgeois democratic institutions are in place, social democratic parties face a series of dilemmas when selecting a political strategy. The first dilemma is whether or not to participate in elections at all. If they participate, they risk incorporation into the machine of state domination; if they abstain from participation, they risk political marginalization. Second, if they decide to participate, they face a dilemma rooted in their electoral base. If they attempt to be a pure working-class party, then they can adopt a consistent set of pro-working-class policies, but they will never get an electoral majority (since the working class is never a majority of the population); if they seek alliances with various segments of the middle class, then they dilute their working-class base and ultimately alienate their working-class support.[14]

Przeworski then shows, using formal mathematical models, that given: (a) the distribution of the population into the class structure, and (b) the historical legacy of past strategies on the patterns of loyalty to and defection from parties by people in different classes, then (c) it is possible to define the maximum and minimum levels of the total vote that are available to the social democratic party at any given time. These define what could be called the "Gramsci bounds" on electoral strategies: the limits of what is possible under the historically embodied constraints. The cumulative effect of past strategies and current structures, then, is an historical trajectory of changing possibilities. Przeworski develops mathematical models of this trajectory of limits for various countries, and then an empirical investigation of the actual trajectory of electoral outcomes that occur within these limits.

A second example is G.A. Cohen's analysis of classical historical materialism. Cohen's task is to try to see what kind of explanation is represented by the Marxist theory of history. He wants to reconcile a number of distinct theses: (1) that the level of development of the forces of production determines the form of social relations of production; (2) that the economic structure (the totality of all relations of production) determines the political superstructure; (3) that the relations of produc-

---

13. See Przeworski, *Capitalism and Social Democracy*; Adam Przeworski and John Sprague, *Paper Stones*, Chicago 1986; and Cohen, *Karl Marx's Theory of History*.

14. The third dilemma occurs if a working-class socialist party were to get elected: should the party try to enact reforms within the constraints of capitalism, in which case it risks abandoning its socialist project; or should it try to initiate a transition to socialism, in which case it risks retaliation from capitalists and accompanying severe economic disruption which, in turn, would erode its electoral base?

tion explain the development of the forces of production; and (4) that the superstructure explains the persistence of the economic structure. Cohen argues that these propositions can be made consistent only if they are linked together through a series of functional explanations. Thus, for example, he argues that for statements (2) and (4) above both to be true, the word "determines" in statement (2) must mean "functionally explains." The superstructure must be functionally explained by the economic base in the following way: the superstructure takes the form that it does because the economic base needs it in order to be reproduced. This may or may not, of course, be a plausible theory either of the relationship between economic and non-economic institutions or of historical development; but it is the necessary form of the argument if the specific elements of the theory as developed by Marx are to be internally consistent.

What is striking in both of these examples is not mainly the abstract substantive claims which they make. After all, Przeworski's argument could be basically viewed as an example of Marx's famous statement that "Men make their own history, but under circumstances not of their choosing," applied to the specific problem of socialist electoral politics. And Cohen's analysis is directly based on Marx's analysis of the "dialectical relation" between forces and relations of production. What is novel in this work is the rigor of the effort at specifying the details of the mechanisms which underlie these more abstract claims. This not only enhances the depth of our understanding of the abstract arguments themselves, but makes it much easier to identify their weaknesses and reconstruct them in light of empirical research.

The importance of choice

The feature of Analytical Marxism that has caused the most controversy, perhaps, is the self-conscious use by certain Analytical Marxists of rational actor models, including mathematical game theory.[15] This has led some people to rename Analytical Marxism "Rational Choice Marxism," and to characterize it as embodying a general commitment to methodological individualism (i.e. to the methodological claim that all social phenomena are in principle explainable exclusively with reference to individuals and their attributes).[16]

---

15. Rational actor models of various sorts have played a particularly prominent role in the work of Jon Elster, John Roemer and Adam Przeworski. Elster, in particular, has argued for the privileged status of such models. See especially Elster's defense of methodological individualism in the introduction of *Making Sense of Marx*, pp. 3–8.

16. See, for example, Alan Carling, "Rational Choice Marxism," *New Left Review*, no. 160, 1986.

This identification of Analytical Marxism with methodological individualism is, I believe, mistaken. Indeed, a number of Analytical Marxists have been explicitly critical of methodological individualism and have argued against the exclusive reliance on models of abstract rationality as a way of understanding human action.[17] What is true, however, is that most Analytical Marxists take quite seriously the problem of understanding the relationship between individual choice and social processes. This does not imply that social processes can be *reduced* to problems of individual intentionality, nor does it imply that instrumental rationality is the ubiquitous basis for intentional action; but it does mean that social theory should systematically incorporate a concern with conscious choice. One way of doing this is through rational actor models of various kinds.

Now, it is certainly possible to acknowledge the usefulness of the intellectual discipline of constructing formal models, and yet reject rational choice models as simply being stupid models. Particularly given the historical identification of rational actor theory with neoclassical economics, what is the attraction of this particular kind of model to many Analytical Marxists? I think the attraction lies in the importance most Analytical Marxists give to a particular analytical task, namely elaborating what is sometimes called the *micro-foundations* of macro-structural theory – that is, analyzing the mechanisms through which individuals come to act the way they do within a set of structurally defined social relations. Whatever else one might want of a social theory, if we want to understand the mechanisms through which a given social cause generates its effects, we must try to understand why individuals act the way they do. And in this context, rational actor models and game theory provide a systematic strategy for analyzing one particularly salient aspect of individual action: action that results from conscious choices in which the costs and benefits are assessed over a range of feasible alternatives within a set of social constraints. If you believe (a) that at least in some important social contexts actors make conscious choices, and (b) that when they make choices they take into consideration the expected consequences of their actions, and finally, (c) that in assessing such consequences they take into consideration the choices of other actors – that is, that they act strategically, not just rationally – then something like game theory and rational choice theory would be an appropriate part of one's repertoire of analytical techniques.

---

17. See, in particular, "Marxism and Methodological Individualism," Andrew Levine, Elliott Sober, and Erik Olin Wright, *New Left Review*, no. 162, 1987, reprinted as chapter 6 in Erik Olin Wright, Andrew Levine, and Elliott Sober, *Reconstructing Marxism*, London 1992. See also the exchange in *Socialist Review*, vol. 19, no. 2, 1989, between Michael Burawoy and Adam Przeworski over the problem of micro-foundations of macro-theory.

The difference between the way Analytical Marxists deploy these kinds of models and the way neoclassical economists and political scientists deploy them lies not in the internal logic of the models themselves, but in the kinds of problems they are used to address and the ways in which the "conditions of existence" of the models are specified. Thus, for example, John Roemer uses rational choice theory to explore the problem of exploitation. In his analysis, the central conditions faced by actors are particular systems of property relations which give different actors monopolies over particular kinds of resources. He then uses the formal mathematical models of rational choice theory to show how exploitation is generated out of such conditions. So while Roemer adopts the formal mathematical apparatus of "bourgeois" models in his work, he asks different questions from neoclassical economists and he characterizes the environment of rational choice in a very different way. As a result, he comes to very different conclusions: far from generating optimal distributional consequences in a market environment, Roemer concludes that individual optimizing strategies systematically generate exploitation and classes.

To be sure, there are limits to the explanatory capacity of formal models built around rational action. Thus, most Analytical Marxists would agree that these kinds of models need to be supplemented in a variety of ways with other kinds of explanations in the construction of social theory. Examples include such things as functional explanations in G.A. Cohen's analysis of the theory of history; subintentional causal explanations in Jon Elster's analysis of the cognitive underpinnings of ideology; and institutional-structural explanations in my work on class formation and Robert Brenner's work on economic crisis. One of the innovations of Analytical Marxism, then, is the attempt to link systematically, within a Marxist theoretical agenda, these sorts of explanatory strategies with the analysis of individual rationality and choice.

What is "Marxist" about Analytical Marxism?

I have stressed in these comments what is "analytical" about "Analytical Marxism." One might ask, when all is said and done, what about it remains "Marxist." Analytical Marxists reject claims about the methodological distinctiveness of Marxism; they adopt the full repertoire of "bourgeois" scientific practices; and they constantly question the core concepts and traditional theses of Marxism. What, then, is Marxist about this theoretical enterprise? I would emphasize three things in answer to this question.

First, much of the work of Analytical Marxists self-consciously works on Marxism as a theoretical tradition. The typical intellectual strategy is to take some core theme or argument in Marxism, establish the necessary conditions for this argument to be sustainable, and then reconstruct the argument in light of the plausibility of those conditions.

Second, the broader agenda of theoretical and empirical questions which Analytical Marxists pose are generally firmly rooted in the discourse and traditions of Marxism. The topics of research – the transition from feudalism to capitalism, the relationship of class structure to class consciousness, the dilemmas of socialist politics, the conditions for solidarity and fragmentation of the working class – clearly take their intellectual coordinates from the Marxist tradition. Even if the *answers* to these questions may deviate considerably from classical Marxist answers, the questions themselves are characteristically Marxist.

Third, the language used to frame answers to these questions is also deeply embedded in Marxist discourse. Class, ideology, consciousness, exploitation, the state, and so on constitute the conceptual repertoire of Analytical Marxism much as they do that of Marxism in general. As Alvin Gouldner has argued, Marxism should be considered what he called an "ideal speech community," an intellectual terrain of dialogue rather than a body of consensually accepted theses. Analytical Marxists work on this terrain and share in this dialogue even if they transform many of the traditionally defended theses.

Finally, and perhaps most problematically given their political heterogeneity, Analytical Marxists broadly share the core normative orientation of Marxism in general. In varying degrees, their work is animated by a commitment to values of freedom, equality, and human dignity, and generally they are sympathetic to some conception of democratic socialism as the institutional vehicle for the realization of these values. While these values may be shared by many post- or non-Marxist radical intellectuals, the linkage between these values, on the one hand, and the theoretical agenda of questions and debate, on the other, systematically anchor Analytical Marxism in the Marxist tradition.

Explaining what it is about Analytical Marxism that makes it Marxist does not, of course, constitute an argument for why one should bother with such an arduous effort at reconstructing Marxism with the intellectual tools of modern social science. Quite apart from a general skepticism about the virtues of science, many radicals are even more skeptical about the virtues of Marxism. Putting the two together might seem a particularly diabolical medicine, more likely to poison than to invigorate radical thought. Why should a radical attempt to revitalize Marxism in this way?

I cannot, in this chapter, provide anything approaching a systematic defense of Marxism as an intellectual tradition within which to produce radical theory. And I should add that not all the theorists who engage in

Analytical Marxism would regard such a defense as particularly important. Some participants in the intellectual project of Analytical Marxism
regard Marxism as simply one of a variety of sources of ideas, concepts,
and tools. Indeed, they may not actually consider themselves to be
"Marxists" of even a weak persuasion. While they may find the intellectual task of analytically reconstructing Marxism to be a productive one, it
is not out of any deep commitment to Marxism as such. It is thus possible
to "do" Marxism (make contributions to the reconstruction of Marxist
theory) without "being" a Marxist (having a general commitment,
political and theoretical, to the Marxist tradition).

In these terms I am among the more intransigently Marxist of the
Analytical Marxists. My defense of Marxism as a theoretical tradition,
therefore, should not be taken as characteristic of Analytical Marxism as
such.

There are two basic reasons why I believe Marxism remains an
essential theoretical framework for radical analysis: (1) The *questions*
that are at the heart of Marxism continue to be critical for any plausible
political project for radical social change; (2) the *conceptual framework*
for tackling those questions continues to produce new and insightful
answers.

First, the questions: there was a time in which many Marxists claimed
that Marxism constituted a fully comprehensive scientific theory of all
facets of social life. The central mechanisms postulated within Marxism
were thought not simply to explain the central dynamics of capitalism as a
system of production or the basic possibilities for class formation, but to
explain everything else of importance as well.

Few Marxist theorists today argue for such grandiose explanatory
pretensions for Marxism. Rather, at the core of Marxism is the problem
of explaining the development of forms of domination and exploitation
that are rooted in the social organization of production, particularly in
the historical epoch of capitalism, in order to understand the possibilities
for the radical transformation of such systems of domination and
exploitation. Marxist theory is preoccupied with understanding the
potentials and dilemmas of, and constraints on, radical social change
imposed by the system of class relations. In the case of capitalism, this
means that Marxism attempts to construct a scientific theory of the
possibility of socialism, where socialism is understood as the central
social form through which capitalist exploitation and domination can be
transcended.

In these terms, Marxists have a distinctively *Marxist* interest in
ideology, the state, culture, gender, race, etc., only in so far as these bear
on the problem of understanding class relations and their potentials for
radical transformation. Of course, the *people* who are Marxists may also

be, for example, feminists, and thus have an interest in gender relations because of a desire to understand the development of gender oppression and the potentials for its transformation independently of the relevance of such concerns for class as such. But Marxism as a theoretical structure does not itself have anything *systematically Marxist* to say about this. (Or, perhaps more precisely, once Marxism has been shorn of insupportable explanatory claims – such as the claim that male domination is to be entirely explained functionally by its role in reproducing class domination – then Marxism as such does not theorize the essential mechanisms that produce and reproduce gender relations.)

Marxism in this sense is "sex-blind." This, however, is not in my judgment a weakness of Marxism; it is a theoretical advance that there is now more precision in its range of theoretical relevance and explanatory capacities.[18] Of course, there may in the future be further scientific advances in which some more general theoretical structure is capable of fully integrating Marxist accounts of class mechanisms and feminist accounts of gender mechanisms into some more comprehensive theoretical system. But there is no necessary reason to believe that this will be possible, and in any case, until such theoretical synthesis occurs it is appropriate to consider class and gender to be distinct mechanisms, each requiring their own set of concepts and explanations.[19]

One might well ask why a person committed to understanding gender oppression or race oppression should care about the Marxist questions. If Marxism – or, at least, Analytical Marxism – no longer pretends to provide a comprehensive explanation of gender domination, why should feminists be interested in Marxism? I believe that a concern with class-based domination and exploitation should be central to the theoretical agenda of political radicals even if their commitments are more preoccupied with problems of race or gender or some other dimension of social life. In so far as projects of radical social change confront constraints embedded in the system of property relations – for example, day care costs money, the availability of these resources depends upon taxes, the

---

18. Feminists often criticize Marxism for being sex-blind, whereas I think that the sex-blindness of Marxism may actually enhance its usefulness for feminists. Marxism should not be a variety of feminism, attempting somehow to subsume the specificity of gender oppression within its concepts. The various attempts, for example, to treat male domination as a species of class domination have largely obscured rather than clarified the relationship between gender and class. It is one thing for feminists to criticize Marxists for being sex-blind in the sense of not recognizing the importance of gender mechanisms in answering the questions which they ask; but it does not follow from this that Marxist concepts as such should be systematically gendered.

19. This argument endorses a variety of what is sometimes called a "dual systems" approach to the relation of class and gender, although I would prefer to call it a "dual mechanisms" approach, since I do not want to insist that class relations and gender relations are each fully integrated into some encompassing "system."

tax base depends upon investment under the control of capitalists – then radicals in general need an understanding of class mechanisms. Marxism is still the theoretical tradition which, in my judgment, has most comprehensively explored those mechanisms.

It is not enough, of course, to defend the Marxist tradition for asking important questions. For Marxism as a theoretical perspective to be relevant today, it is also important to defend the conceptual framework for producing answers to the questions it asks. At the core of the Marxist tradition is a set of relatively familiar concepts: class structure, exploitation, class struggle, class formation, mode of production, economic structure, the state, ideology. Each of these concepts has come under systematic scrutiny in recent years, and as a result there has been considerable progress in specifying their explanatory potentials. As a result, while Marxists have generally narrowed their explanatory pretensions over the past decade or so, there has also been a complementary deepening of the answers to the questions they pose using this repertoire of concepts.

The theoretical contributions by the participants in the series on "Production and Democracy" in the *Socialist Review* amply illustrate this vitality of the Marxist tradition.[20] Michael Burawoy's work on the labor process and factory regimes has significantly advanced our knowledge of the mechanisms through which cooperation is forged within production by showing how the adaptive strategies of workers and the responses of capitalists jointly shape a set of "rules of the game" within which the interests of workers and capitalists are coordinated.[21] Sam Bowles and Herb Gintis's work on the political nature of exchange relations in capitalism has given much more precision to the role of power in a competitive economy by showing how control over assets inherently generates asymmetries of power within exchange.[22] Adam Przeworski's work on social democracy, discussed earlier, has powerfully illuminated the dilemmas posed to working-class politics in democratic capitalism by

---

20. Michael Burawoy, "Should We Give Up on Socialism?" *Socialist Review*, vol. 19, no. 1, 1989, pp. 58–76; and "Marxism without Micro-foundations," *Socialist Review*, vol. 19, no. 2, 1989, pp. 53–86; Adam Przeworski, "Class Production and Politics: a reply to Burawoy," *Socialist Review*, vol. 19, no. 2, pp. 87–111; John Roemer, "Visions of Capitalism and Socialism," *Socialist Review*, vol. 19, no. 3, pp. 93–100.

21. See Michael Burawoy, *The Politics of Production*, London 1985. Michael Burawoy has, at times, distanced his own work from "Analytical Marxism," first, because he doubts the usefulness of formal rational actor models, and second, because he is generally skeptical about the hard claims to "science" made by Analytical Marxists. Nevertheless, in spite of these disclaimers, I believe that his work does satisfy the four criteria for Analytical Marxism which I laid out at the outset of this chapter. For an exchange between Michael Burawoy and myself on the status of Marxism as a science, see *The Debate on Classes*, London 1990, Part II.

22. Sam Bowles and Herbert Gintis, "Contested Exchange," *Politics & Society*, 1990.

showing how democratic institutions force socialist parties to choose between an erosion of socialist ideals (if they seek class alliances to expand their electoral base) or permanent marginalization (if they remain faithful to radical visions of working-class interests). And my own work on class structure, I believe, has helped to deepen our understanding of the middle class within advanced capitalist societies by analyzing how this class is constituted as a contradictory location within class relations. This body of work testifies to the continued capacity of research using Marxian conceptual tools to produce new answers to enduring questions.

The Impact of Analytical Marxism

The challenges facing the Marxist tradition of social theory today are of an unprecedented magnitude. Many people on the left have proclaimed Marxism moribund, seeing its core concepts and theoretical arguments as increasingly irrelevant either as a guide to understanding the world or to changing it. Analytical Marxism constitutes one significant response to this challenge. It argues that in order to revitalize Marxism and reconstruct its theoretical power, it must enthusiastically adopt the most sophisticated tools of contemporary social science. And, if Marxism hopes to play an active role inside the academy in countering the ideological dominance of conservative and liberal currents of social research, it has to adopt the methodologically most powerful weapons available or risk permanent isolation and marginalization.

Has this strategy worked? What kind of real impact has Analytical Marxism had, either in the university or in the broader world of radical politics? Analytical Marxism is only about fifteen years old as a self-consciously constituted perspective, and thus it is probably premature to try to make a systematic assessment of its effects. Furthermore, as a partisan advocate of Analytical Marxism, it would in any case be hard for me to weigh the evidence dispassionately. Nevertheless, I think that there are at least some indications that this approach to Marxist theory has begun to have some impact beyond its immediate circle of supporters.

In spite of the decline worldwide in Marxist scholarship, the work of Analytical Marxists is increasingly appearing in publications around the world oriented towards progressive audiences outside the academy, and Analytical Marxist ideas are beginning to have an influence on public discussions on the left.[23] In more academic terms, a number of journals

---

23. Translations of Analytical Marxist work have appeared in Italian, Spanish,

have devoted considerable space to articles and symposia revolving around Analytical Marxist work, and numerous publications have appeared containing extended critiques of Analytical Marxism, which is also an indicator that it is becoming more influential.[24] At a more institutional level, several of the central advocates of Analytical Marxism have gained positions of considerable institutional importance within the universities in which they work.[25]

Whether this institutional presence constitutes "success" or "co-optation," of course, is a matter of debate. There are many radicals who will accuse this new breed of Academic Marxists of careerism and opportunism.[26] It is certainly the case that assuming these kinds of institutional roles does pose risks and may both reflect and generate serious compromises of political commitments. The same can be said about the basic methodological strategy of Analytical Marxism: just as adopting the political weapons of capitalist democracy risks incorporating socialists into the normal regulative functions of the capitalist state, so adopting the scientific practices of conventional social science risks neutralizing the revolutionary aspirations of Marxism. Above all, there is the risk of narrowing the field of legitimate questions to those that are tractable with these sophisticated tools. Statistically rigorous data anal-

---

Swedish, French, German, Dutch, Portuguese, Russian, Chinese, Polish, Hungarian, Korean, and Japanese. As an example of Analytical Marxist ideas entering general discussions on the left, in the recent publication by the British Communist Party, *Facing the Future*, there was an explicit discussion of the concept of "contradictory class locations," although there was no attribution of the concept.

24. Two issues of the journal *Politics & Society* have been devoted entirely to discussions of Analytical Marxist work – one issue on John Roemer's analysis of class and exploitation in 1985 and a second issue on Sam Bowles and Herbert Gintis's work on contested exchange, in 1990. *Critical Sociology*, the *Berkeley Journal of Sociology* and *Theory and Society* have each contained symposia on problems of Analytical Marxism, while one whole issue of *The Canadian Journal of Philosophy* was devoted to Analytical Marxism in 1989. The *Socialist Review* has recently published a series of essays within this perspective, and numerous Analytical Marxist articles and critiques of Analytical Marxism have appeared in the *New Left Review*, *Philosophy and Public Affairs*, *The Review of Radical Economics*, and other journals. Examples of books containing extended critiques of Analytical Marxism include G. Carchedi, *Class Analysis and Social Research*, London 1987; Paul Kamolnick, *Classes: a Marxist Critique*, Dix Hills 1988; Stephen Resnick and Richard Wolff, *Knowledge and Class*, Chicago 1987.

25. Examples include Robert Brenner, the director of the Center for Comparative History and Social Theory at UCLA; John Roemer, the head of the Program in Economics, Justice and Society at the University of California, Davis; and myself, director of the A.E. Havens Center for the Study of Social Structure and Social Change at the University of Wisconsin. While none of these centers can be considered "Institutes of Analytical Marxism" – they all try to serve the needs of a relatively broad progressive community in their universities – they nevertheless represent a much higher level of institutional support for this kind of theoretical enterprise than existed in the past.

26. Russell Jacoby, in *The Last Intellectuals*, New York 1987, makes this kind of accusation in a particularly strident and unsympathetic way.

ysis tends to restrict investigations to problems that are easily quantifi-
able; rational choice theory tends to direct attention to those problems of
strategic interaction that can be formally modeled within the repertoire
of game theory models. Such potential restriction on the domain of
inquiry imposed by the choice of scientifically rigorous methods poses
serious threats to the political vitality of radical thought.

These risks need to be acknowledged, and resisted. But to respond to
them by refusing to build enclaves of radical scholarship within leading
universities robs Marxism of the capacity to play an effective role in the
academy; and to cope with these risks by rejecting these analytical and
scientific methods altogether undermines the ability of Marxism to
enhance its theoretical understandings of the world in ways which will
enable it, once again, to play an effective role in politics as well.

Marxism as Social Science

In 1989, the *Berkeley Journal of Sociology* invited a number of people to comment on an exchange between myself and Michael Burawoy which had been published in the 1987 issue of the journal.[1] The original exchange revolved around the scientific and theoretical status of my book *Classes*. In an interview with a group of graduate students at the University of California, Berkeley, which was published as the opening item in the dialogue between myself and Burawoy, I had defended the attempt in that book of pursuing Marxist questions with quantitative research techniques. Burawoy criticized my position, arguing that my vision of science was inattentive to the social conditions for the production of knowledge and that this had especially critical implications for my aspirations to produce a science that was faithful to Marxism as an emancipatory theory. I then replied, defending a version of scientific realism and arguing that academic Marxism, isolated to some extent from the pressures of popular struggles, had the potential of making certain distinctive kinds of contributions to knowledge relevant for emancipatory projects of social change.

The 1989 *BJS* symposium on this earlier exchange included commentators who were much more hostile to the whole enterprise of trying to build a serious Marxist social science. In this chapter, I engage two themes that emerged in different ways in a number of the contributions to the symposium: first, the claim in several of the essays that the exchange between myself and Michael Burawoy was simply a rehash of the old-fashioned debate between "scientific" and "critical" Marxism; and second, the claim that the preoccupations of our debate are largely

---

1. See Erik Olin Wright, "Reflections on Classes," and Michael Burawoy, "The Limits of Wright's Analytical Marxism and an Alternative," in the *Berkeley Journal of Sociology*, vol. XXXII, 1987. This exchange was subsequently reprinted as chapter 2 in my book, *The Debate on Classes*, London 1989.

irrelevant given the broader supersession of Marxism as a plausible perspective for any kind of radical social theory, scientific or otherwise. With respect to the first claim, I will argue that our debate does not revolve around a polarized opposition between science and critique, but rather concerns two contrasting emphases in the construction of Marxism as a science. With respect to the second issue, I will argue that Marxism remains a productive, knowledge-producing theoretical tradition and that its relevance is not diminished by the proliferation of a range of post-Marxist radical theoretical approaches. I will not primarily engage these themes in the form of a point-by-point discussion of the various contributions to the symposium, but will rather take a few of the claims of these contributions as a point of departure for a more general discussion of the issues.

Marxism as a Social Science

Ben Agger writes:

> The controversy over Marxism's scientificity, raging for over half a century, has been settled: Lukács, the Frankfurt school, the Parisian existential-Marxists all vanquish the Engels/Stalin model of a "dialectic of nature" . . . Quantitative Marxism is nothing new, except to Quantitative non-Marxists; it merely refurbishes the stagnant "dialectical materialism" used by socialist authoritarians to justify one political perversion or another. . . . Whichever side we are on – positivist Marxism or Western Marxism – all of this has been said before.[2]

This characterization of the issues in my exchange with Burawoy rests on an unjustified identification of contemporary aspirations for Marxism to be a social science with previous uses of the rhetoric of "science" within Marxism as an ideology of intellectual domination, particularly by elites within political parties. This treatment of the issues reflects a deep irony in the use of the word "science" within the Marxist tradition: Marxists who have most stridently insisted on the scientificity of Marxism have often adopted theoretical practices which are quintessentially anti-scientific. "Scientific Marxism" often functioned more like a secular theology than a scientific discipline: Marxism became Marxology; classical texts were canonized; and the central arguments of the "science" were impervious to transformation.

---

2. Ben Agger, "Is Wright Wrong (Or Should Burawoy Be Buried?): Reflections on the Crisis of the 'Crisis of Marxism'," *Berkeley Journal of Sociology*, vol. XXXIV, 1989, p. 187.

This kind of theoretical practice has nothing to do with "science" in any philosophical tradition, and certainly has nothing to do with "positivism."[3] This is not to say that all substantive theses contained within such pseudo-scientific Marxism were necessarily false, but simply that the theoretical practices and methods which were deployed to defend those theses were often profoundly anti-scientific.

One of the striking features of some of the current efforts to reconstruct Marxism as a social science is precisely the commitment to take its scientificity serious. It would, of course, be arrogant to insist that before the present renaissance in Marxist theory, there was no awareness of the anti-scientific character of much of what passed for Marxist science. Indeed, when Marx himself declared "I am not a Marxist" he was in part affirming the need for a genuinely scientific practice. Nevertheless, throughout much of the history of Marxism, the claims to scientificity have been largely ritualistic and hardly congruent with the actual practices. Whatever else might be our differences, both Michael Burawoy and I are committed to the view that Marxism should aspire to the status of a science and that it should take that aspiration seriously. Neither of us treat Marxism primarily as a hermeneutical practice for understanding the meaning of social practices, nor as a strictly philosophical practice for cultural critique. Both of us believe that Marxism should aspire to produce explanations, and that any given explanation we produce may turn out to be wrong. Contrary to Agger's suggestion, this position has nothing to do with Stalinist "scientific Marxism."

Now, affirming a commitment to "science" leaves unspecified exactly what is meant by "science," and this is, of course, a hotly contested issue in philosophy. Michael Burawoy, at least, believes that on the question of how science itself should be understood we are in significant disagreement, while I think that our positions are not in fact so divergent.

As I argued in the original exchange in the *Berkeley Journal of Sociology*, I adopt what is generally described as a *realist* view of science. This involves the following basic view of the scientific enterprise: science attempts to identify the underlying *mechanisms* which generate the empirical phenomena we experience in the world. Our ability to gain

---

3. Many commentators on Marxism seem to believe that since positivist approaches to science often seek invariant "laws" in the phenomena they study, and since orthodox Marxism also speaks of the "laws of history," it must therefore be the case that this kind of Marxism is guilty of positivist scientific practice. It may be guilty of positivist *rhetoric*, but the theoretically rigid orthodoxies of "scientific socialism" are completely antithetical to science, whether positivist or anti-positivist. One of the hallmarks of this anti-scientific practice is the way in which citations of Marx's (or Lenin's or someone else's) texts displace the systematic analysis of data and development of arguments as a way of defending theoretical positions.

knowledge of these mechanisms is complicated by two properties of the relationship between our observations of the effects of the mechanisms – our "experiences" – and the mechanisms themselves. First, we live in an open system in which many mechanisms are simultaneously operating. This means that the effects of one mechanism may be counteracted by another. There is not, therefore, an invariant relationship between the existence of a mechanism and empirical manifestations of its effects.[4] Secondly, our observations of anything are simultaneously shaped by mechanisms internal to the process of observation itself (which include such things as our systems of classification and description, as well as our technologies of observation) and mechanisms which directly generate (cause) the phenomenon in question.[5] Because of this duality, even apart from the problem of the complexity of living in an open-system, it is impossible ever to inductively discover truths about mechanisms *simply* by generalizations from pure empirical "facts," since those facts are necessarily shaped by the observation process itself. And this, in turn, implies that in order for observations to be intelligible, they must be embedded in theories about these mechanisms.

Thus, I reject the view of naïve empiricism that we can observe the world without categories already embedded in theories. Observations cannot be theory-neutral, and therefore our theories can never be simple inductive generalizations from pre-theoretical "facts." But I also reject the anti-realist view that our observations are wholly constituted by the categories of thought, by the discourses we use in describing the world. Scientific theories attempt to construct explanations based on real mechanisms that exist in the world independently of our theories, even though our observations of those mechanisms and their effects depend in part upon the theories themselves.

I believe that, his protestations notwithstanding, in practice Burawoy accepts a view of scientific practice that is essentially congruent with

---

4. It also follows from this complexity that the empirical observation of an hypothesized effect cannot be taken as definitive proof of the existence of the proposed mechanism, since it is possible that two (or more) distinct kinds of mechanisms could generate the same empirical effects (experiences). Loïc Wacquant's claim in his essay in this symposium that the kind of realism I propose is guilty of the "fallacy of affirming the consequent" is incorrect: scientific realism does not imply that observations of effects constitute definitive proof of the operation of a given mechanism, since multiple mechanisms are always present in open-systems.

5. Dick Walker, in his essay, "In Defense of Realism and Dialectical Materialism: a Friendly Critique of Wright and Burawoy's Marxist Philosophy," in the 1989 *Berkeley Journal of Sociology* symposium, states that the control of "observational error" (his words) was not an important issue in scientific realism. I do not think that this is correct: mechanisms internal to the process of observation are among the most important "contingent" mechanisms implicated in the use of data (experience) to evaluate claims about causes.

these views. There is nothing inherently anti-realist about Burawoy's adoption of Lakatos's approach to the development of science in terms of research programs and theoretical cores. In my judgment, Burawoy's central concern in his discussions of the philosophy of science is giving an account of the process through which scientific *questions* are productively generated: these emerge from the puzzles posed by research programs as they encounter anomalies in the world, where an anomaly is understood as a set of observations which are in some way or another inconsistent with the existing theories of the program.[6] A program is progressive if it is capable of recognizing such puzzles and generating new explanations in a non-arbitrary way for dealing with them, where to be "non-arbitrary" means that the new propositions are in some sense derived from the internal principles of the "core" of the program rather than added on in an *ad hoc* manner. This Lakatosian view of the *question*-generating machine of science is entirely consistent with the realist claim that the objective of science is to produce *answers* to these questions that take the form of explanations revolving around the identification of effect-generating mechanisms.

Where then do we differ? Two issues seem to me to be especially important: the first concerns the kinds of puzzles with which we are preoccupied, and the second concerns our response to a set of dilemmas posed by the sociology of knowledge.

While both of us accept the importance of working within a research program with a relatively consistently articulated theoretical "core," and both of us believe that the ultimate theoretical objective is producing explanations rooted in mechanisms consistent with that core, we are preoccupied with rather different kinds of puzzles. My work has been concerned mainly with puzzles generated by the internal logic of the *concepts* of the core of Marxism, whereas Burawoy has been concerned with puzzles generated by *predictions* of the core. Thus, above all, I have worried about the concept of class structure, trying to accommodate the non-polarized reality of "middle classes" within a conceptual framework built around a polarized concept of class. The middle class is a puzzle or anomaly within such a conceptual field, and I have proposed various ways of providing a non-arbitrary conceptual solution. This is not, as Loïc Wacquant asserts in his essay in the symposium, an attempt to "solve on paper a question which is not resolved in reality"; rather, it is

---

6. Perhaps a slightly more precise way of saying this is that *if* one wants one's research to have a cumulative effect on knowledge, then the questions which drive the research need to be generated by such puzzles. Much research, of course, may not self-consciously be tied to the puzzles of a research program. The result is that the specific knowledge generated by the research is unlikely to add to any body of theoretical knowledge.

an attempt to generate a conceptual repertoire that gives precision to the ways in which it is not "resolved" in reality.[7] This is what the concept of "contradictory locations" attempts to do. Burawoy, in contrast, is directly concerned with the puzzles posed by the failure of classical Marxist predictions of a revolutionary working class in advanced capitalism. He has engaged in a wonderfully rich array of empirical investigations of workers acting under different constraints in different times and places in order to figure out why it is that workers in capitalism are so consistently non-revolutionary.

Another way of putting this is that my work has revolved around the "independent variables" of the Marxist core – the central explanatory concepts, especially class itself – whereas Burawoy's work has revolved around the central "dependent variable" of Marxism – especially patterns of class formation. My intuition has been that I could not effectively embark on the task of confronting in a serious way the explanation of class formation until I got the conceptual apparatus used in those explanations straightened out; Burawoy's assumption is that the only way to straighten out such concepts is to launch headlong into the dirty work of generating explanations themselves.

This brings me to the sociology of knowledge point. Both of us, I think, accept the very general point that in one way or another the kind of knowledge we produce is shaped by the social constraints within which we live. And both of us believe that bourgeois academic institutions impose enormous pressures on scholars to produce knowledge that does not pose threats to existing forms of oppression and exploitation. As Marxists wanting to produce a particular kind of knowledge – knowledge that, we hope, will contribute in some way to emancipatory possibilities – we thus have somehow to situate ourselves in a social setting in such a way that these pressures are to some extent counteracted. Where we differ, I think, is in our view as to how to accomplish this.

Burawoy feels that the only viable strategy to counter the academicizing forces of intellectual work in a university is to be directly engaged in the world and struggles of the people one studies. By being a participant

---

7. See Loïc Wacquant, "Social Ontology, Epistemology and Class: On Wright's and Burawoy's Politics of Knowledge," *Berkeley Journal of Sociology*, vol. XXXII, 1987, p. 174. Contrary to Wacquant's characterization of my position, at this level of abstraction I do not think that my views differ at all from Pierre Bourdieu's. Bourdieu's distinction between "classes on paper" and "real classes" is exactly parallel to my distinction between class structure (determined by the patterns of objective relations and resources) and class formation (socially constituted groups organized within a class structure around these relations and resources). The real struggles of actors over social identities and categories are, in these terms, struggles over class formation; but – as Bourdieu also argues – the probabilities of success and stability in such struggles for class formation are determined by the underlying class structure itself.

observer in the world of ordinary workers, one's identity is partially unhinged from the normative coordinates of the academy. This engagement accomplishes two critical tasks. First, it provides a methodological vehicle for generating the necessary kinds of data to answer the questions about which Burawoy is most interested – questions about the limits and possibilities of radical working-class formation. As a participant observer actively engaged in the world he studies, Burawoy in effect conducts a long series of mini-experiments, making daily conjectures about what will happen if he does X and then "testing" these hypotheses on the shop floor. Second, and particularly important in the present context, this kind of engaged fieldwork provides the social setting for sustaining a commitment in a serious way to the questions themselves. Participant observation thus serves a double purpose: it partially counters the pressures of the academy, enabling a radical scholar to ask the right questions, and it provides a social setting for obtaining the data necessary for producing the best answers.[8]

I am not convinced that, at least at this moment in history, the institutional pressures on conformity to bourgeois values are so strong that Burawoy's solution is the only one possible. In any event, for better or worse, I have certainly adopted a different strategy. Instead of weakening my ties to the academy, I have tried to counter the pressures by creating within the academy a dense network of radical scholarship which openly and consistently affirms emancipatory values. As a graduate student I helped found the Union of Marxist Social Scientists and the West Coast Socialist Social Science Conference; as a faculty member at the University of Wisconsin I have helped build the Class Analysis and Historical Change Program; and, more recently, with a number of colleagues I have helped found a left-wing research center, the Havens Center for the Study of Social Structure and Social Change. Each of these projects of institution-building was self-consciously designed to generate an environment of intellectual accountability in which norms of political radicalism would have a legitimate place.

It would be absurd to argue that this strategy of creating institutional enclaves of radical social thought inside established universities can effectively eliminate pressures for conformity. But neither does personal engagement with workers in factories and unions dissolve the pressures

---

8. To state this point in a slightly different way, I believe that Burawoy's commitment to qualitative methods in general and participant observation in particular does not directly follow from any general philosophical beliefs about the nature of social science, but rather from a particular substantive view about the social structural conditions for the production of knowledge on the one hand, and a view about the nature of the decisive mechanisms responsible for explaining variations in class formation on the other (i.e. mechanisms that are embedded in the lived experiences of workers within production).

from grant agencies and tenure committees. I suppose that the model of building institutional enclaves of radical scholarship within which different values have effective power is like the strategies of "advanced democracy" or "non-reformist reforms" advocated by democratic socialists in the 1970s: this strategy acknowledges that reforms are achievable within existing institutions that allow for genuinely new possibilities of action but which, nevertheless, remain compatible with the reproduction of the institutions themselves. The strategy of constructing an alternative form of intellectual accountability through personal engagement outside the university, on the other hand, implies that such reforms are ultimately illusions which, far from creating an institutional space within which radical intellectuals can effectively work, have the effect of co-opting those intellectuals and neutralizing their radicalism.

In the end I do not know which is the more effective strategy. Both seem plausible; both contain real risks.

Theoretical Cores and Eclecticism

Judith Stacey and Linda Collins strongly affirm the virtues of theoretical eclecticism:

> Our commitment to comprehending and resisting domination and injustice in their all too variegated guises leads us to greater theoretical eclecticism than Wright or Burawoy. Having passed through different stages of Marxist political discourse along our individual paths to our current research and politics, each of us has lost interest in the terms of their *BJS* debate. Our work on gender, race and community requires different, perhaps less rooted, anchors than Marxism alone provides.[9]

Similarly, Loïc Wacquant asks why should we restrict our effort at theory construction to Marxism as such:

> If the end-purpose of class theory is to explain the structure, formation and trajectory of classes as historical forces, and if we believe that the social universe comprises complex structures wholly or partly independent of our knowledge of them, why should we *a priori* limit our investigations of them by holding on to Marxist tenets, however defined, rather than launch into an all-out search using the full gamut of theoretical resources at hand?[10]

Eclecticism is certainly an appealing doctrine of intellectual practice.

---

9. Linda Collins and Judith Stacey, "Salvation or Emancipation? Reflections on the Wright/Burawoy Exchange," *Berkeley Journal of Sociology*, vol. XXXIV, 1989, p. 52.

10. Wacquant, "Social Ontology, Epistemology and Class," p. 167.

Sticking to a strong, integrated theoretical core often gets social theorists into trouble, for the world is complex and ambitious theories always try to push the limits of simplification. It is much easier to respond to each new complexity with a patchwork of relatively unconnected conceptual elements than to constantly strive for coherence and theoretical integration. There is no doubt that much of the time an eclectic approach will be less vulnerable to charges of dogmatism, oversimplification, rigidity, and other academic sins. But is eclecticism a desirable universal principle for building theories and advancing knowledge?

Imagine the following two possible worlds of theoretical debate on social questions. In the first world, most theorists are committed to one or another of a series of well-articulated, systematic theoretical paradigms (or research programs, to use the Lakatosian expression favored by Burawoy). Each of these paradigms is built around a core of central questions, assumptions, concepts, and general theses. To be committed to such a paradigm does *not* mean that one is "dogmatic" in the cognitive sense of rigidly adhering to a set of ideas that are immune from challenge; but it does imply a certain stubbornness in the defense of core elements of a paradigm, a reluctance to abandon ship whenever it springs a leak. On occasion, these divergent approaches may attempt to explain the same empirical phenomena, and when this happens the theorists working within these different approaches may engage in sustained debate; but often, they are asking different questions, and thus do not directly confront each other.

In the second world, theorists all take an eclectic stance towards such paradigms. Theorists are not committed in general to developing and defending coherent, conceptual cores in their theories, but rather believe that the best way to build our understanding of social phenomena is to use whatever concepts and arguments seem most appropriate for each specific empirical problem without worrying about the compatibility of such concepts with some overarching "framework." This does not imply that the theorists in question are opposed to explanation as such, but simply that they reject the methodological view that it is desirable to embed explanations of specific phenomena within more general explanatory principles.

In which of these worlds is our knowledge of social phenomena most likely to advance? In which world is there a better chance that our learning process will have a cumulative character to it? I think knowledge is more likely to advance in a cumulative way in a world with many theorists committed to systematic, tightly organized paradigms, than in a world made up exclusively of eclectics. This does not imply that I would prefer a world made up entirely of theorists who accept my own perspective. I think that it is much healthier to work as a Marxist

sociologist in a world with radical feminist sociologists who are committed to the pervasive explanatory centrality of gender and reject class
analysis altogether, and with neoclassical economists who affirm the
centrality of economic processes but deny that they should be theorized
in class terms, than to work on an intellectual terrain inhabited entirely
by Marxists (let alone entirely by Analytical Marxists!).

I believe that the intellectual terrain with the greatest vitality for
exploring social questions is likely to be an intensely pluralistic one, in
the sense that no single approach overwhelmingly dominates intellectual
life; but on this pluralistic terrain, knowledge is more likely to advance if
the different perspectives each attempts, self-consciously, to elaborate
their underlying assumptions, to formulate their concepts in as coherent
a way as possible, and to develop a systematic set of general theses using
these concepts and assumptions. This is hard work. Eclecticism might
itself be one of the theoretical approaches contending on this terrain, but
it would be parasitic on the more tightly organized theoretical paradigms,
since there must be something from which to pick and choose in order to
construct eclectic explanations. Eclecticism would thus not be a privileged methodological stance, but simply one strategy among several.[11]

This general view of the conditions under which knowledge is likely to
advance is not equivalent to epistemological relativism. To defend the
virtues of a pluralistic theoretical terrain is not to argue that all theoretical positions are equally valid. Evidence and argument can be brought to
bear to "adjudicate" among rival explanations *when the rivals attempt to
explain the same empirical phenomena.* The point is that the outcome of
such contestation of rival perspectives is more likely to produce a
cumulative trajectory of knowledge, rather than simply a fragmented
resolution of a specific debate, if the positions in dispute are built around
systematic, coherent theoretical frameworks.

To argue that it is desirable to have an intellectual environment within
which some people are committed to elaborating a distinctively Marxist
approach does not imply that in the concrete analysis of specific problems. Marxists should refuse to consider causal processes that fall outside
of a Marxist framework. As argued in the previous chapter, Marx*ism* is
largely sex-blind in so far as its core categories are defined independently
of gender relations, but this does not imply that when Marx*ists* analyze a

---

11. The premiss of the argument advanced here is that the kind of realist explanation
outlined earlier is possible. One can, of course, deny the very possibility of realist social
knowledge altogether, and thus deny the possibility of knowledge having a "cumulative"
character. Perhaps all we can do is *describe* social phenomena from particular cognitive
points of view, rendering them meaningful to us because of our normative concerns. If this
is so, then there would be no particular virtue in trying to construct general explanatory
theoretical frameworks around a core of coherently integrated concepts and assumptions.

concrete empirical problem their analyses must be sex-blind. Marxists can also be feminists, even if Marxism and feminism cannot be melded into a unified theoretical framework, at least given the current state of knowledge.[12] If we want to understand the absence of solidarity in a working-class community, for example, it may be necessary to study both the sorts of mechanisms specified in Marxist theory – forms of organization of the labor process, mechanisms of hegemonic incorporation by capitalism, fragmentation of labor markets, etc. – as well as mechanisms unspecified by Marxism as such, such as gender relations or ethnic divisions. The importance of the *question* itself is driven by Marxism, which places working-class formation at the center of its analysis; and the theoretical *relevance* of these non-class mechanisms is established by their articulation to the class-based mechanisms. In the actual deployment of class analysis to investigate concrete empirical problems, therefore, Marxism is compatible with a kind of anchored eclecticism.[13]

An analogy with medical science may help to clarify these arguments about the relationship between Marxism, feminism, and other frameworks of emancipatory social theory.[14] In medicine it is often useful to distinguish the *clinical* practice of medicine from the *scientific* practice of medicine. A scientific endocrinologist does research on the structure and processes of the body's endocrine system. In developing the general theories of this system and its functioning, an endocrinologist will draw on, for example, the genetics theory, but only in so far as this is relevant for answering the questions posed by the study of hormones. This in no way implies that the only theoretical relevance of genetics in general is its bearing on the endocrine system, but simply that this is the relevance for the explanatory purposes of an endocrinologist. In clinical medicine, a physician tries to diagnose a concrete illness in a concrete human body in order to cure it (i.e. to paraphrase Marx, understand the symptoms in order to transform them). For this task the physician draws on the available theories of a wide variety of illness-producing mechanisms, not for the purpose of advancing our scientific understanding of those mechanisms, but for the purpose of solving a particular concrete prob-

---

12. By a "unified framework" I mean a theoretical structure within which class and gender are two components logically integrated through some overarching principle rather than simply added together. The attempts at formulating such integrated frameworks of which I am aware are quite unpersuasive and typically have the character of either subsuming gender under class analysis or class under gender analysis.

13. The best Marxist historical and sociological research, from Marx's own historical writings to contemporary Marxist scholarship, has always adopted this kind of flexible strategy, linking a wide array of non-class factors to the class and economic causes that are at the core of Marxist theory.

14. This analogy is developed at some length in Erik Olin Wright, Andrew Levine, and Elliott Sober, *Reconstructing Marxism*, London 1992, pp. 180–82.

lem. In this sense, in the practice of clinical medicine the physician engages in a certain kind of eclecticism by drawing on the diverse theories of different biological mechanisms. The development of those theories themselves, however, proceeds in a much less eclectic manner.

Now, it may be the case that certain of these mechanisms might in general be much more "important" than others in the sense that they are implicated in many more kinds of diseases or more powerfully shape the course of development of diseases. Just as Marxists have often made strong claims about the general centrality of class in the production of social "illness," some medical scientists have argued, for example, that the immune system is really the key to understanding disease processes across a wide spectrum of quite distinct illnesses. If this were true, it might provide a justification for focusing our research energy on deepening our theoretical understanding of that kind of mechanism, and it might suggest to a physician that in beginning a diagnosis for certain illnesses, a good place to begin would be to analyze the immune system.

It is also possible that because of explanatory zeal and professional interests, a proponent of a particular disease-production mechanism might exaggerate its explanatory scope and importance, in the extreme case elevating a single kind of mechanism to the status of the central determinant of all illness. At times, Marxists have certainly been guilty of such explanatory imperialism when they claim that class is the most important cause of everything. Combating such explanatory imperialism is an important task of science. But arguing for a more precisely formulated specification of the explanatory reach of class analysis does not imply that class is simply one factor in a long list of social causes, no more important than any other in explaining the major dilemmas and contradictions of contemporary society. Class may not be *the* central cause of *everything* social and still be *a* central cause of *most* social phenomena of interest to radicals. And, so long as it is recognized that class is a pervasive social cause, then social clinicians interested in diagnosing specific empirical problems with an eclectic tool kit have an interest in the preservation and development of Marxism as the social science of class analysis.

10

Explanation and Emancipation in Marxism and Feminism

Both Marxism and feminism are emancipatory theoretical traditions in that they envision the possibility of eliminating from social life certain forms of oppression.[1] The two traditions differ, however, in the extent to which theorists within each take for granted the *viability* of their core emancipatory projects: Marxists have often treated the viability of communism – a society without class oppression – as problematic; feminists rarely question the viability of a society without male domination. Of course, feminists frequently engage the problem of the social, political, and cultural obstacles to eliminating male domination, and different feminists have different visions of what life in a world without male oppression would be like. But what is not generally discussed is the viability of a society within which male domination has been eliminated. For reasons which we will explore below, there is much skepticism among people who share the radical egalitarian *values* of Marxists that a classless society with advanced technologies is viable; there seems to be much less skepticism among people with feminist values that a society without male domination is viable. Feminists generally take it for granted that social life does not *require* male domination; Marxists are forced to defend the claim that social life under conditions of developed technology does not need some form or other of class denomination.

The central objective of this chapter is to explore this contrast between these two traditions of emancipatory social theory. My motivation for doing so comes primarily from the Marxist side of the comparison. At the core of the project of reconstructing Marxism as a social

---

1. I am using the term "emancipation" as the most general way of framing the normative objectives of radicals. A variety of more specific values can be subsumed under this general expression: self-realization, happiness, meaningfulness, sexual fulfillment, material welfare, etc. "Oppression," then, is a situation in which a group is unjustly deprived of one or more of these values; emancipation is the elimination of the relevant form of oppression.

theory is the problem of the relationship between its emancipatory vision and its explanatory structure. My hope is that a comparison with the feminist theoretical tradition will help to give greater precision to our understanding of the dilemmas which Marxism faces today. The point of the comparison of Marxism and feminism in this chapter, therefore, is not to indict feminists for their relative silence on the problem of the viability of feminism's emancipatory project, nor to show that Marxists are somehow more sophisticated because they worry about these issues. Rather, the point is to use the contrast between the theoretical preoccupations of these two traditions as a way of revealing certain salient properties of the theoretical terrain on which they work.

Before we approach these issues, however, we need to clarify several key concepts we will be using throughout the analysis: Marxism, feminism, oppression, and emancipatory viability.

Marxism and Feminism as Emancipatory Theories

It is far from easy to produce compact, non-controversial definitions of "Marxism" and "feminism." The boundaries of each are contested, both by intellectuals committed to these traditions and by their critics. For the purposes of this chapter, I do not think that it is necessary to provide complete definitions of either; it will be sufficient to work with a fairly stylized description of their underlying theoretical structures. I will, accordingly, treat Marxism and feminism as emancipatory traditions of social theory built around the critical analysis of particular forms of oppression – class oppression and gender oppression respectively – rather than as well-bounded, integrated explanatory theories.[2] They are *emancipatory* theories in that both theoretical traditions believe that the forms of oppression on which they focus should be and can be eliminated; both see the active struggle of the oppressed groups at the core of their theory as an essential part of the process through which such oppression is transformed; and intellectuals working within both tradi-

---

2. It may be controversial to some people to characterize feminism as an emancipatory tradition directed against *gender* oppression rather than simply against the oppression of *women*. Certainly, until recently feminists did not explicitly embed their understanding of the oppression of women in a theory of gender relations, and thus earlier feminists generally characterized their struggles as strictly against the oppression of women as such. Many contemporary feminists, however, understand the ramifications of male domination within gender relations more broadly than simply as an issue of men dominating and oppressing women. Male homosexuals, for example, are also generally viewed as oppressed under existing gender relations, and while it is a more complex (and contentious) argument, I think that many heterosexual men can also be viewed as oppressed within gender relations. There is no need to work through these issues in the present context.

tions believe that the central reason for bothering to do social theory and research is to contribute in some way to the realization of their respective emancipatory projects. Where they differ, in these terms, is in the kind of social oppression which anchors their emancipatory and theoretical projects.

In making the distinction between Marxisms and feminisms in terms of their pivotal concern with different forms of oppression, I am making no assumptions about the autonomy, one from the other, of these two forms of oppression in the world. Clearly, in actual societies there are systematic, reciprocal effects between gender relations and class relations in all sorts of ways. Understanding such reciprocal effects between class and gender is at the heart of much socialist feminism, whether in the form of "dual systems theory" or more unitary theories of class and gender.[3] Nevertheless, unless one is prepared to abandon the separate categories of "class" and "gender" altogether and replace them with a new amalgamated category, "clender," I believe that it is important to distinguish class and gender analytically as two dimensions of social relations which interact rather than treat class/gender as a unitary category. Once such a distinction is made, then the question of the feasibility of eliminating each of these aspects of social oppression can be posed. The *answer* may be that one cannot be eliminated without the other, as some socialist feminists have stressed, but that should be a discovery rather than a premiss of the categories themselves.

Defining Marxisms as emancipatory theories for the elimination of class oppression and feminisms as emancipatory theories for the elimination of gender oppression leaves open precisely what is packed into the concept of "oppression" within each tradition. Obviously, depending precisely on how oppression is defined, the project of eliminating oppression can become a utopian fantasy or a practical political program. If, for example, we define oppression in typical liberal terms as a situation in which different categories of people have different *formal rights*, then it would be a relatively non-contentious matter to argue that class and

---

3. In the terms of the present discussion, socialist feminism can be thought of as a hybrid of the two emancipatory traditions we are examining. Throughout this discussion I will not make a distinction between "socialist feminism" and "Marxist feminism," since both of these attempt to take seriously the problem of the interconnection between class and gender. The classical statement of "dual systems theory" is Heidi Hartmann's essay, "The Unhappy Marriage of Marxism and Feminism," in Lydia Sargent, ed., *Women and Revolution*, Boston 1981, pp. 1–41. A critique of dual systems theory which attempts to frame a more unitary theory of class and gender is Iris Young, "Beyond the Unhappy Marriage: a critique of dual systems theory," in Sargent, pp. 43–70. For a general discussion of varieties of feminism which discusses the difference between socialist feminism and Marxist feminism, see Alison Jaggar and Paula Rothenberg Struhl, eds, *Feminist Frameworks*, New York 1984, and Alison Jaggar, *Feminism and Human Nature*, Totowa 1983.

gender oppression can be eliminated. Once workers have the franchise and full rights to organize collectively, and once ascriptive barriers to equal opportunity have been eliminated, class oppression will have disappeared. Once women are accorded full citizenship and reproductive rights, and anti-discrimination procedures are firmly in place, gender oppression will be eliminated.[4] On the other hand, if one takes a maximalist view of what it would mean to eliminate oppressions, then eliminating particular forms of oppression may indeed seem utopian. In the Marxist tradition, for example, there are those who have claimed that class oppression will exist so long as there is any division of labor whatsoever between mental and manual labor, between conception and execution. It is hard to imagine how a technologically advanced society could actually function under such principles.

For the purpose of the analysis of this chapter, I will adopt a conception of eliminating oppression that is more radical than the liberal conception but less extravagant than a maximalist understanding. Oppression will be defined as a situation in which the relevant categories of social actors (people within the social relations of production and within gender relations) systematically differ in terms of social power and material welfare.[5] The emancipatory project of eliminating oppression then means the equalization of power and welfare across the relevant social categories.[6] In the rhetoric of the Marxist tradition, this corresponds to the elimination of alienation and exploitation – eliminating power differentials linked to the social relations of production and inequalities in income that go beyond differences in needs. This amounts to the elimination of classes. The emancipatory future envisioned in traditional Marxism – communism – is a classless society. In the case of gender oppression this definition of emancipation implies eliminating power and welfare differentials between men and women. This goes far beyond equal rights, since it implies instituting a wide range of social changes (e.g. public provision of childcare, equality of labor market

---

4. For a discussion of liberal feminism, see Jaggar, chapters 3 and 7.

5. The problem of defining oppression is aggravated in the present context, since we are comparing the emancipatory projects of eliminating two different kinds of oppression: class and gender. In order to make sense of the comparison we need to discuss these two oppressions in analytically comparable terms. It would make no sense, for example, to compare a liberal conception of gender oppression (eliminating gender inequalities of rights) with a more radical conception of class oppression (eliminating classes altogether).

6. The idea of equality of "welfare" is complicated, given that people differ so greatly in their non-material endowments and needs. The normative ideal of equality of welfare therefore usually takes the more modest practical form of equality of income (or access to external resources), modified by some provisions for inequalities of income required to deal with various kinds of disabilities (i.e. "to each according to need"). For the present purposes of comparing Marxism and feminism as emancipatory and explanatory theories, we can bracket these difficult philosophical problems.

position, changes in work organization to eliminate gender differences in the burden of childrearing, etc.) necessary to give men and women equal real power.

Many feminists, of course, hold much more complex visions of gender emancipation than simply equality of power and welfare. Some believe in the possibility of dismantling gender relations altogether; others see emancipation as centered on making certain purported "female differences" the central organizing principles of social life (e.g. nurturing); and still others place issues of sexuality, especially the problem of homophobia, at the center of the emancipatory project. These are all interesting and important issues, and a fully elaborated discussion of the varieties of feminist emancipatory ideals would have to explore the implications of these alternatives. Nevertheless, all of these different feminisms share the thin notion of emancipation as the elimination of gender inequality of power and welfare, and thus for the purposes of our comparison with Marxism I will rely on this understanding of emancipatory objectives.

With this working definition of oppression, the question of the viability of an emancipatory project can be restated as follows: could a society within which power and welfare were not differentiated by class and/or gender be sustainable? Or would such a society necessarily contain self-destructive contradictions which will tend to unravel the emancipatory objectives or make them simply unattainable in the first place? The goal of this chapter, then, is to explore the relationship between the kind of explanatory theories characteristic of the Marxist and feminist traditions and the nature of these emancipatory projects. Again, this is a stylized and limited characterization of the emancipatory vision of Marxism and feminism. There are many emancipatory issues within each theoretical tradition that are not directly encompassed within this definition: the problem of autonomy and self-realization in Marxism; questions of sexuality, identity and difference in feminisms. Nevertheless, equality of power and welfare are sufficiently central to the emancipatory agenda of all Marxisms and feminisms that comparing the two traditions in these terms will be help to clarify certain important differences in the explanatory tasks which they confront.

The Silence on the "Viability" of Emancipatory Objectives in Feminism

In order to establish the credibility of the project of gender emancipation, feminist intellectuals have focused primarily on three tasks. First, much writing has been devoted to demonstrating that gender relations can properly be described as relation of domination and oppression. A great deal of feminist empirical work is devoted to providing evidence that women are systematically harmed in many ways by the gender relations within which they live, and thus that those relations can be described as oppressive. Second, feminists have been concerned to establish that these relations are not unalterably given by biology, but are socially (or, some theorists would prefer, culturally) constructed. Clearly, the indictment of gender relations as oppressive would be vitiated if the disadvantages women suffer were completely determined by biology. Much attention has therefore been devoted to demonstrating the great variability in the forms of oppression of women across time and place in order to give credibility to the claim that such oppression is socially generated. Third, modern feminists have analyzed the various social, economic, and cultural processes in contemporary societies which undermine and/or reproduce existing forms of gender oppression and thus create the context for transformative struggles, especially through the agency of women. Discussions of these three clusters of issues have been at the heart of the development of modern feminism.

Very little attention has been directly given, however, to the problem of the practical viability of a society within which gender oppression has been eliminated. As already noted, much effort has been devoted to demonstrating that gender relations are socially constructed, but this is not equivalent to demonstrating that gender emancipation is viable. Indeed, it is possible that male domination *could* be biologically based *and* that male domination can be eliminated. Biologically, human beings are omnivores but this does not prevent people from adopting a strictly vegetarian diet. Biologically, human beings have sexual drives, but this does not prevent the social creation of celibate religious orders. Whatever one's judgment is on the question of the biological roots of gender relations, the problem of demonstrating the eliminability of male domination is thus not equivalent to demonstrating that male domination is socially constructed.

Of course, much discussion has gone into the analysis of the obstacles to actually creating such a society. It is important, however, not to confuse a claim that the obstacles to *achieving* an emancipatory alternative are enormous, perhaps even insurmountable under contemporary conditions, with the claim that the alternative itself is not *viable*.[7] Feminists differ considerably in the extent to which they believe that such

---

7. Consider the contrast between the achievability and viability for socialism. It could be the case (a) that counterfactually, if capitalism were destroyed and workers democratically controlled the means of production, the economy would run efficiently and equitably, and thus socialism would be deemed viable, and also (b) that capitalists would rather destroy the world through a nuclear suicide than give up power. Under these conditions socialism is viable, but unattainable.

obstacles are either primarily located in cultural and sexual practices that shape the formation of deeply rooted gender subjectivities, or mainly located in economic and political institutions of power and privilege. Feminists also disagree over whether gender domination can be gradually eroded through an incremental process of reform or whether radical ruptures in the system of male domination are needed.[8] But the viability of the emancipatory objective itself is not subjected to systematic, critical scrutiny.[9] Feminists do not ask the question, "are there contradictions within egalitarian gender relations which might render a society without male domination non-reproducible?" It is as if demonstrating that *existing* gender relations are oppressive and socially constructed is equivalent to showing that a society within which male domination has been eliminated would be viable.

This silence on the part of feminists occurs in an ideological context in which there is relatively little skepticism among people who hold radical egalitarian values about the viability of eliminating male domination. Even among leftist radicals who are not particularly sympathetic to feminism as a tradition of theory, there is relatively little skepticism in the contemporary period about the practical viability of a society without male domination. To be sure, there is often a lot of skepticism by non-feminist leftists about the viability of distinctively feminist *politics*, since many Marxists believe that the liberation of women can only succeed if subordinated to the allegedly "more fundamental" task of transforming class relations. And there is certainly skepticism about some radical feminist claims concerning the range of ramifications of eliminating gender oppression (for example, the claim that bureaucratic hierarchy is a distinctively male form of administrative organization, and thus that eliminating male domination would imply – and require – an elimination of all hierarchy). But, at least in the contemporary period, relatively little skepticism is directly expressed at the possibility of eventually eliminating differences in welfare and power based on gender.

---

8. For a discussion of the history of feminist thought which touches on the problem of incremental reform vs. ruputural breaks in male domination, see Hester Eisenstein, *Contemporary Feminist Thought*, Boston 1983.

9. The one context in which the issue of the viability of gender emancipation is indirectly posed is in socialist feminist discussions about whether or not *capitalist* society is viable without gender oppression. It is often argued that capitalism *needs* male domination for various reasons, and that thus this particular form of society is not reproducible without gender oppression. Such arguments, however, all concern the viability of *capitalism* without male domination; there is no discussion of whether or not a post-capitalist society without male domination is viable.

The Viability of Classlessness

The contrast between the relative silence on the problem of the viability of gender emancipation and the extensive discussions of the viability of communism (understood as a full classless society), and even of socialism (understood as a society in which the working class democratically controls the means of production and class divisions are declining) is striking. Many radical intellectuals on the left, including Marxists committed to radically egalitarian values, doubt that class inequalities could ever be completely eliminated. A variety of familiar arguments have been advanced against the viability of classlessness. First, it is often argued that in order for a complex economy to maintain even minimal efficiency, significant material incentives (and sanctions) are needed, particularly for people occupying positions of great responsibility requiring high levels of skill. While logically it might not be the case that such incentive-inequalities would have to threaten classlessness, there would be strong tendencies for the recipients of such incentives to use the leverage of their positions to extort economic premiums from the larger community.[10] While perhaps less onerous than the inequalities based on property ownership in capitalism, such extortion in a "socialist" society would constitute exploitation rooted in command over productive resources (skills and responsible jobs in this instance) and would thus challenge the emancipatory project of classlessness.[11]

Second, skepticism is often expressed about the possibility of genuinely democratic control over the means of production. While it might be possible in quite small firms for ordinary workers to play an active role in organizational decision-making, many people argue that in large firms such involvement would necessarily be superficial at best. Perhaps workers could have a say in choosing managers, but the actual running of large, complex corporations – including the practical exercise of much

----

10. An "incentive" is an amount of extra income necessary to compensate a person for the extra effort involved in acquiring skills or performing arduous and stressful work (which, for example, might accompany high levels of responsibility). An "extortion," on the other hand, is an increment of income above and beyond what is necessary to compensate a person for this extra effort. Strictly speaking, incentive payments are needed in order to maintain rough equality in overall welfare across persons (i.e. people need to be compensated for the extra "disutility of labor"), whereas extortion generates inequality in real welfare. In these terms, "extortion" is equivalent to "exploitation." For a discussion of these conceptual issues, see Erik Olin Wright, *The Debate on Classes*, London 1989.

11. The characterization of the incomes of people who command high levels of skill or responsibility as "exploitation" is derived from the work of John Roemer. See especially Roemer, "New Directions in the Marxian Theory of Class and Exploitation," *Politics & Society*, vol. 11, no. 3, and *A General Theory of Exploitation and Class*, Cambridge, Mass. 1982.

operational power – would have to be under the control of managers and executives. This, again, would tend to generate class inequalities.

Finally, particularly in the aftermath of the stagnation and collapse of the state socialist economies, many leftist intellectuals argue that because of the massive information problems in a complex industrial society, centralized planning of the details of production is not possible. Given that centralized allocation of capital is not possible, then some kind of market mechanism for the allocation of capital goods is needed to coordinate production. But once markets in investments (rather than simply in consumer goods) are allowed to function in even limited ways, they will tend to generate class inequalities. While there could be considerable democratic social control over the parameters of the system of production, once markets are allowed to play a significant role in allocating capital, something very much like capitalism would tend to re-emerge. This would be the case even if firms took the form of workers' cooperatives, since under conditions of market competition such co-operatives would behave pretty much like capitalist firms.

A range of plausible arguments can be used to defend the emancipatory project of a classless society against these attacks. Against the first claim it can be argued that gradually, over time, the balance between extortion and incentive could shift in favor of incentives, particularly as the economic security of people increases and high-quality public goods replace important elements of private consumption. Against the second claim it can be argued that through education, work teams, shorter working weeks, and other changes, meaningful democratic participation becomes much more possible even within large organizations, and thus the effective power differentials associated with hierarchy might decline over time. Finally, against the third claim it could be argued that while market mechanisms might of necessity play an important information role in allocating capital, the inegalitarian consequences of such allocations can be systematically neutralized by an activist, socialist state. Taxation, redistribution, and regulation could be designed in such a way as to prevent the relatively decentralized, cooperatively managed firms from degenerating into capitalist enterprises.

My point here is thus *not* that the arguments against the possibility of eliminating class oppression are convincing. Rather, the point is that these doubts are raised by people on the left, people sympathetic to the emancipatory egalitarian values themselves. At this time in history, parallel arguments are not generally made by egalitarians with respect to gender oppression. Of course, there many be *anti*-egalitarians of various sorts for whom a society without male domination would be seen as non-viable. Certainly many right-wing religious fundamentalists would see such a society as destroying the basic fabric of social life, leading to chaos

and disintegration. Within the community of people sharing egalitarian
emancipatory values, however, there is little skepticism about the viability of a radical emancipatory project for the elimination of gender
domination and inequality, while there is considerable skepticism about
the elimination of class oppression.

One hundred years ago the situation was quite different. Radical class
theorists took it as obvious that class inequality and domination were
becoming increasingly unnecessary and could be superseded in a post-
capitalist society. Capitalist development was seen as creating such high
levels of concentration and centralization of production, with such high
levels of surplus, that workers would be able to transform the solidarities
and interdependencies they experienced within production into an egalitarian reorganization of the society as a whole. All they needed to
accomplish this was power. Feminists in the last century, on the other
hand, rarely envisioned a society without a quite substantial gender
division of labor and even gender inequality. While recognizing that the
potentials of women were blocked by the forms of male domination
existing in their society, particularly as these were embodied in legal
restrictions on the rights of women, the emancipatory project did not
generally pose the possibility of a future of radically egalitarian relations
between men and women.[12]

At the close of the twentieth century, second-wave feminism envisions
a future that ranges from complete equality of rights of men and women
to the elimination of all gender inequalities in power and welfare
(although not necessarily the elimination of all gender differences). No
feminists imagine that male *domination* in even vestigial form is essential
for social life. Many Marxists, on the other hand, have come to doubt the
feasibility of the most egalitarian forms of their historic emancipatory
class project, partially as a result of the failures of authoritarian state
socialist systems and partially as a result of theoretical development
within Marxism itself.

Why is the viability of the feminist emancipatory alternative to male
domination seen as so unproblematic compared to the Marxist emancipatory project? One possibility is that this simply reflects the historical
context for the development of the two intellectual traditions. Marxism
has not only had one hundred-plus years of sustained debate, but has also
borne witness to a massive historical "experiment" in applying certain of
its core ideas to the actual design of social institutions. Whether or not
one endorses or condemns these experiments as authentic embodiments
of Marxist ideals, they have deeply affected the intellectual climate

---

12. This characterization of nineteenth-century feminism was suggested to me by Linda
Gordon (personal communication).

within which the problem of class emancipation can be discussed. Perhaps after a hundred years of development of systematic feminist social theory, and in the aftermath of an equivalent attempt at instituting radical gender equality, there would be similar skepticism about its viability.

While undoubtedly the current skepticism among leftists about class-lessness has been significantly shaped by the historical experience of the authoritarian socialist states, I do not think that the silence on the problem of viability within feminism can be attributed mainly to the absence of massive societal experiments in gender emancipation or the relatively recent vintage of systematic feminist theory. Rather, I believe there is a crucial difference in the character of the emancipatory projects themselves which provides a plausible grounding for feminist confidence that gender emancipation is a viable social project. In particular, class and gender differ in terms of the relationship between lived micro-experiences within existing relations and the macro-institutional changes required for emancipation.

Micro- and Macro-Contexts of Emancipatory Projects

In the everyday practices of living in patriarchal societies, in a variety of ways people can experience prefigurative forms of gender equality.[13] First of all, in the historical experience of contemporary women there has been a steady trajectory of transformation of gender relations in an egalitarian direction. Without suggesting that male domination is on its last legs, or even that new forms of gender inequality have not emerged, the opening up of greater personal opportunities and political possibilities for women is a critical part of the lived experience of women in the twentieth century.[14] Furthermore, in the more recent past there has been

13. To say that a person experiences a "prefigurative form" does not imply that in a male dominated society either men or women can really experience "what it would be like" to live in a gender-egalitarian society. To experience a partial form of X is not the same as experiencing a fully developed form of X for a limited time or in a limited context. The point being made here is that within oppressive gender relations it is possible for people to experience glimpses of more egalitarian relations, glimpses which contribute to the credibility of the alternative.

14. There are feminists who insist that male domination has "simply" been reconstituted in a new and equally oppressive form – from private patriarchy constructed particularly within the family to public patriarchy constructed particularly within the labor market and the state. In this view, the transformations that have occurred in the past fifty years do not represent any real progress towards more egalitarian gender relations. While it is undeniable that new forms of male domination have emerged, reflected in such things as the feminization of poverty, new forms of job segregation, and the double shift of paid and domestic labor, in terms of the overall distribution of welfare and power in capitalist democracies, I believe that the trajectory of gender relations has been in a generally egalitarian direction in recent decades.

added to this experience of a trajectory of social change, the experience of the collective political efficacy of women engaged in transformative politics. The women's movement itself generates a range of experiences of solidarities among women which are prefigurative of a society in which women are not dominated by men. If for no other reason, therefore, a simple extrapolation into the future of trends of the recent past suggests the viability of a world without gender oppression.

But this is not all. Gender oppression itself has a peculiar structure in that even inside the existing relations within which men dominate women there are elements of prefigurative experiences of symmetry and equality. Women have male children whom they nurture; boys have mothers whom they love. And even in the relations of husbands and wives within traditional "patriarchal" relations, alongside practices which are oppressive, reflecting relations of domination, there are elements of reciprocity and companionship which prefigure, even if in a limited way, the potential for egalitarian relations. This is part of the specific complexity of gender domination – the way it packages together in variable degrees and forms domination and equality, oppression and reciprocity.[15] The elimination of gender oppression can thus be partially experienced in micro-contexts in a society within which gender domination remains. The practical plausibility of eliminating gender oppression altogether is therefore experienced, if still in partial and limited ways, within existing societies.

It could be objected that the same is true about the elimination of class domination. After all, in the practical cooperation among workers on the shop floor and in the solidaristic struggles against bosses, workers could be said to experience prefigurative forms of socialist – or even communist – relations. Such solidaristic and cooperative experiences have certainly been important in drawing people to the socialist movement, and they do provide some existential basis for the plausibility of the Marxist emancipatory project. Why, then, aren't such experiences a practical demonstration of the viability of a classless society?

There are two issues that distinguish prefigurative emancipatory gender experiences from prefigurative emancipatory class experiences. First, in the case of gender, the prefigurative symmetrical experiences include experiences that bind people together across gender categories. In the case of class, the prefigurative emancipatory experiences are not between workers and capitalists, but exclusively among workers.

---

15. The way in which this internal complexity of gender relations, combining oppression and reciprocity, prefigures egalitarian gender relations was emphasized to me by Linda Gordon in a discussion of an earlier draft of this chapter.

Second, and more important for the present context, there is a different relationship between micro-experiences and macro-changes in the case of class and gender: whereas it is relatively easy to extrapolate from the micro-setting of prefigurative non-oppressive gender interactions to an image of a society without gender oppression, it is much more problematic to extrapolate from the micro-settings of class solidarity to a model of society without class domination. The reason for this is that socialist (and communist) production requires active macro-level *coordination*, with macro-level institutional arrangements which generate distinctive macro-level dynamics. The solidarities experienced in the interpersonal practices of class struggle and the micro-settings of the labor process, therefore, do not translate in any simple way into the institutional mechanisms of planning, information flows, allocation of capital, and price setting. There is nothing comparable at the macro-institutional level for gender practices.

This is emphatically *not* to suggest that macro-institutional arrangements are unimportant for gender relations. Gender is not simply a micro-interpersonal phenomenon in contrast to class, which is both a micro- and a macro-social phenomenon. The laws of the state, the structure of labor markets, and the division of labor, to cite several examples, all affect gender practices in significant ways and are systematically shaped by gender relations. And it is also undoubtedly the case that in order to create and reproduce a society without gender domination, state institutions would have to enforce various laws against discrimination and violence structured around gender. There would have to be extensive public provision of childcare services and reorganization of work to eliminate gender differences in the burden of childcare, since childrearing plays such a central role in sustaining gender inequalities. Particularly in a transition period towards a society without gender oppression it would probably be necessary to have quite pervasive forms of state intervention in issues around gender, although much of this intervention could perhaps be of an extremely decentralized sort. All of these interventions imply that gender egalitarianism requires certain kinds of macro-social arrangements.

Nevertheless, even though gender relations are not simply equivalent to micro-practices and experiences (and thus their transformation requires various kinds of macro-structural arrangements), there is still an important difference from the parallel situation of eliminating class oppression. The emancipatory gender interventions of the state are all directed at the micro-settings of gender practices; they would not have to solve any problems of the system-level coordination of different gender practices as such in order for the society to be reproducible. What is the gender equivalent of long-term macro-economic planning of investments? Or of international flows of commodities? Or of coordination of intermediate goods in a highly interdependent production process? All of these macro-institutional issues potentially call into question the idea of a classless society. There do not seem to be any parallel system-integration dilemmas posed by gender equality. It is for this reason that the extrapolation from particular micro-experiences of eliminating gender oppression to the society as a whole seems so plausible; macro-institutional arrangements may have to intervene systematically at the micro-level, but there are no distinctively *gender* contradictions of the macro-coordination as such.

Now, it *could* in principle be the case, contrary to what I have just argued, that the extrapolation from the micro- to the macro- is illegitimate in the case of emancipatory gender practices, just as it seems to be for class practices. There are two kinds of possibilities worth considering. First, it could be the case that the kinds of state interventions and other institutional arrangements discussed above – work reorganization, child-care, real labor market equality, etc. – could only be possible (for financial and other reasons) under socialist conditions. Capitalism may be incompatible with the institutional conditions for complete gender emancipation.[16] *If*, then, it turns out that socialism itself is not viable for the reasons adduced earlier, this would imply that an extrapolation from the micro-prefigurative experiences of gender equality to society as a whole would also be illegitimate. This would not, however, be due to any distinctive contradiction inside of the project of gender emancipation as such. Rather, the non-viability of gender emancipation would be due to a macro-failure in the project of class emancipation.

There is a second possibility, however, in which the macro-institutional dilemmas of eliminating gender oppression are rooted directly in gender relations as such. For example, suppose it is the case that if male domination were eliminated, biological reproduction would drop drastically. For reasons that are not now understood (this concocted argument goes), the cultural values that support having children require gender inequality to be sustained. In a society without gender oppression, therefore, few women would have children, and thus demographic collapse would occur. The very reproduction of society, therefore, would be threatened by the elimination of gender oppression. Under such conditions, gender-based macro-institutional arrangements would have to be organized to ensure adequate breeding and such arrangements

---

16. Such a claim need not imply that male domination serves some essential *function* for capitalism. Male domination – like pollution and environmental degradation – could even be harmful for capitalism and yet eliminating male domination could be impossible in capitalist societies because of cost and other constraints.

might well contradict the emancipatory objectives of the feminist project.

While this argument may be ridiculous, it has the same form as the efficiency-collapse effects postulated by the absence of class inequality: the unintended consequences of the elimination of a form of oppression undermine the material conditions necessary for sustaining the society and thus sustaining the emancipatory project itself. The critical point is that whereas in the Marxist context there are credible arguments of this sort raised by class-egalitarians that call into question the viability of the Marxist emancipatory project, such arguments are not raised (at least not by egalitarians) against gender equality.

It is important to be very clear on what is being claimed here. I am not denying that macro-social phenomena are deeply *gendered* in the sense that their form and consequences are shaped by gender relations in a variety of ways. Nor am I saying that there are no gender obstacles to transforming macro-institutions. The power that men wield economically, politically, and culturally constitutes large obstacles to the transformation of the macro-institutions that contribute to sustaining male dominance, just as the power of capitalists constitutes a significant obstacle to transforming the macro-institutions of capitalism. None of this implies, however, that there are any inherent gender dilemmas posed by the transformation of those macro-institutions. In the absence of credible arguments that macro-arrangements free of gender domination would self-destruct *for gender reasons*, it is therefore perfectly reasonable to extrapolate from the prefigurative experiences of gender equality at the micro-level to the society as a whole. With such extrapolations in hand, then the core feminist theses – existing relations are oppressive and these relations are socially constructed – seem to imply the practical viability of the emancipatory transformation of the relations.

Classical Marxism and the Viability of Socialism/Communism

Unlike the issue of the viability of a society without male domination, socialist theorists have never been able completely to by-pass the problem of the feasibility of socialism. And Marxists have often felt it necessary at least to make gestures towards arguments for the viability of communism (complete classlessness). In classical Marxism, this issue was handled in a particularly elegant – if ultimately unsatisfactory – way through the development of a theory of history, generally referred to as "historical materialism." Even though most Marxists today reject the rather deterministic cast of classical historical materialism, it is nevertheless worth reviewing the core arguments of the classical theory since the way it solves the problem of linking the emancipatory project to an explanatory theory remains an important part of the Marxist intellectual terrain.[17]

Historical materialism can be divided into what might be called the "General Theory of History," which attempts to chart and explain the overall trajectory of human history, and the "Special Theory of Capitalist History," which more modestly tries to explain the trajectory of capitalist development from its emergence to its demise. While the Special Theory is of more relevance for understanding the problems contemporary Marxism faces in defending its emancipatory project, it will be helpful to first briefly review the General Theory itself.

Since the internal logic of the General Theory of History has been recently subjected to such rigorous scrutiny by G.A. Cohen, I will only sketch out the central contours of the argument here.[18] Within historical materialism, the history of humankind is seen as developing in a systematic way through a series of stages defined by their distinctive social organizations of production. Each stage is characterized by a particular combination of forces of production and relations of production, and the central dynamics of the system come from the ways in which the forces and relations of production interact. More specifically, Cohen has elaborated this interaction in the following form:

1. The forces of production have a tendency to develop in history. This Cohen calls the "Development Thesis."

2. At any given level of development of the forces of production, there is some set of relations of production which will be optimal for the further development of the forces of production.

3. There will be a tendency for those relations of production which are optimal for the development of the forces of production to be selected (through an unspecified process of class struggle) because they are optimal.

---

17. To avoid misunderstanding, it is important to avoid equating "Marxism" with "historical materialism." Historical materialism is a particular way of theorizing the overall trajectory of historical development. Much of what is intellectually valuable in the Marxist tradition does not depend upon the validity of this general theory of history. Marxism is also a form of class analysis of social institutions. While Marxist class analysis is embedded in an understanding of historical *variation*, it need not presuppose a theory of historical *trajectory* (i.e. a theory of the inherent tendencies for historical variations in class relations to follow some developmental path). For a further discussion of the relationship between class analysis and historical materialism, see Erik Olin Wright, Andrew Levine, and Elliott Sober, *Reconstructing Marxism*, London 1992, Part I; and chapter 12 below.

18. See G.A. Cohen, *Karl Marx's Theory of History: a defense*, Princeton 1978. For an appreciative critique, see Wright, Levine, and Sober, chapter 2.

4. The relations that exist, therefore, have the form they do because that form of relations best facilitates the development of the forces of production.[19] This is the essential statement of the functional explanation of the relations of production by the forces of production.

5. Within all class-based relations of production, there is a limit to the maximum possible development of the forces of production, and thus eventually the further development of the forces of production will be blocked (or, to use Marx's term, "fettered").

6. When such fettering occurs, the now dysfunctional relations of production will be replaced (according to thesis 3 above) with new relations of production capable of unfettering the subsequent development of the forces of production.

If the General Theory of historical materialism could be shown to be true, then it would offer a powerful analytical tool for sustaining the Marxist emancipatory project. Capitalism, after all, is a class-based mode of production, and thus according to (4) will eventually fetter the development of the forces of production. When it does so, according to (5) those relations will eventually be replaced by new ones which will unfetter the forces. Eventually, therefore, a society without class exploitation is predicted by the theory since class modes of production eventually exhaust their capacity to develop the forces of production.[20]

The problem is that there is little reason to believe the General Theory as such. That is, at the level of abstraction of "relations of production" and "forces of production" it is hard to imagine what mechanism could exist which guarantees the eventual fettering of the forces of production by all class-based relations of production. Marx certainly never provided an actual argument for an inherent tendency for fettering at that level of abstraction, and neither does Cohen in his reconstruction of Marx's argument.

The validity of the generalizations within the General Theory, there-

---

19. One can slightly soften this statement without undermining its essential structure, by saying: "The *probability* of a given set of relations existing is determined by *the extent to which* those relations are optimal for the further development of the forces of production. There is therefore a *tendency* for the relations to be what they are because they facilitate the development of the forces." The probabilistic form retains the functional form of Cohen's interpretation of historical materialism without implying a unique, deterministic historical trajectory.

20. Even if Marx was wrong that capitalism was the last form of class society, and a new form of class society would replace capitalism according to thesis (5), still eventually that society would also fetter the forces of production according to thesis (4) and thus would eventually be replaced. Unless one believes that there is an indefinite number of new class modes of production, therefore, eventually a society without classes will occur.

fore, depends upon the validity of the various Special Theories of the history of the different modes of production that comprise the trajectory of the General Theory. That is, there is a special Theory of Pre-class Society History, a Special Theory of Feudal History, and a Special Theory of Capitalist History. For each of these theories there may be convincing arguments for the inevitability of fettering and transformation.[21] In particular, for present purposes, the critical issue is the validity of the Special Theory of Capitalist History.

Marx put a great deal of effort into developing the Special Theory of the fettering of forces of production within capitalism. His strongest arguments are contained in the quasi-deterministic theory of the long-run *non*viability of capitalism based on his famous "Law of the Tendency of the Falling Rate of Profit."[22] Without going into the technical details of the argument of the falling rate of profit, Marx argued that by virtue of the inherent competitive dynamics of capitalism, combined with the difficulties capitalists face in extracting labor effort from workers, there will be a systematic tendency in capitalism for capitalists to substitute machines for labor (or, as he put it, for the "organic composition of capital to rise"). However, according to Marx's analysis of the labor theory of value, the rate of profit is fundamentally a function of the amount of surplus labor time performed in production. By substituting machines for labor-power, therefore, capitalists reduce the amount of labor time in production available for exploitation, and this ultimately erodes the rate of profit. The decline in the average rate of profit, in turn, makes capitalism as a whole more and more vulnerable, since random shocks, tendencies for overproduction, etc., will more easily push the rate of profit to zero or below.

The key point is that *if* there is an inherent, forceful tendency for the rate of profit to fall, and *if* the available "counter-tendencies" cannot ultimately block this decline, then there is a high probability that eventually capitalism will stagnate and the forces of production will become fettered, since in capitalism the only source of resources for new investment and innovation come from capitalistic profits. If the Law of Tendency held true, therefore, capitalism would ultimately become

---

21. If each of these Special Theories were shown to be valid, then collectively they could provide the justification for the generalization contained within the General Theory of History, but they would still not provide a defense of the General Theory as such since there is no independent theoretical argument for the explanatory mechanisms in the general theory itself.

22. I refer to this theory as "quasi-deterministic" since Marx is careful to describe a set of counter-tendencies to the general tendency he proposes. While he does argue that in some unspecified long run these counter-tendencies cannot permanently block the primary tendency, nevertheless most of his arguments simply imply the strong probability that the rate of profit will fall, not that that fall is inevitable.

unreproducible as a social order. This does not mean that socialism would only occur in the aftermath of the catastrophic collapse of capitalism. People may become committed to socialism out of the belief that capitalism will collapse, and through such commitments bring about the demise of capitalism before it would have self-destructed. In any event, the theory provides a strong basis for predicting the eventual non-sustainability of capitalism as a social order.

The thesis of the likely long-term nonviability of capitalism due to its self-destructive internal contradictions is crucial for the traditional Marxist theory of socialism, The burden on the theory to demonstrate positively the superiority of socialism (let alone communism) over capitalism is reduced if it can be demonstrated that ultimately capitalism itself is nonviable. Socialism could be plagued with all sorts of inefficiencies, dilemmas, and uncertainties, and yet be preferable to moribund capitalism. Furthermore, if indeed capitalism becomes nonviable and thus ceases itself to be an alternative to socialism, then the political will to cope with dilemmas internal to socialism and creatively devise novel solutions would increase, thus rendering socialism itself more attractive. Given that his theory of the laws of motion of capitalism predicts its eventual non-reproducibility, Marx could perhaps be excused for refusing to elaborate blueprints or even systematic arguments for the sustainability of socialism/communism as the alternative to capitalism. It was enough to say that the workers would be in control and that through their creative energies, through trial and error and systematic experimentation, the precise institutional forms of socialism, and later communism, would be produced.

Unfortunately, the debates over the labor theory of value in recent years have raised very serious issues with the Law of the Tendency of the Rate of Profit to Fall. Not only have the general claims of the labor theory of value to explain the rate of profit in terms of labor value been seriously challenged, but even within the terms of the labor theory of value, the specific claim that there is any tendency for the "organic composition of capital" to rise indefinitely (and thus for the rate of profit to have a tendency to fall) has been shown to be at best very problematic and at worst simply wrong.

There may, of course, be other kinds of dynamic tendencies within capitalism, besides the hypothesized tendency of the rate of profit to fall, which could potentially provide a basis for predicting the eventual socialist transformation of capitalism. Indeed, Marx himself often advanced other arguments besides the strong theory of capitalist nonviability driven by the falling rate of profit, most notably his frequent reference to the contradiction between the increasing social character of production and the enduring private character of capitalist appropriation. The increasing social character of production signaled the increasing capacity of workers themselves to organize production and deploy the means of production for the satisfaction of human needs and the expression of human creative energies; the enduring private appropriation by capitalists blocked the realization of this potential by directing production towards the goal of private profits and the expansion of capital.[23] The tendency for this "contradiction" to increase does not itself depend upon the falling rate of profit (although the falling rate of profit would render this contradiction more destabilizing); it merely depends upon a claim about the trajectory of organizational forms of capitalist production. Socialism, then, becomes the solution to this contradiction by creating a new social form of appropriation compatible with the already developed social character of production.

G.A. Cohen also elaborates a view of capitalist development and its "distinctive contradictions" that does not hinge on the falling rate of profit.[24] He proposes that while capitalism may not actually fetter the sheer *growth* of the forces of production in the manner postulated in historical materialism, it fetters the *rational use* of those forces of production (through waste, a bias for consumption over leisure, ecological damage, etc.). What Cohen calls "use fettering," then, could provide the rationale for socialism, at least if one were convinced that socialism would "unfetter" the rational use of the means of production.

Marx may be correct that as capitalism develops there is an increasing contradiction between social production and private appropriation, and Cohen may well be correct that capitalism suffers increasingly from use fettering. But these processes would only lead one to predict the eventual triumph of socialism if it could also be shown that they constituted powerful motivations for people (especially workers) to struggle to overthrow capitalism in favor of socialism. In the case of the theory of the tendency of the falling rate of profit, much weaker motivational assumptions are needed, since in the long run capitalism itself becomes unreproducible. Neither of the alternative formulations of capitalism's distinctive contradictions – social production/private appropriation and use fettering – by themselves imply that capitalism as an economic system has any tendency to become unsustainable, and thus they only become effective arguments for socialism (let alone communism) if socialism can be shown to be superior to capitalism. This, again, requires a positive theory of the viability of the emancipatory alternative to capitalism.

---

23. In Marx's words from volume III of *Capital*: "The contradiction between the general social power into which capital develops, on the one hand, and the private power of the individual capitalist over these social conditions of production, on the other, becomes ever more irreconcilable . . . "

24. G.A. Cohen, *Karl Marx's Theory of History: a defense*, Princeton 1978.

This failure to develop a convincing theory of the fatal fettering of the forces of production in capitalism matters because, as already suggested, it is a far from simple task to demonstrate convincingly the practical superiority of socialism over capitalism, particularly in the aftermath of the collapse of social experiments carried out in the name of socialism. Capitalism may be damaging to masses of people, oppressive and exploitative; it may embody contradictions between the deeply social-cooperative character of its productive forces and its system of private appropriation; and it may block the rational deployment of those forces of production to meet human needs. Yet people may still prefer actually existing capitalism to an alternative with uncertain characteristics and dynamics whose viability is open to serious challenge by sympathetic (let alone hostile) critics. In the absence of a credible theory of the inherent tendency for capitalism to move towards catastrophic collapse, a positive theory of the viability of socialism and communism becomes essential.

The importance of this task is widely recognized by socialists. Even in the heyday of the intellectual sway of relatively deterministic versions of Marxism, there was some discussion of the problem of the design of socialist institutions and of the conditions under which socialism could be sustainable. In recent years there has been a proliferation of serious theoretical and empirical work exploring these issues. No comparable body of theory and research on the problem of the viability of eliminating gender oppression has yet developed within feminism. This is *not* an indictment of the theoretical work of contemporary feminists. Rather, it is a reflection of the different theoretical agendas imposed by the differences in two emancipatory projects.

Inplications for the Form of Explanatory Theory

At the core of the Marxist tradition is a set of quasi-deterministic theories in which the "laws of motion" of social systems tend to propel social change along specific trajectories. Sometimes these deterministic arguments are relatively strong, as in classical historical materialism. Other times they are considerably weakened, taking the form of arguments about underlying tendencies and counter-tendencies which only generate probabilities of particular courses of development rather than unique paths. And sometimes – especially in certain strands of contemporary Marxism – determinism is rejected altogether in favor of a theoretical framework emphasizing the open interplay of structure and agency. Capitalism, as a result, is seen as having no inherent tendencies of development. Even in this case, however, anti-deterministic arguments are constantly in a dialogue with the more deterministic (sometime called "economistic") variants of Marxism, since determinism is such an integral part of this intellectual tradition.

Feminism, in contrast, has characteristically taken the form of a much more agent-centered theory, in which there is no particular tendency for social change to move along a given trajectory. With a few exceptions, feminists do not posit "laws of motion" of patriarchy of even a probabilistic character towards self-destruction. The prospects for women's liberation depend crucially on consciousness raising and on culturally oriented emancipatory struggles. The problem of determinism is generally not a central preoccupation.[25]

If the analysis of this chapter is correct, then perhaps one of the reasons why Marxism has often taken a relatively deterministic form is precisely because such deterministic arguments helped to pre-empt a serious problem confronting emancipatory class theories, namely the credibility of the radical egalitarian alternative embodied in the revolutionary project. Marx certainly relied heavily on the "scientific" argument that socialism is the necessary culmination of laws of motion of capitalism as a way of discrediting and dismissing the moral arguments for socialism of the "utopian socialists" and the various proposals extant in his era for blueprints of a socialist society. Workers would join the revolution because socialism is inevitable and hastening its arrival was in their interests, not because of an abstract belief in its morality or the credibility of its institutional design.[26]

---

25. There are, of course, some feminists who deploy more deterministic frameworks for analyzing variations in gender relations, especially within those strands of feminist theory that are most heavily influenced by the Marxist tradition. For example, although she clearly rejects class determinism, Mary O'Brien, in *The Politics of Reproduction*, Boston 1981, translates the Marxist notion of a "dialectic" between the forces and relations of production into an account of the dialectic of forces and relations of reproduction to produce a relatively deterministic account of the transformation of gender relations. A similar kind of argument is found in Shulamith Firestone, *The Dialectic of Sex*, New York 1971. Judith Chafetz's book, *Gender Equity: an Integrated Theory of Stability and Change*, Newbery Park 1990, is a more sociological work on gender inequality that also has a somewhat deterministic cast. These kinds of deterministic arguments, however, are outside of the central thrust of most feminist theory which emphasizes the relatively open, non-deterministic character of the future of gender relations.

26. It might seem a paradox that workers would join a movement for socialism when they believed that capitalism will destroy itself by its own internal dynamics, thus making socialism inevitable. G.A. Cohen, in *History, Labour and Freedom*, Oxford 1989, explains this paradox by arguing that the prediction of the inevitable demise of capitalism is itself made on the basis of the theory of workers' rational agency. That is, the supersession of capitalism by socialism is inevitable precisely because workers respond to the conditions of capitalism in a rational way. The analysis presented here goes further than Cohen's argument by arguing that the *theory* of the inevitability of the demise of capitalism was essential for rending socialism/communism credible, and that workers would therefore be less likely to join a revolutionary movement if they feel that the viability of socialism is an open question.

Feminist theory does not so acutely face this problem, and thus feminists have less reason to be attracted to such deterministic theoretical currents. Given that the emancipatory project has relatively high existential validity to feminists, and given the plausibility of extrapolating from individual micro-level experiences to society as a whole, the viability of a society without gender domination and oppression is generally not viewed as deeply problematic by people who share the normative commitments of feminists. There is thus no pressure from the emancipatory goals of feminism to come up with a deterministic theory of the internal contradictions of patriarchy which push it on a trajectory towards its self-destruction.

Whether or not these differences in the nature of their emancipatory projects actually help explain the tendencies towards determinism in Marxian socialist theory and non-determinism in feminism, the fact remains that historical materialism did provide a convenient solution to a very difficult problem for Marxist theory. The theoretical advances in recent years, however, have seriously undermined the credibility of both the General Theory of Historical Materialism and the Special Theory of Capitalist History. This certainly does not in and of itself imply that the emancipatory project of Marxism is bankrupt, nor that the explanatory capacity of Marxism as a tradition of social theory has been exhausted. But it does mean that the task of developing a more systematic, positive theory of a classless society is imperative if this emancipatory project is to regain credibility.

11

Marxism After Communism

In both the popular press and the scholarly media the collapse of regimes ruled by communist parties is often equated with the collapse of Marxism as a social theory. However, while there is unquestionably an historical linkage between Marxism and capital-C Communism, they are not interchangeable. Marxism is a tradition of social theory, albeit a social theory that has been deeply embedded in efforts to change the world. What is more, it is a tradition of social theory within which it is possible to do social science – that is, identify real causal mechanisms and understand their consequences. Capital-C Communism, on the other hand, is a particular form of social organization, characterized by the eradication or marginalization of private ownership of productive resources and high levels of centralization of political and economic power under the control of relatively authoritarian political apparatuses, the party, and the state. Such parties and states used Marxism as a legitimating ideology, but neither the collapse of those regimes, nor their failure to live up to the normative ideals of Marxism are, in and of themselves, proofs of the bankruptcy of Marxism as a tradition of social scientific practice.[1]

Indeed, there is a great irony in the claim that the demise of communist regimes based on command economies implies the demise of Marxism. The core ideas of classical Marxism as developed in the late nineteenth century would lead one to predict that attempts at revolution-

---

1. It has been argued, especially by political conservatives, that there is an inherent connection between the nature of Marxism as a social theory and the pathologies of state bureaucratic socialism. Marxism produces the Gulag. The social effects of a complex body of ideas like "Marxism," however, can never simply be derived from the logic of the theory *per se*, but are always highly contingent on the social constraints and dilemmas in which actors accepting the theory find themselves. Just as Christianity as a religious tradition played an important role in such varied social practices as the Spanish Inquisition and the American civil rights movement, so Marxism as a social theory will have different consequences for social practice depending upon the social forces and context in which it is embedded.

ary ruptures with capitalism in backward, non-industrialized countries would ultimately fail to accomplish their positive objectives. Orthodox historical materialism insisted that socialism only becomes possible when capitalism has exhausted its capacity for development of the forces of production – when it is a fetter on the future development of society's productive capacity.[2] All Marxists, including Lenin, believed this prior to the Russian Revolution. The anomaly from the point of view of classical Marxism, therefore, is not that the state bureaucratic command economies have failed and are in a process of transition to capitalism, but that they survived for as long as they did. This reflects a basic silence in classical Marxism: it contains no theory of the temporal scale of its predictions. But the important point in the immediate context is that the collapse of communist states is not a refutation of Marxism; it is at most a refutation of Leninist voluntarism, of the belief that by revolutionary will and organizational commitment it is possible to build socialism on inadequate material foundations.

Yet, even though strictly speaking the collapse of communist regimes does not imply a refutation of Marxism as a social theory, nevertheless the events of the late 1980s have helped to accelerate a growing sense of self-doubt and confusion on the part of many radical intellectuals about the viability and future utility of Marxism. I continue to believe that Marxism remains a vital tradition within which to produce emancipatory social science, but I also feel that in order for Marxism to continue to play this role it must be reconstructed in various ways. In the rest of this chapter I want to sketch briefly the basic contours of this reconstruction, focusing especially on the problem of class analysis.

Three Nodes of Marxism

Before discussing the project of reconstruction itself, it is first necessary to map out the central contours of what it is that is being reconstructed – that is, what is "Marxism"? The answer to this question, of course, can become an exercise in stupid doctrinal scholasticism: what is a *true* Marxist as opposed to a phoney Marxist. The Marxist tradition is littered with the debris of battles over this kind of question. My intention here is not to define a set of beliefs which one must hold in order to be properly counted as a "Marxist," but rather to map out the basic coordinates of the Marxist tradition as a way of giving focus to the task of reconstruction.

---

2. For the clearest and most systematic elaboration of this classical claim, see G.A. Cohen, *Karl Marx's Theory of History: a defense*, Princeton, New Jersey 1978.

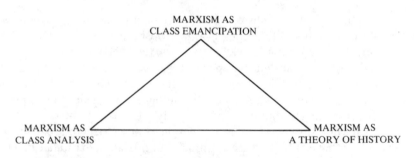

Figure 11.1   The Three Nodes of Marxism

To do this I think it is useful to see the Marxist tradition as being built around three conceptual nodes.[3] These I will call Marxism as *class analysis*,[4] Marxism as a *theory of historical trajectory*, and Marxism as an *emancipatory normative theory*. These three nodes are illustrated in Figure 11.1. Let me briefly define each of these and their interconnections, and then indicate what I see to be the central tasks of reconstruction within them.

The contrast between Marxism as class analysis and Marxism as a

---

3. There are other ways of defining the contours of the Marxist tradition. From different sides of the methodological fence Alvin Gouldner in *The Two Marxisms*, New York 1979 and Louis Althusser in *For Marx*, London 1977, for example, see the central line of demarcation within the Marxist tradition lying between deterministic-scientific Marxism and voluntarist-humanist Marxism. Others have distinguished between "vulgar Marxism" and non-reductionist Marxism. In contrast to schemas which analyze the Marxist tradition in terms of epistemological and methodological commitments, the proposal that the Marxist tradition should be mapped in terms of these three nodes emphasizes the substantive preoccupation of different styles of Marxism. For a more elaborate discussion of these nodes of Marxist theory, see Erik Olin Wright, Andrew Levine and Elliott Sober, *Reconstructing Marxism*, London 1992, chapter 8. It should be noted that in that earlier treatment the "theory of historical trajectory" node was referred to as "Marxism as scientific socialism."

4. Robert Brenner has argued (personal communication) that "class analysis" is too narrow a characterization of the "explanatory node" of Marxism. In particular, class analysis does not adequately encompass the problem of *alienation*. While alienation generated inside the capitalist labor process might be subsumed under class analysis, alienation rooted in markets and competition (also theorized under the rubric "commodity fetishism") cannot. Such alienation would exist even if we had a market economy consisting entirely of worker-owned and run cooperatives. In Brenner's view, market-generated alienation is as powerful an explanatory principle within Marxism as class-generated exploitation. He thus proposes substituting the concept of "social property relations" for "class analysis" as the encompassing term to capture the core explanatory logic of Marxism. Class analysis would then be one among several aspects of the analysis of social property relations. In my usage of the terms here, the analysis of market competition within capitalism is treated as one dimension of class analysis, namely the analysis of the forms of competitive interaction among agents *within* specific classes – labor markets for the working class and commodity markets for the capitalist class.

theory of history can be clarified by the use of an analogy from medicine. Consider the following two disciplines: endocrinology and oncology. Endocrinology is what might be called an "independent variable disci- pline." If you are an endocrinologist you are allowed to study a vast array of problems – sexuality, personality, growth, disease processes, etc. – so long as you explore the relationship between the endocrine system and those explananda. Endocrinology is disciplined in its explanatory vari- ables – the hormone system – but promiscuous in its dependent variables. Furthermore, in endocrinology it is not an embarrassment to discover that for some problems under investigation hormones turn out not to be very important. It is an advance in our knowledge of endocrinology to know what hormones do not explain, as well as to know what they do. Oncology, in contrast, is a dependent variable discipline. As an oncolo- gist you can study any conceivable cause of cancer – toxins, genetics, viruses, even psychological states. Oncology is disciplined in its depend- ent variable but promiscuous in its independent variables. And, in oncology, it is not an embarrassment to discover that certain potential causes of cancer turn out to be not very important.

In these terms, Marxism as class analysis is like endocrinology – it is independent variable Marxism – and Marxism as a theory of history is like oncology – dependent variable Marxism. As class analysts Marxists can study virtually anything. You can do a class analysis of religion, war, poverty, taste, crime. As in endocrinology, it should not be an embar- rassment to discover that class is not very important for certain problems – this, too, is an advance in our knowledge about class. For example, in a recent study on the relationship between class and the sexual division of labor in the home in the United States and Sweden, in spite of valiant efforts on my part to show that class was important, I concluded that the class composition of the household had very little to do with the distribution of housework between husbands and wives in either country. Yuppie husbands and working-class husbands did equally little work. The resulting paper, "The Noneffects of Class on the Gender Division of Labor in the Home," is, I hope, a contribution to class analysis by virtue of helping to clarify the limits of the explanatory reach of class.[5]

The distinctive dependent variable of Marxism is history or, perhaps somewhat more precisely, *historical trajectory*. In its most ambitious form this is the overall epochal trajectory of human history from the prehistory of human civilization, through the present and into the future. In its more modest form, it is the trajectory of capitalist development, from its origins within precapitalist feudal societies through its dynamic

5. *Gender and Society*, June 1992.

development and towards its eventual demise. In both cases Marxism attempts to theorize the inherent tendencies of historical change to follow a particular trajectory with a specific kind of directionality.[6]

Marxism as an emancipatory normative theory is the third, and in some ways the least elaborated, node of the Marxist tradition. Indeed, there have been Marxists – including Marx himself in places – who have denied the relevance of moral theory altogether. Nevertheless, the emancipatory dimension of Marxism is important and helps to frame much of what makes Marxist class analysis and Marxist theories of history distinctive. The heart of the emancipatory theory of Marxism is the idea that the full realization of human freedom, potential, and dignity can only be achieved under conditions of "classlessness" – the vision of a radically egalitarian society in terms of power and material welfare within which exploitation has been eliminated, distribution is based on the principle "to each according to need, from each according to ability," and the control over society's basic productive resources is vested in the community rather than in private ownership.

There are many different ways in which this egalitarian emancipatory ideal has been elaborated. Sometimes the stress is on the communitarian aspects of the ideal, sometimes on the issue of self-actualization and individual freedom, sometimes on the issue of material egalitarianism and the end of exploitation. In the strongest versions of the Marxist emancipatory vision, classlessness is treated as the necessary and sufficient condition for the realization of emancipatory goals. Most contemporary Marxists would take a more modest position, seeing classlessness as a necessary, but not sufficient, condition, thus opening the door for an autonomous role for gender and other non-class issues in a project of human emancipation. In any case, what makes these normative issues distinctively Marxist is the commitment to classlessness as the necessary condition for the realization of these values.

Working-class politics – the collective organization of social forces in pursuit of working-class interests – has traditionally constituted the unifying link among the three nodes of Marxism. The emancipatory

---

6. In these terms, Marxism is much more ambitious than Darwinian evolutionary biology in its attempts to explain historical change. Darwin never attempted to treat the trajectory of biological history as having any directional tendency of development. Its trajectory is the result of the contingent connection between accidental environmental factors and universal laws of adaptation. Classical Marxism, in contrast, argues that human history in general – or at least the history of capitalism in particular – has a relatively determinate trajectory. In this sense, the Marxist theory of history more resembles the theory of the development of a single organism from conception to birth through maturation than it resembles the theory of evolution. For a systematic comparison of the Marxist theory of historical materialism and the Darwinian theory of biological evolution, see Wright, Levine, and Sober, chapter 3.

normative theory defines the ultimate values of radical working-class politics; the theory of history generates its broad, long-term objectives; and class analysis provides the basis for its strategies. If the point is actively to change the world, not merely to interpret it, then Marxism is above all about using *class analysis* to understand the political processes for the realization of *historically* possible *emancipatory* goals.

The Interconnections among the Three Nodes of Marxism

The interconnections among these nodes are an essential part of what makes Marxism a distinctive intellectual enterprise.[7] Consider class analysis. What is most distinctively "Marxist" about Marxist class analysis? It is not the view that capitalists and workers exist in a class relation based on ownership of the means of production and sale of labor power. Nor is it the claim that this relation generates material inequalities and conflicts. This much one finds in Weber's class analysis. The crucial property of Marxist class analysis which differentiates it from Weberian analysis is its linkage to the normative problem of class emancipation and a theory of historical trajectory. The emancipatory normative theory is directly implicated in one of the core concepts of Marxist class analysis: exploitation. "Exploitation" is simultaneously an explanatory concept and a morally charged term. As an explanatory concept, exploitation is meant to identify one of the central mechanisms through which class structure explains class conflict. Class relations are thought to explain conflict in part because classes do not simply have *different* material interests which are contingently conflictual; their material interests are *intrinsically antagonistic* by virtue of being based on exploitation. Identifying such class relations as exploitative also implies a moral judgment about the inequalities generated within those relations. Exploitation does not simply define a "transfer of labor" from one social group to another, but a transfer that is deemed unjust or illegitimate. The emancipatory ideal of radical egalitarianism – ending class exploitation – is thus implicated in the very conceptualization of class itself.

---

7. Not all Marxists would accept this characterization of the "terrain of Marxism." Some Marxists, especially those who work in the more Hegelian tradition of theorizing, would object to the language of "mechanisms," "independent variables," and "dependent variables." Instead, Marxism's core concepts are seen as rooted in a notion of totality which cannot be meaningfully decomposed into "causes" and "effect." Still, even in Hegelian Marxism, class analysis figures prominently in the conceptualization of the totality, and the central point of theorizing the totality is to understand the "unfolding of history" towards the emancipation of the proletariat. Hegelian Marxism can therefore be seen as engaging these three nodes albeit with a very different philosophical stance towards the problem of theoretical construction than the one I am using here.

One could, of course, construct a form of class analysis in which the concept of classlessness was simply a normative ideal of radical egalitarianism without any belief in the possibility of achieving this normative ideal. This would give the class analysis a moral edge, but there would be no implication that this alternative to capitalism was actively posed by capitalism itself. This is where the link between class analysis and the theory of historical trajectory comes in. The theory of history attempts to show that there are inherent tendencies inside capitalism which pose socialism as an alternative. There are various forms of such claims, from highly deterministic ones (capitalism necessarily destroys itself through its own contradictions and is inevitably superseded by socialism) to much softer versions, in which the development of capitalism simply poses the possibility of socialism, perhaps making that possibility more and more viable, but not more and more of a necessity. In any case, this link between class analysis, class emancipation, and historical trajectory is crucial for the distinctive, critical force of Marxism: class analysis is not just a moral condemnation of capitalism rooted in its link to an emancipatory ideal; it is also an empirical critique of capitalism rooted in its account of the historical generation of real alternatives.

In classical Marxism, these three theoretical nodes mutually reinforced each other in an extremely tight manner. Marxism as class emancipation identified the disease in the existing world. Marxism as class analysis provided the diagnosis of its causes. Marxism as the theory of historical trajectory identified cure. Without class analysis and the theory of history, the emancipatory critique of capitalism would simply be a moral condemnation – what Marx derisively called "utopian socialism" – while without the emancipatory objective, class analysis would simply be an academic speciality. The three nodes constituted a unitary theory in which class analysis provided the necessary and sufficient explanatory principles for the theory of historical trajectory towards an emancipatory future. The enormous appeal of Marxism came in part from the unity of these three elements, for together they provided a seemingly firm basis for the conviction that eliminating the miseries and oppression of the existing world was not simply a utopian fantasy, but a practical political project.

In recent years, along with a considerable deepening of our understanding of each of these nodes taken separately, there has been a gradual erosion of their unity and integration. Today, relatively few Marxists still believe that class analysis alone provides a sufficient set of causes for understanding the historical trajectory of capitalism, and even fewer feel that this historical trajectory is such that the likelihood of socialism has an inherent tendency to increase with capitalist development. From a comprehensive and relatively self-contained paradigm of social science which aspired to explain all social phenomena relevant to emancipatory social change. Marxism is moving towards a more loosely coupled conceptual framework that provides an account of a range of specific causal mechanisms that help explain those phenomena.

This decline in the integration of its theoretical components has contributed to the sense of intellectual crisis in the Marxist tradition. The loosening of its theoretical structure, however, need not signal the impending demise of Marxism; on the contrary, the less rigid framework may open up new avenues of theoretical development within each of the nodes of the Marxist tradition. Such a reconstruction is especially important given the intellectual climate created by the collapse of the command economies ruled by communist parties.

The Challenge to Marxism Posed by the Collapse of Communism

Even though a good case can be made that the collapse of the command economies is consistent with the predictions of classical Marxism, these great historical transformations nevertheless pose a challenge for all three nodes of Marxism. The Marxist emancipatory ideal, the theory of history, and Marxist class analysis all depend in one way or another on the plausibility of socialism as an alternative to capitalism. If the collapse of these regimes undermines the theoretical arguments about the feasibility of transcending private property and capitalist class relations, then these elements of Marxism are seriously threatened. While the demise of the command economies does not prove that there are no viable emancipatory alternatives to capitalism, it does potentially call such claims into question, depending upon one's diagnosis of exactly why the command economies reached such a crisis and impasse.

Neo-Marxists had been very critical of the Soviet Union long before the present attempt to construct capitalism. The guts of the standard neo-Marxist critique revolved around the problem of democracy: in the absence of meaningful democracy, socialist economic institutions could not be constructed and sustained. Many neo-Marxists thus felt that a profound democratization of social and political institutions would be able to lend viability to the socialist project, at least under conditions of highly developed forces of production. Rather than seeing the core problem of command economies as the absence of private ownership of capital, we argued that it lay in the absence of workers' democracy.

Hardly anyone in Russia and Eastern Europe seems to believe this. What is more, many radical intellectuals in the West who share the egalitarian values traditionally associated with Marxism are also today skeptical about the viability of democratic socialism, let alone commun-

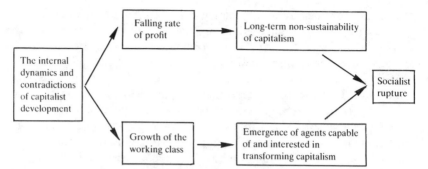

Figure 11.2   Traditional Marxist Argument for Socialism

ism.[8] Even if one believes that the empirical evidence remains highly ambiguous on these matters, it is difficult nevertheless to sustain the concepts of socialism and communism with the certainty that once characterized Marxism. Without such concepts, however, the whole enterprise of Marxist class analysis falters.

As explained in the last chapter, classical Marxism had a brilliant solution to the problem of establishing the credibility of socialism as a form of social production: it turned the problem upside down and tried to prove the long-term *non*viability of capitalism. The story is quite familiar, as illustrated in Figure 11.2. It is based on two causal chains, both rooted in the internal dynamics of capitalist development. One causal chain leads from the contradictions of capitalist development through the falling rate of profit to the fettering of the forces of production within capitalism and thus the long-term non-sustainability of capitalism; the other causal chain leads through the growth of the working class to the increasing capacity of agents capable of transforming capitalism. The coincidence of these two causal chains makes a rupture in capitalism desirable and possible.

If this story were correct, then it would perhaps be less essential to have a positive theory of socialism as an alternative to capitalism. If capitalism is non-reproducible in the long run and if agents exist (workers) who have a clear interest in democratic control over social production and a capacity to seize power, then perhaps the problem of demonstrating the viability of socialism can be bracketed. Unfortunately, both of the causal chains in this argument no longer seem secure, even to many theorists still working within the Marxist tradition. The

---

8. The issue here is not socialism as an immediately achievable political project, but its viability as a successful, sustainable alternative to developed capitalism under any plausible historical conditions.

thesis of the long-term non-reproducibility of capitalism – the inherent, endogenous tendency towards deepening, and eventually catastrophic, crises rooted in the falling rate of profit – is certainly problematic, as is the claim that capitalism produces a sufficiently homogeneous class of proletarians to constitute its gravediggers.

In this context, then, the failure of the command economies and the tentative embrace of capitalism by many people in those societies is troubling to democratic socialists. While these societies were not socialist in the sense of society's productive resources being democratically controlled by workers, they had suppressed capitalist property, and their failure is thus consistent with the claim that private ownership of capital is essential for incentives and efficiency in developed economies.

The future of Marxism thus faces two significant challenges: first, there is the theoretical challenge posed by developments within radical social theory, including the Marxist tradition itself, which have led to a rejection of totalizing versions of Marxism, and second, there is the political challenge posed by the dramatic historical developments of recent years which call into question the feasibility of a critical theory normatively anchored in socialism. Some people might think that these challenges will ultimately lead towards a dissolution of Marxism as a coherent intellectual tradition. There are certainly voices in the post-Marxist, post-modernist camp who reject all explanatory ambitions for class analysis as epistemologically illegitimate and believe that efforts of reconstructing Marxism are last-gasp efforts by recalcitrants unwilling to face the facts. Such counsels of despair should, I believe, be resisted. While there may be no going back to the confident assurances of Marxism as a comprehensive paradigm of everything, it is also the case that any serious attempt to understand the causes of oppressions in order to enhance the political projects aimed at their elimination must include as part of its core agenda the analysis of class. And for this, a reconstruction of Marxism is essential.

In what follows I will briefly discuss ways of recasting the tasks of each of the nodes of the Marxist tradition, and then turn to a more sustained discussion of certain problems in class analysis.

Reconstructing the Nodes of Marxism

Marxism as the theory of historical trajectory

The central *function* of the theory of historical trajectory within Marxism is to provide a grounding for the claim that socialism – and ultimately communism – are not simply moral ideals, but empirically viable alternatives to capitalism. Historical trajectory was taken as an explanandum not primarily for its own sake as an object of intellectual curiosity, but because it provided the foundation for scientific socialism.

The question, then, is whether this function can be satisfied without embracing the problems of trying to construct such an ambitious theory of history. Two departures from the traditional model are particularly promising.[9] First, the explanandum can be shifted from historical *trajectory* to historical *possibility*. Instead of trying to explain the overall trajectory of human history, or even the trajectory of capitalism, as a more or less determinate sequence of stages, it may be more useful to focus on the ways in which alternative futures are opened up or closed off by particular historical conditions. A theory of historical possibility might develop into a stronger theory of historical trajectories, but it does not presume that sequences follow a single trajectory as opposed to a variety of possible trajectories.

Second, instead of understanding historical variation in terms of discrete, qualitatively discontinuous modes of production as in classical Marxism, historical variation can be analyzed in terms of more complex patterns of decomposition and recombination of elements of modes of production.

Consider capitalism and socialism. Capitalism is a society within which capitalists own the means of production and workers own their labor power; socialism is a society within which workers collectively own the means of production while still individually owning their labor-power. In traditional Marxist conceptions of modes of production you have either one or the other, except perhaps in periods of unstable transition. (Of course, in a socialist society one might still have vestiges of some capitalist enterprises and in a capitalist society there can be some state enterprises and even worker-owned enterprises, but any given unit of production would be capitalist or socialist.)

An alternative conceptualization sees the category of "ownership" as consisting of a complex set of rights and powers, and entertains the possibility that these rights and powers can be broken apart, that they need not form a unitary gestalt. Within a given system of production, certain rights can be socialized while others remain private. Individual firms can therefore have a mixed ownership character. Even in American capitalism, the heartland of relatively pure capitalism, certain aspects of private property rights are partially socialized through such things as health and safety regulations and environmental protection. Such a situation, as suggested in chapter 6, might be termed an "interpene-

---

9. For an extended discussion of these and other modifications of classical historical materialism, see Wright, Levine, and Sober, chapter 5.

tration" of modes of production. Rather than seeing the historical trajectory of capitalism primarily in terms of the ruptural division of capitalism versus socialism, this way of thinking about economic structure opens up the possibility for a much wider set of variations among capitalisms and socialisms in which different patterns of interpenetration become the salient problem for analysis. In analyzing the historical development of capitalist societies, then, the issue becomes one of trying to theorize the development of different trajectories (in the plural) of such interpenetrations of modes of production.

Marxism as a theory of class emancipation

The shift in the account of historical variation from a sequence of discrete modes of production to patterns of interpenetration of modes of production suggests a parallel shift in the normative theory of class emancipation. Instead of seeing "classlessness" as the practical normative principle motivating Marxist theory, this principle might better be thought of as "less classness." This implies a shift from an idealized end state to a variable process. Capitalisms vary in the degree of exploitation and inequality that characterizes their class structures and in the extent to which socialist elements have interpenetrated the system of production. Private ownership of capital can be more or less constrained through democratic empowerment of workers, and through socialized control over various dimensions of property rights. Classlessness still remains as a utopian vision, but the operative norm that provides the basis for the empirical critique of existing institutions is the reduction in classness.

A focus on less classness also opens the door for a much broader variety of theoretical models of practical emancipatory objectives. Let me give two recent examples. As discussed in chapter 7, one proposal for the reform of the welfare state in advanced capitalism is to replace most income-support programs with an unconditional "basic income grant" (or BIG).[10] The idea is quite simple: every citizen is given a subsistence grant of basic income sufficient to have a "historically and morally" decent standard of living, unconditional on the performance of any contribution to the society. The grant of basic income is like the grant of basic education and basic health: a simple right of citizenship. Such a grant effectively breaks the linkage between separation from the means

---

10. A particularly lively discussion of basic income was launched by the publication of an essay by Robert Van der Veen and Philippe Van Parijs, "A Capitalist Road to Communism," *Theory and Society*, no. 15, 1986, pp. 635–55. For a provocative collection of essays evaluating the normative and practical issues involved in basic income, see Philippe Van Parijs (ed.), *Arguing for Basic Income: ethical foundations for a radical reform*, London 1992.

of production and separation from the means of subsistence which is the hallmark of proletarianization in capitalism. Marxists, following Marx, have always assumed that it was inherent in capitalism that, by virtue of the separation from ownership of the means of production, workers would also be separated from the means of subsistence and would thus be forced to work for a living. This is what it means to call workers "proletarians." What the BIG proposal hopes to accomplish is a significant erosion of the coercive character of capitalism by making work much more voluntary, and thus at least partially deproletarianizing the working class. There are, of course, many possible objections, both ethical and practical, to BIG. The point here is that this kind of proposal is opened up within a reconstructed theory of class emancipation once the normative core is understood in terms of less classness, rather than exclusively in terms of classlessness.

A second illustration of the new kinds of models of emancipatory objectives is represented in John Roemer's controversial work on the problem of public ownership and the meaning of "socialism."[11] Roemer argues that it is inconceivable that any technologically advanced society can function with the minimum necessary efficiency without a substantial role for markets in both consumption goods and capital. He therefore believes that the idea of a centrally planned socialism is no longer viable. But how can you have real markets, especially in capital, without having private ownership? How can the idea of "market socialism" be made coherent? His proposal is basically quite simple. Very briefly, it amounts to creating two kinds of money in a society – money for the purchase of consumption goods and money for the purchase of ownership rights in firms (stock-money). Stock-money is initially distributed equally to all adults and a mechanism exists for the individuals in each new cohort of adults to receive their per capita share of stock-money. The two kinds of money are non-convertible; you cannot cash in your wealth in commodity money for stock-money. This prevents people who have a high income from their jobs becoming wealthy owners. You are allowed to buy and sell stocks with your stock-money, and thus there is a stock market. Firms obtain new capital through loans from banks, which are publicly owned.

There are various other details and refinements of this idea, but basically it amounts to creating a mechanism in which it becomes impossible for people to become wealthy owners of the means of production. Ownership is "socialized" in the sense that every person has

---

11. See John Roemer, "Can there be Socialism after Communism?" *Politics and Society*, no. 20, 1992, pp. 261–76 and *A Future for Socialism*, Cambridge, Mass. 1992.

close to the per capita share of ownership of means of production and credit institutions are democratically controlled. In other respects, markets function with only the usual kinds of regulations one finds in capitalist economies.

Is this socialism? Does it further the emancipatory goals that socialists have traditionally supported? These are important and controversial questions. But again, as in the case of BIG, models of this sort enter the purview of a normative theory of class emancipation once the preoccupation shifts to less classness.

Marxism as class analysis

To understand the tasks facing a reconstructed class analysis it is useful to distinguish between two understandings of what class analysis can realistically hope to achieve. Consider the problem of explaining various aspects of gender oppression – let's say the unequal division of labor in the home. One view is that Marxists should aspire to a general class *theory* of gender and thus of gender inequalities. To return to the analogy between Marxism and medicine, this would be equivalent to proposing an endocrinological theory of cancer in which hormones would be viewed as the most fundamental determinant of cancer. Similarly, a class theory of gender oppression implies that class is in some sense understood as the most fundamental or important cause of gender oppression. This need not imply that all aspects of gender oppression are explainable by class; rather it suggests that at an appropriate level of abstraction, class explains the most important properties of gender oppression.

An alternative view is that Marxists should engage in the class *analysis* of gender oppression without prejudging ahead of time whether or not a full-fledged class theory of gender is achievable. A class analysis implies examining the causal connections between class and gender and their mutual impacts on various explananda, such as gender ideologies, women's poverty, or sexual violence. This implies a provisional recognition that gender processes are rooted in autonomous causal mechanisms irreducible to class, and that the task of class analysis is to deepen our understanding of their interactions in explaining specific social phenomena. Now, it may happen that out of the discoveries of the class analysis of gender oppression, it may eventually be possible to construct a class theory of such oppression. While such an eventuality seems unlikely given our present knowledge of these processes, it is not logically precluded.

Reconstructing class analysis, therefore, involves a shift from an a priori belief in the primacy of class in social explanations to a more open stance toward exploring the causal importance of class. It might appear that this way of treating class analysis relegates class to the status of simply one factor among many. Does this not lead to a kind of causal pluralism characteristic of some currents in "post-modernist" social theory, in which everything causes everything and nothing is accorded special explanatory importance?[12] Such a conclusion might be warranted if we had recently arrived from outer space and never studied anything about human social life. The fact is, however, that we know a great deal about social life, both from casual observation and from systematic research, and one of the things we know is that class is massively important for understanding many social phenomena. Class is a powerful causal factor because of the way in which class determines access to material resources and thus affects the use of one's time, the resources available to pursue one's interests, and the character of one's life experience within work and consumption. Class thus pervasively shapes both material interests and capacities for action. This is to suggest not that class is universally the most important determinant of everything social, but that it is presumptively important for a very wide range of phenomena. More specifically, class is likely to be especially important in explaining the possibilities for and obstacles to human emancipation, since on virtually any construal of the problem, emancipation requires fundamental reorganizations of the use of society's material resources, surplus, and time. Such projects, therefore, inevitably involve in a central way class politics – political struggles over property relations and control of the social surplus. The central task of class analysis, then, is to give greater precision to the causal structure of class phenomena and the relationship between class and other social phenomena relevant to the normative goals of Marxism.

Elements of a Reconstructed Class Analysis

My work on reconstructing class analysis has revolved around a relatively simple model of the interconnections among the core concepts of class analysis: class structure, class formation, and class struggle. This model is illustrated in Figure 11.3. The basic idea of this model, as explained in chapter 3, is that class structures impose *limits* upon, but do not uniquely determine, both class formations (i.e. the collective organization of class forces) and class struggles; class formations *select* class struggles within

---

12. Or, in some versions of post-modernist social theory, nothing explains anything and everything is simply a matter of perspective.

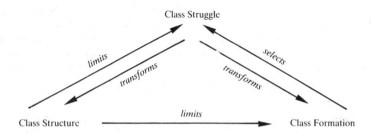

Figure 11.3 Model of Class Structure, Class Formation and Class Struggle

the limits imposed by class structures; class struggles in turn have *transformative* impacts on both class structures and class formations.[13] This is not a purely structural model, for the conscious practices of actors – class struggles – transform the social structures which limit those practices. But it is also not an agent-centered model, for those struggles are seen as systematically constrained by the structures within which people live and act. Structures limit practices, but within those limits practices transform structures.

This model defines, at best, an agenda of problems to be solved. Content needs to be put into each of the terms and mechanisms need to be elaborated for each of the connections specified in the model. My own work on these issues has been preoccupied primarily with one element of the model: class structure. I have argued that in order to have a solid foundation for understanding the relationship between class structure and class formation, and of both of these to class struggles, we first need a coherent concept of class structure. Traditional Marxist concepts of class structure suffered, I have argued, from two major problems. First, they were too *abstract* for many empirical problems. The conventional Marxist concept of class structure posits polarized, antagonistic classes defined within pure modes of production – slaves and slavemasters, lords and serfs, capitalists and workers. But for many concrete empirical problems, many locations in the class structure, especially those loosely called the "middle class," do not seem to fit such a polarized view of classes. Second, traditional Marxist concepts of class structure tended to be too macro. They described the overall structures of societies, but did not adequately map onto the lives of individuals. My objective, then, was to

---

13. The model in Figure 11.3 can be considered the core macro-model of class analysis. There is a parallel micro-model which links class *locations* to class *consciousness* and class *practices* of individuals.

produce a Marxist concept of class structure which would link concrete and micro-levels of analysis to the more abstract macro-concepts.

I will illustrate this problem of concept formation through two specific conceptual issues: the problem of the *middle class* and the problem of *class alliances*.[14]

The middle class

The "middle class" poses an immediate problem for Marxist class analysis: if the abstract concept of class structure is built around polarized classes, what does it mean to be in the "middle?" In the 1970s, when I began to work on this problem, there was, in my judgment, no satisfactory answer to this question. I proposed a new concept as a way of dealing with these kinds of locations: *contradictory locations within class relations*. The basic logic was quite simple. Previous attempts at solving the problem of the middle class all worked on the assumption that a given micro-*location* within the class structure (a location filled by an individual) had to be in one and only one class. Thus the middle class was treated as part of the working class (a new working class), part of the petty bourgeoisie (a new petty bourgeoisie), or as an entirely new class in its own right (a professional-managerial class). I argued that there was no need to make this assumption. Why not entertain the possibility that some class locations – jobs actually performed by individuals – were simultaneously located in more than one class? Managers, for example, could be viewed as simultaneously capitalists and workers – capitalists in so far as they dominated the labor of workers, workers in so far as they did not own the means of production and sold their labor-power to capitalists.

The idea of contradictory locations seemed to provide a more coherent solution to the problem of the middle class, a solution that was consistent with both the abstract polarized class concept and the concrete complexities of real class structures. Nevertheless, there were a number of significant conceptual problems with this approach.[15] This led me in the mid 1980s to propose a second solution to the problem of the middle class. This solution revolved around the concept of "exploitation."

---

14. In the original version of this chapter published in the *New Left Review*, a third problem was discussed, the problem of the so-called "underclass." Since the discussion of the underclass appears in the final section of chapter 2 above, it has been deleted here.

15. These problems are discussed at length in Erik Olin Wright, *Classes*, London 1985, chapter 2. The most salient of them is that the concept of domination replaced exploitation as the core criterion for class locations within the concept of "contradictory locations."

Exploitation can be loosely defined as a process by which one group is able to appropriate part of the social surplus produced by another group. Any society, I argued, is characterized by a variety of mechanisms of exploitation. Capitalist societies do not simply have distinctively capitalist forms of exploitation based on unequal ownership of means of production. They also contain what I called, based on the work of John Roemer, "skill exploitation" and "organization exploitation."[16] In skill exploitation, owners of scarce skills are able to extract a rent component in their wages. This is basically a component of the wage above and beyond the costs of producing and reproducing the skills themselves.[17] It thus embodies part of the social surplus. In organization exploitation, managers are able to appropriate part of the surplus through the power which they command inside the bureaucratic structures of capitalist production. Using this notion of differentiated mechanisms of exploitation, the "middle class" could be defined as those locations in the class structure which were exploited on one mechanism of exploitation but were exploiters on another. Professional and technical employees, for example, can be seen as capitalistically exploited but skill exploiters. They thus constitute "contradictory locations within exploitation relations."

Both of these proposals break with the idea that individual class locations must have a homogeneous class character, and in this way they introduce greater concrete complexity than earlier concepts of "class location." In other respects, however, both of these proposals still adopt a quite restricted view of what it means to occupy a class "location." In particular, they both define locations statically and restrict the concept of class locations to jobs. A fully elaborated micro-concept of how individual lives are tied to class structure needs to break with these restrictions by developing the idea of *mediated* class locations and *temporal* class locations.[18]

---

16. See John Roemer, *A General Theory of Class and Exploitation*, Cambridge, Mass. 1982.

17. The concept of "surplus" is not easy to define rigorously. The conventional idea in the Marxist tradition is that the total social product can be divided into two parts. One part – the necessary product – is the part needed to cover all of the costs of production, including the costs of producing workers (or, as Marxists have traditionally called it, the "value of labor-power"). The surplus, then, is the difference between the total product and the necessary product. The difficulty with this definition comes in when we try to define precisely the "costs of producing labor-power." If such costs are equated with the empirical wages of employees, then, by definition, no employee can be an exploiter. If, however, wages are seen as potentially containing "rents" derived from various kinds of barriers to entry in labor markets, then wages can contain pieces of surplus.

18. For a more extensive discussion on the concepts of mediated and temporal class locations, see my essay "Rethinking, Once Again, the Concept of Class Structure," chapter 8 in Erik Olin Wright et al., *The Debate on Classes*, London 1989.

The concept of mediated class locations recognizes that people are linked to the class structure through social relations other than their immediate "jobs." People live in families, and via their social relations to spouses, parents and other family members, they may be linked to different class interests and capacities. This problem is particularly salient in households within which both husbands and wives are in the labor force but may occupy different job-classes. A schoolteacher married to a business executive has a different "mediated" class location than a schoolteacher married to a factory worker. For certain categories of people – full-time housewives and children, for example – mediated class locations may be the decisive way in which their lives are linked to class. For others, mediated class locations may be less salient. In any case, the patterning of mediated class locations is potentially an important way in which class structures vary.

Temporal class locations refer to the fact that many jobs are embedded in career trajectories which in various ways involve changes in class character. Many managers, for example, begin as non-managerial employees, but the fact that they are on a managerial career track changes the class interests tied to their statically defined location. Moreover, many middle-class employees have a sufficiently high rent component in their wage (i.e. earnings above what is needed to reproduce their labor-power) that they can turn a significant amount of savings into capital through various kinds of investments. Such a capitalization of employment rents is itself a special kind of temporal dimension to class locations, for it enables highly paid middle-class employees over time to tie their class interests directly to the bourgeoisie. This does not mean that they become capitalists, but rather that their class location assumes an increasingly capitalist character over time.

All of these complexities are attempts at defining systematically the linkages between individual lives and the class structure in ways that enrich the general mode of determination in Figure 11.3. In that model, class structures are seen as imposing limits on the process of class formation. There are two basic mechanisms through which this limitation occurs: first, class structures shape the material interests of individuals and thus make it more or less difficult to organize certain arrays of class locations into collective organizations; and second, class structures shape the access to material resources and thus affect the kinds of resources that can be deployed by collective organizations within class struggles. Both of the proposed concepts of the middle class, as well as the concepts of mediated class locations and temporal class locations, attempt to provide a more fine-grained map of the nature of the material interests and resources available to individuals by virtue of their linkage to the class structure and thereby facilitate the analysis of the process of class formation.

Class alliances and multiclass movements

One of the main objectives in elaborating these refinements in the concept of class structure is to facilitate the analysis of class formations and class politics. One crucial dimension of class formation is the problem of class alliances. Class alliances are situations in which people from different class locations come together to engage in collective action against a common class enemy by reaching, in one way or another, some kind of compromise on the differences in their class interests. A class alliance is thus to be contrasted with what can be termed a "multiclass movement" in which the actors agree to ignore class differences in order to form a solidaristic movement for some political objective. National liberation movements, for example, frequently place class differences among their supporters on a back burner in the name of "national unity." No real attempt is made to forge a class compromise between bourgeois, middle-class, working-class, and peasant participants in the struggle. They are united in their opposition to a colonial power, but their unity is not grounded in any significant attempts at reconciling their conflicting class interests.

This contrast between multiclass movements and class alliances is, of course, somewhat stylized. Many situations involve variable mixes between these two ideal types. Nevertheless, the analytical distinction is important both politically and theoretically. In many situations, multiclass movements are easier to form than class alliances, but equally, they frequently founder by virtue of the unresolved class tensions within them. Class alliances, on the other hand, may be harder to forge, but once forged may be more durable since conflicts of interest have been compromised rather than ignored.

The various complexities in the analysis of class structure we have been discussing can help to illuminate specific problems in the formation of class alliances. Consider the problem of alliances involving the middle class with either the capitalist class or the working class. People in the middle class and the working class are both exploited by capitalists; they are both employees dependent upon the labor market for their livelihoods. They thus share some common class interests vis-à-vis capital which constitutes a basis for a class alliance. On the other hand, as skill and organization exploiters, middle-class employees earn salaries that contain a component of surplus which they are interested in protecting. Particularly when this component is large, people in the middle class have the capacity to capitalize their surplus and thus link their class interests directly to those of capitalists. These conflicting forces mean that within class struggles the middle class will be pulled between class formations involving alliances with workers or with capitalists. There are

254   INTERROGATING INEQUALITY

historical moments when the middle class seems to ally strongly with the bourgeoisie, as in Chile in the overthrow of the Allende regime, and other circumstances in which segments of the middle class forge fairly durable alliances with workers, as in Sweden in the period of the heyday of Social Democratic Party rule. An important task of class analysis is to sort out the conditions under which one or the other of these patterns of alliance occurs.

The underclass, as discussed in chapter 2, poses quite different problems for the analysis of class alliances. It might seem natural that the underclass and the working class would tend to form class alliances, but there are many obstacles to this occurring. In their efforts to protect the jobs of workers and increase their wages, the labor movement often creates barriers within labor markets which act to the disadvantage of people in the underclass. In many historical cases, the underclass has been a source of scab labor in strikes and in other ways it has been manipulated by capitalists against workers. Thus, while both workers and the underclass share an interest in the state providing job training, regulating capital, and increasing employment opportunities, in many contexts they see each other on opposing sides. Again, one of the tasks of class analysis is to understand the conditions which make solidaristic movements combining the working class and the underclass feasible.

The last twenty-five years have witnessed an extraordinary development of theory and research within the Marxist tradition. Our understanding of a host of Marxist problems – including such things as the labor theory of value, the theory of history, the dynamics of capitalist development, the transition from feudalism to capitalism, the contradictions of the capitalist state, the mechanisms of consent formation within production, and the problem of the middle class in capitalist societies – has been fundamentally transformed. These are solid achievements.

It is ironic, then, that in the context of such advances Marxism should be pronounced dead as an intellectual force in the world. Mark Twain once remarked, on reading his own obituary in the newspaper, that "the reports of my death are highly exaggerated." What look like the death throes of Marxism to hostile critics may be simply growing pains as Marxism matures as a social scientific theory of class and its effects. One thing, however, is certain: class politics will continue to be a central dimension of social struggles, since the forms of ownership and control of society's productive resources have such a pervasive impact on so many social issues. And, if class politics is a central dimension of social struggle, then class analysis will have an important role to play in developing adequate theoretical tools for radicals. What remains to be seen, however, is the extent to which such class analysis will be embedded in a broader theoretical configuration that contains the normative commitments of class emancipation and the explanatory aspirations of a theory of historical possibilities.

References

Agger, Ben, "Is Wright Wrong (Or Should Burawoy Be Buried)?: Reflections on the Crisis of the 'Crisis of Marxism'," *Berkeley Journal of Sociology*, vol. XXXIV, 1989.

Alford, Robert and Roger Friedland, *The Powers of Theory*, Cambridge, Cambridge University Press, 1985.

Althusser, Louis, "Ideology and Ideological State Apparatuses," in Althusser, *Lenin and Philosophy*, New York, Monthly Review Press, 1971.

Althusser, Louis, *For Marx*, London, New Left Books, 1977.

Aminzade, Ron, *Class, Politics, and Early Industrial Capitalism*, Binghamton, NY, SUNY Press, 1981.

Bachrach, Peter and Morton S. Baratz, "Two Faces of Power," *American Political Science Review*, vol. 51, December 1962.

Banfield, Edward, *The Unheavenly City*, New York, Little, Brown, 1970.

Becker, G.S., *The Economics of Discrimination*, Chicago, University of Chicago Press, 1971.

Becker, G.S., *Human Capital*, New York, National Bureau of Economic Research, 1975.

Bettelheim, Charles, *Economic Calculation and Forms of Property*, New York, Monthly Review Press, 1975.

Bettelheim, Charles, *Class Struggles in the USSR*, New York, Monthly Review Press, 1976.

Bhaskar, Roy, *A Realist Theory of Science*, Sussex, Harvester Press, 1978.

Bhaskar, Roy, *The Possibility of Naturalism*, Atlantic Highlands, NJ, Humanities Press, 1979.

Block, Fred, *Revising State Theory: Essays in Politics and Postindustrialism*, Philadelphia, PA, Temple University Press, 1987.

Bobbio, Norberto, "Are there Alternatives to Representative Democracy?," *Telos*, no. 35, 1978.

Bowles, Sam and Herbert Gintis, *Schooling in Capitalist America*, New York, Basic Books, 1976.

Bowles, Sam and Herbert Gintis, *Democracy and Capitalism*, New York, Basic Books, 1986.

Bowles, Sam and Herbert Gintis, "Democratic Demands and Radical Rights," *Socialist Review*, 19:4, 1989.

Bowles, Sam and Herbert Gintis, "Contested Exchange," *Politics & Society*, 18:2, pp. 165–222, June 1990.

Brenner, Bob, "The Agrarian Roots of European Capitalism," in T.H. Aston and C.H.E. Philpon (eds), *The Brenner Debate*, Cambridge, Cambridge University Press, 1985.

Burawoy, Michael, "The Politics of Production and the Production of Politics," in *Political Power and Social Theory*, vol. 1, Maurice Zeitlin (ed.), Greenwich, CT, JAI Press, 1979.

Burawoy, Michael, "Terrains of Contest," *Socialist Review*, no. 58, 1981.

Burawoy, Michael, "The Hidden Abode of Underdevelopment," *Politics & Society*, 11:2, 1982.

Burawoy, Michael, *The Politics of Production*, London, Verso, 1985.

Burawoy, Michael, "The Limits of Wright's Analytical Marxism and an Alternative," *Berkeley Journal of Sociology*, vol. XXXII, 1987.

Burawoy, Michael, "Should We Give Up on Socialism?," *Socialist Review*, 19:1, pp. 58–78, 1989a.

Burawoy, Michael, "Marxism Without Micro-foundations," *Socialist Review*, 19:2, pp. 53–86, 1989b.

Burnham, James, *The Managerial Revolution*, Bloomington, Indiana University Press, 1941.

Capp, Al, *Li'l Abner Meets the Shmoo*, Princeton, WI, Kitchen Sink Press, 1992.

Carchedi, G., *Class Analysis and Social Research*, London, Basil Blackwell, 1987.

Carling, Alan, "Rational Choice Marxism," *New Left Review*, no. 160, 1986.

Chafetz, Janet, *Gender Equity: an Integrated Theory of Stability and Change*, Newberry Park, CA, Sage, 1990.

Clawson, Dan, *Bureaucracy and the Labor Process*, New York, Monthly Review Press, 1980.

Cliffe, Tony, *State Capitalism in Russia*, London, Pluto Press, 1974.

Cohen, G.A., *Karl Marx's Theory of History: a Defence*, Princeton, NJ, Princeton University Press, 1978.

Cohen, G.A., "The Labor Theory of Value and the Concept of Exploitation," *Philosophy and Public Affairs*, 8:4, pp. 338–60, 1979.

Cohen, G.A., "Reply to Elster on Marxism, Functionalism, and Game Theory," *Theory and Society*, 11:4, pp. 483–95, 1982.

Cohen, G.A., "The Structure of Proletarian Unfreedom," in John Roemer (ed.), *Analytical Marxism*, Cambridge, Cambridge University Press, 1986.

Cohen, G.A., *History, Labor and Freedom*, Oxford, Oxford University Press, 1989.

Cohen, Joshua and Joel Rogers, *On Democracy*, New York, Penguin, 1983.

Cohen, Joshua and Joel Rogers, *Secondary Associations and Democratic Governance*, Cambridge, Cambridge University Press, 1992.

Collins, Linda and Judith Stacey, "Salvation or Emancipation? Reflections on the Wright/Burawoy Exchange," *Berkeley Journal of Sociology*, vol. XXXIV, 1989.

Dahrendorf, Ralph, *Class and Class Conflict in Industrial Societies*, Stanford, CA, Stanford University Press, 1959.

Djilas, Milovan, *The New Class: an Analysis of the Communist System*, New York, Praeger, 1957.

Domhoff, G. William, *The Powers that Be*, New York, Random House, 1979.

Domhoff, G. William, *Who Rules America Now?*, Englewood Cliffs, NJ, Prentice Hall, 1983.

Domhoff, G. William, *The Power Elite and the State*, Hawthorne, NY, Aldine de Gruyter, 1990.

Eisenstein, Hester, *Contemporary Feminist Thought*, Boston, MA, G.K. Hall, 1983.

Elster, Jon, *Logic and Society*, New York, John Wiley, 1978.

Elster, Jon, "Roemer vs. Roemer," *Politics & Society,* 11:3, 1981.

Elster, Jon, *Making Sense of Marx*, Cambridge, Cambridge University Press, 1985.

Fantasi, Rick, *Cultures of Solidarity*, Berkeley, University of California Press, 1988.

Firestone, Shulamith, *The Dialectic of Sex*, New York, William Morrow, 1970.

Giddens, Anthony, *The Class Structure of the Advanced Societies*, New York, Harper & Row, 1973.

Giddens, Anthony, *A Contemporary Critique of Historical Materialism*, Berkeley, University of California Press, 1981.

Giddens, Anthony, *The Nation State and Violence*, Berkeley, University of California Press, 1985.

Gilbert, Dennis and Joseph Kahl, *The American Class Structure*, Homewood, IL, The Dorsey Press, 1982.

Goldthorpe, John H., *Social Mobility & Class Structure in Modern Britain*, Oxford, Oxford University Press, 1980.

Gouldner, Alvin, *Patterns of Industrial Bureaucracy*, Glencoe, IL, The Free Press, 1954.

Gouldner, Alvin, *The Two Marxisms*, New York, Seabury Press, 1979.

Gouldner, Alvin, *The Future of Intellectuals and the Rise of the New Class*, New York, Seabury Press, 1980.

Hartmann, Heidi, "The Unhappy Marriage of Marxism and Feminism," in Lydia Sargent (ed.), *Women and Revolution*, Boston, MA, South End Press, pp. 1–41, 1981.

Hindess, Barry and Paul Hirst, *Pre-Capitalist Modes of Production*, London, Routledge & Kegan Paul, 1976.

Hindess, Barry and Paul Hirst, *Marx's Capital and Capitalism Today*, London, Routledge & Kegan Paul, 1977.

Jacoby, Russell, *The Last Intellectuals*, New York, Basic Books, 1987.

Jaggar, Alison, *Feminist Politics and Human Nature*, Totowa, NJ, Rowan & Allenheld, 1983.

Jaggar, Alison and Paula Rothenberg Struhl (eds), *Feminist Frameworks*, New York, McGraw-Hill, 1984.

Jencks, Christopher, *Rethinking Social Policy, Race, Poverty and the Underclass*, Cambridge, MA, Harvard University Press, 1992.

Kamolnick, Paul, *Classes: a Marxist Critique*, Dix Hills, General Hall, 1988.

Konrad, George and Ivan Szelenyi, *Intellectuals on the Road to Class Power*, New York, Harcourt Brace Jovanovich, 1979.

La Vida: A Puerto Rican Family in the Culture of Poverty, New York, Random House, 1966.

Landecker, Werner S., *Class Crystallization*, New Brunswick, NJ, Rutgers University Press, 1981.

Lenski, Gerhard, *Power and Privilege*, New York, McGraw-Hill, 1966.

Levi, Margaret, *Of Rule and Revenue*, Berkeley, University of California Press, 1988.

Levine, Andrew, *Arguing for Socialism*, London, Routledge & Kegan Paul, 1984.

Levine, Andrew, *The End of the State*, London, Verso, 1987.

Levine, Andrew, Elliott Sober and Erik Olin Wright, "Marxism and Methodological Individualism," *New Left Review*, no. 162, 1987.

Levine, Andrew and Erik Olin Wright, "Rationality and Class Struggle," *New Left Review*, no. 123, 1980.

Lewis, Oscar, *Five Families: Mexican Case Studies in the Culture of Poverty*, New York, Basic Books, 1959.

Lindblom, Charles, *Politics and Markets*, New York, Basic Books, 1977.

Lukes, Steven, *Power: A Radical View*, London, Macmillan, 1974.

McMurtry, John, *The Structure of Marx's World View*, Princeton, NJ, Princeton University Press, 1978.

Mandel, Ernest, "Ten Theses on the Social and Economic Laws Governing the Society Transition Between Capitalism and Socialism," *Critique*, no. 3, 1974.

Marcuse, Herbert, *One-Dimensional Man*, Boston, MA, Beacon Press, 1964.

Marshall, Gordon, Howard Newby, David Rose and Carolyn Vogler, *Social Class in Modern Britain*, London, Hutchinson, 1988.

Marx, Karl, *Capital: A Critique of Political Economy*, vol. III, trans. Ben Fowkes, Harmondsworth, Penguin, 1976.

Miliband, Ralph, *The State in Capitalist Society*, New York, Basic Books, 1969.

Miller, Richard W., *Analyzing Marx: Morality, Power and History*, Princeton, NJ, Princeton University Press, 1984.

Mouffe, Chantal, "Hegemony and Ideology in Gramsci," in Chantal Mouffe (ed.), *Gramsci & Marxist Theory*, London, Routledge & Kegan Paul, 1979.

Murray, Charles, *Losing Ground*, New York, Basic Books, 1984.

O'Brien, Mary, *The Politics of Reproduction*, Boston, MA, Routledge & Kegan Paul, 1981.

Offe, Claus, "Structural Problems of the Capitalist State: Class Rule and the Political System: On the Selectiveness of Political Institutions," in Klaus von Beyme (ed.), *German Political Studies*, vol. 1, Newberry Park, CA, Sage, 1974.

Offe, Claus and Volker Ronge, "Theses on the Theory of the State," *New German Critique*, no. 6, Fall 1975.

Offe, Claus and Helmut Wiesenthal, "Two Logics of Collective Action: Theoretical Notes on Social Class and Organizational Form," in *Political Power and Social Theory*, vol. 1, Maurice Zeitlin (ed.), Greenwich, CT, JAI Press, pp. 67–116, 1980.

Orloff, Ann and Theda Skocpol, "Why Not Equal Protection? Explaining the Politics of Public Social Spending in Britain, 1900–1911, and the United States, 1880s–1920," *American Sociological Review*, 49:6, pp. 726–50, 1984.

Parkin, Frank, *Marxist Class Theory: a Bourgeois Critique*, New York, Columbia University Press, 1979.

Peterson, Paul E., "The Urban Underclass and the Poverty Paradox," in Christopher Jencks and Paul E. Peterson (eds), *The Urban Underclass*, Washington, DC, The Brookings Institution, pp. 3–28, 1991.

Piven, Francis Fox and Richard Cloward, *Why Americans Don't Vote*, New York, Pantheon, 1988.

Politics & Society, Special Issue on John Roemer's Theory of Class and Exploitation, 11:2, 1982.

Poulantzas, Nicos, "The Problem of the Capitalist State," New Left Review, no. 58, pp. 67–78, 1969.

Poulantzas, Nicos, *Political Power and Social Classes*, London, New Left Books, 1973.

Poulantzas, Nicos, *Classes in Contemporary Capitalism*, London, New Left Books, 1975.

Przeworski, Adam, "Material Interests, Class Compromise, and the Transition to Socialism," *Politics & Society*, 10:2, 1980a.

Przeworski, Adam, "Social Democracy as a Historical Phenomenon," *New Left Review*, no. 122, 1980b.

Przeworski, Adam, "The Material Bases of Consent: Economics and Politics in a Hegemonic System," in *Political Power and Social Theory*, vol. 1, Maurice Zeitlin (ed.), Greenwich, CT, JAI Press, 1981a.

Przeworski, Adam, "Exploitation, Class Conflict and Socialism: the Ethical Materialism of John Roemer," *Politics & Society*, 11:3, 1981b.

Przeworski, Adam, *Capitalism and Social Democracy*, Cambridge, Cambridge University Press, 1985.

Przeworski, Adam, "Class, Production, and Politics: A Reply to Burawoy," *Socialist Review*, 19:2, pp. 87–111, 1989.

Przeworski, Adam and John Sprague, *Paper Stones*, Chicago, University of Chicago Press, 1986.

Reich, Michael, *Racial Inequality*, Princeton, NJ, Princeton University Press, 1981.

Resnick, Stephen and Richard Wolff, *Knowledge and Class*, Chicago, University of Chicago Press, 1987.

Roemer, John, "New Directions in the Marxian Theory of Class and Exploitation," *Politics & Society*, 11:3, 1981.

Roemer, John, *A General Theory of Exploitation and Class*, Cambridge, MA, Harvard University Press, 1983.

Roemer, John, "Should Marxists Be Interested in Exploitation?," *Philosophy and Public Affairs*, 14, pp. 30–65, Winter 1985.

Roemer, John (ed.), *Analytical Marxism*, Cambridge, Cambridge University Press, 1986.

Roemer, John, *Free to Lose*, Cambridge, MA, Harvard University Press, 1988.

Roemer, John, "Visions of Capitalism and Socialism," *Socialist Review*, 19:3, pp. 93–100, 1989.

Roemer, John, "Can There Be Socialism After Communism?," *Politics & Society*, 20:3, 1992.

Roemer, John, *A Future for Socialism*, Cambridge, MA, Harvard University Press, 1994.

Rogers, Joel, "Don't Worry, Be Happy: Institutional Dynamics of the Postwar Decline of Private Sector U.S. Unionism," *Wisconsin Law Review*, 1990.

Rogers, Joel, *Silenced Majority*, New York, forthcoming.

Ryan, William, *Blaming the Victim*, New York, Pantheon, 1971.

Ryan, William, *Equality*, New York, Pantheon, 1981.

Skocpol, Theda, "Political Response to Capitalist Crisis: Neo-Marxist Theories of the State and the Case of the New Deal," *Politics & Society*, 10:2, 1980.

Skocpol, Theda, "Bringing the State Back in: False Leads and Promising Starts in Current Theories and Research," in Peter Evans, Theda Skocpol and Dietrich Reuschemeyer (eds), *Bringing the State Back In*, Cambridge, Cambridge University Press, pp. 3–37, 1985.

Smith, Vicki, *Managing the Corporate Interest*, Berkeley, University of California Press, 1990.

Szymanski, Al, "Racial Discrimination and White Gain," *American Sociological Review*, vol. 41, pp. 403–14, 1976.

Szymanski, Al, *Is the Red Flag Flying?*, London, Zed Press, 1979.

Therborn, Göran, *What Does the Ruling Class Do When It Rules?*, London, Verso, 1978.

Van der Veen, Robert and Philippe Van Parijs, "Capitalism, Communism, and the Realm of Freedom: A Formal Presentation," *Louvain-la-Neuve Working Paper*, no. 8501, 1985.

Van der Veen, Robert and Philippe Van Parijs, "A Capitalist Road to Communism," *Theory and Society*, 15:5, pp. 635–55, 1986.

Van Parijs, Philippe, *Evolutionary Explanation in the Social Sciences: an Emerging Paradigm*, Totowa, NJ, Rowan & Littlefield, 1981.

Van Parijs, Philippe, "A Revolution in Class Theory," in Erik Olin Wright *et al.*, *The Debate on Classes*, London, Verso, pp. 191–212, 1989.

Van Parijs, Philippe (ed.), *Arguing for Basic Income: Ethical Foundations for a Radical Reform*, London, Verso, 1992.

Wacquant, Loïc, "Social Ontology, Epistemology and Class: On Wright's and Burawoy's Politics of Knowledge," *Berkeley Journal of Sociology*, vol. XXXII, 1987.

Walker, Dick, "In Defense of Realism and Dialectical Materialism: a Friendly Critique of Wright and Burawoy's Marxist Philosophy," *Berkeley Journal of Sociology*, vol. XXXIV, 1989.

Willis, Paul, *Learning to Labour*, New York, Columbia University Press, 1981.

Wilson, William Julius, *The Declining Significance of Race*, Chicago, University of Chicago Press, 1982.

Wilson, William Julius, *The Truly Disadvantaged: The Inner City, the Underclass and Public Policy*, Chicago, University of Chicago Press, 1987.

Wood, Ellen Meiksins, "The Separation of the Economic and Political in Capitalism," *New Left Review*, no. 127, 1981.

Wright, Erik Olin, *Class, Crisis and the State*, London, New Left Books, 1978.

Wright, Erik Olin, *Class Structure and Income Determination*, New York, Academic Press, 1979.

Wright, Erik Olin, "Varieties of Marxist Conceptions of Class Structure," *Politics & Society*, 9:3, 1980.

Wright, Erik Olin, "The Status of the Political in the Concept of Class Structure," *Politics & Society*, 11:3, 1981.

Wright, Erik Olin, *Classes*, London, New Left Books/Verso, 1985.

Wright, Erik Olin, "Reflections on Classes," *Berkeley Journal of Sociology*, vol. XXXII, 1987.

Wright, Erik Olin, "The Comparative Project on Class Structure and Class Consciousness: an Overview," *Acta Sociologica*, 32:1, pp. 3–22, Spring 1989.

Wright, Erik Olin *et al.*, *The Debate on Classes*, London, Verso, 1990.

Wright, Erik Olin *et al.*, "The Non-effects of Class on the Gender Division of Labor in the Home," *Gender and Society*, 6:2, pp. 252–82, June 1992.

Wright, Erik Olin, Andrew Levine and Elliott Sober, *Reconstructing Marxism*, London, Verso, 1992.

Wright, Erik Olin and Joachim Singlemann, "Proletarianization in the American Class Structure," *American Journal of Sociology*, vol. 88, supplement, 1982.

Young, Iris, "Beyond the Unhappy Marriage: a Critique of Dual Systems Theory," in Lydia Sargent (ed.), *Women and Revolution*, Boston, MA, South End Press, pp. 43–70, 1981.

Name Index

Agger, Ben 200–01
Alford, Robert 20, 89, 93–4
Allende, Salvador 254
Althusser, Louis 54, 99, 236n
Aminzade, Ron 138
Aston, T.H. 180n

Bachrach, Peter 93n
Banfield, Edward 35
Baratz, Morton S. 93n
Bardhan, Pranab 180
Becker, G.S. 27n
Bettelheim, Charles 115n
Bhaskar, Roy 183n
Block, Fred 95
Bobbio, Norberto 98n
Bourdieu, Pierre 204n
Bowles, Sam 14, 20, 72–3, 76, 78, 80–82, 84, 87, 180, 195, 197n
Brenner, Robert 14, 180, 185, 191, 197n, 236n
Burawoy, Michael 13–14, 19, 68n, 69–70, 72, 77n, 82n, 190n, 195, 199–207
Burnham, James 116n

Capp, Al 43n
Carchedi, G. 197n
Carling, Alan 189n
Chafetz, Judith 232n
Clawson, Dan 136n
Cliffe, Tony 115n
Cloward, Richard 102n
Cohen, G.A. 14, 27n, 43n, 60n, 106n, 114n, 118, 154, 180, 185–9, 191, 226–7, 230, 232n, 235n
Cohen, Joshua 103n, 180n, 186
Collins, Linda 206

Dahrendorf, Ralph 63, 89n
Darwin, Charles 238n

Djilas, Milovan 116n

Eisenstein, Hester 217n
Elster, Jon 2, 14, 22, 91n, 154n, 180, 184nn, 189n, 191
Engels, Friedrich 200
Esping-Andersen, Gosta 104

Fantasia, Rick 80n
Firestone, Shulamith 232n
Friedland, Roger 20, 89, 93–4

Giddens, Anthony 89n, 95
Gilbert, Dennis 89n
Gintis, Herbert 20, 72–3, 76, 78, 80–82, 84, 87, 180n, 195, 197n
Goldthorpe, John H. 89n
Gordon, Linda 220n, 222n
Gouldner, Alvin 86n, 130–32, 192, 236n
Gramsci, Antonio 75, 98n, 100, 188

Hartmann, Heidi 213n
Hauser, Robert 11
Havens, A.E. 197n, 205
Hieder, Karl 4
Hindess, Barry 118n
Hirst, Paul 118n

Jacoby, Russell 197n
Jaggar, Alison 213n, 214n
Jencks, Christopher 37n

Kahl, Joseph 89n
Kamolnick, Paul 197n
Konrad, George 130–31

Lakatos, Imre 203
Landecker, Werner S. 89n
Lenin, V.I. 70, 96n, 201n, 235
Lenski, Gerhard 24, 89n

263

Subject Index

abstraction, levels of 102n, 162n
accumulation 100, 124–7, 141–2
achievement models of inequality 30
alienation 158, 236n
altruism 159
Analytical Marxism 14, 178ff.
  impact of 196–7
  main concepts of 186
  Marxist character of 191–6
  origins of 179–81
  and scientific norms 182–5
  use of models in 187–9
anarchism 156n
anomalies, scientific 203
asymmetrical reciprocity, *see*
  domination
atomization 97–8
attributes, monadic and relational 22,
  24
authority 54, 63, 76, 81, 92n

basic income grant, *see* universal
  grant
bourgeoisie, *see* capitalists

capital,
  and accumulation 125
  constraint of private ownership of
    245
  cultural 131–2
  and exploitation 45
  mobility of 163
  organic composition of 228

capital flight, and universal grant 163,
  168, 171
capitalism,
  and accumulation 127
  alternative futures of 116, 154–6
  contradictions of 109, 113
  definition of 45, 120ff.
  emergent tendencies of 148–51, 240
  interpenetration with communism
    143–4
  interpenetration with statism
    140–42
  and labor process 82
  legitimation of 150
  longevity of 241
  and mixed property rights 244–5
  non-viability of 113, 228–31, 242–3
  and oppression 49
  and surplus labor 121–2
  and universal grant 160
capitalist state, *see* state, class
  character of
capitalists,
  dependence on workers of 90
  and domination 64, 128
  interests of 78
  and interests of entire society 100
  and managers 83
  and poverty 38
  and power 94–6, 103
  preferences of, and universal grant
    162, 164

definition of 45
and labor process 86
Marxist analysis of 250
Marxist vs. Weberian approaches
to 92
mixed economy 167
models, and Analytical Marxism
187–9
modes of production,
articulation of 134–8, 147
Asiatic 118n
colonial 70
definition of 117–18
dominant 146–8, 152
interpenetration of 136 ff.
and social change 68
and totality 118
monopoly capitalism 103
multiclass movements 253–4

Native Americans 40, 48–9
neo-conservative theories of the state
100–01
new class, theories of 131–2
Non-Bullshit Marxism Group 14–15
norms, non-strategic and labor
process 74, 81

oppression,
and class 43
definition of 39–40, 211, 213–14
economic 41
gender, see gender oppression
and interests 42
and underclass 49

paradigms 8, 207
participant observation 204–5
patriarchal despotism 83
pluralism, theoretical 208–9
politics,
and class structure 51–2
and production 69–70
relation to Marxist and Weberian
approaches to class 92
post-Marxism 8, 12–13
post-modernism 12, 243, 248
poverty,

culture of poverty models 34–5
explanations of 32–9
individualist models of 33
systemic explanations of 37–9,
49–50
underclass theories of 36
power,
definition of 22–3, 93
negative 96–7
short-side 72
systemic, variation in class
character of 103
practice, definition of 54–5
production relations, political
dimensions of 68, 119, 127–9
productivity, and capitalism 159
profits 100, 162–3, 166–8
proletarianization 122, 151, 246
proletariat, see working class
property relations 122, 149, 166
property rights,
and exploitation 55–6, 59, 60
mixture of 143–4, 244–5
and universal grant 163

quantitative methodology, and
Marxism 10–11, 200

rational choice theory 189–91
rationality,
and exploitation 42
strategic, definition of 74
strategic, and labor process 81
realism, see science, realist view of
reductionism 104–5
reference groups 13–15
rent component in wages 67n, 251,
252–3
reproduction, biological 224
reserve army of labor 168
rights, and class and gender 213–14

science,
and Marxism 182–5, 200–05
realist view of 183, 201–3
skills,
and exploitation 66
of workers, and labor process 81–2